Constellations

The Life and Music of John Buckley

Constellations
The Life and Music of John Buckley

by Benjamin Dwyer

with a Foreword by Barra Ó Séaghdha

Carysfort Press

A Carysfort Press Book in association with Peter Lang

Constellations: The Life and Music of John Buckley
by Benjamin Dwyer

with a Foreword by Barra Ó Séaghdha

First published as a paperback in Ireland in 2011 by
Carysfort Press Ltd
58 Woodfield
Scholarstown Road
Dublin 16
Ireland

ISBN 978-1-78997-085-2

© 2011 Copyright remains with the author.

Typeset by Carysfort Press Ltd

eprint

This book is published with the financial assistance of
The Arts Council (An Chomhairle Ealaíon) Dublin, Ireland

Caution: All rights reserved. No part of this book may be printed or reproduced or utilized in any form or by any electronic, mechanical, or other means, now known or hereafter invented including photocopying and recording, or in any information storage or retrieval system without permission in writing from the publishers.

Contents

Acknowledgements   ix
Foreword   xi

Introduction   1

1 | Beginnings (1951-1972)   3

Early Years and Background
Introduction to Music
School Days
The Move to Dublin

2 | Early Works (1973-1976)   15

Teacher and Composer
Contemporary Music in Ireland in the 1970s
New Developments

SELECTED ANALYSIS: 24

Sonata for Cor Anglais and Piano (1973)
Three Pieces for Solo Flute (1973)
Wind Quintet (1976)

3 | Between the Celtic and the Avant-garde (1977-1987)   37

Part 1: Towards Ireland
Recognition
Studies in Cardiff
Myth and Modernism

SELECTED ANALYSIS: 43

Taller than Roman Spears (1977)
Oileáin (1979)
I Am Wind on Sea (1987)

Part 2: Towards Europe
Early Successes
Connecting with Cage and Lutoslawski

SELECTED ANALYSIS: 71

Concerto for Chamber Orchestra (1981)
Time Piece (1982)

4 | Educational and Peripheral Works (1982-1998)   81

Ennis Composition Summer School
Educational Works

5 | Consolidation (1988-1996)   93

Expanding Horizons
The Scene in Ireland
The Late 1980s and Early 1990s

SELECTED ANALYSIS: 109

Symphony No. 1 (1988)
A Thin Halo of Blue (1990)
The Words Upon the Window Pane (1991)
Concerto for Organ and Orchestra (1992)

6 | Towards a New Refinement (1997-2005)   139

The Late 1990s and the New Millennium

SELECTED ANALYSIS: 146

Concerto for Alto Saxophone and String Orchestra (1997)
Tidal Erotics (1999)
In Winter Light (2004)

7 | Constellations (2005-2010)   161

as far as the eye can see
Coda

Bibliography   171

Appendices I-VI   179

1: Catalogue of Compositions
2: *Abendlied–* (text)
3: *Rivers of Paradise –* (text)
4: *The words upon the window pane –* (Libretto)
5: *Te Deum* (text)
6: Discography

Index   *319*

Acknowledgements

I am indebted to many people and institutions that assisted me in the writing of this monograph.

I would like to express my gratitude to St Patrick's College, Drumcondra (Dublin City University) for its financial support of this project. I want to acknowledge the encouragement of the Royal Irish Academy of Music in providing financial assistance towards the publication of this book. Deborah Kelleher, Director of the Royal Irish Academy of Music, has been very supportive of my work in all its areas.

Many professional colleagues of mine who know and work with John Buckley assisted me greatly. They include Ciaran Bennett, Anthony Byrne, Darby Carroll, Bobby Chen, Rhona Clarke, Frank Corcoran, Denis Costello, Raymond Deane, William Dowdall, Roger Doyle, Susan Doyle, Kenneth Edge, Brian Farrell, John Feeley, Fergus Johnston, Aylish Kerrigan, Timo-Juhani Kyllönen, John McLachlan, Darragh Morgan, Martin O'Leary and Gavin O'Sullivan. Their perceptive comments and performances of Buckley's work helped me greatly to contextualize Buckley's music. The Contemporary Music Centre (Dublin) provided access to scores, books and other archival material, which was extremely useful. Thanks are due to Tina Kinsella, Barra Ó Séaghdha and Kimberly Campanello, who read through early drafts of *Constellations* and made insightful suggestions and constructive criticisms.

Versions of some of the commentary in this publication first appeared in *The Musical Times* (winter 2010) under the title 'From the Celtic to the Abstract: Shifting Perspectives in the Music of John Buckley'. I'd like to thank Hugh Maxton for giving me permission to publish his libretto *The Words Upon the Window Pane*.

Thanks also go to Tony Carragher for the cover photo and photos 6 and 7 inside.

I would like to add a special thanks to Dr Lorraine Byrne Bodley for her tremendous support for this project and her ongoing commitment to seeing a broad and healthy engagement with music in Ireland among composers, musicologists and music lovers alike. I want to further thank Dr Dan Farrelly and Carysfort Press (Dublin). Dan's undertaking of the publication of a book relating to contemporary Irish music demonstrates his belief in the need for such a work to exist.

I am indebted as ever to my family, and in particular, my father Benjamin, for the constant encouragement shown to me during the long gestation of this monograph.

Finally, however, my greatest appreciation goes to John Buckley and his wife Phil. John has been as helpful as one could wish. He made himself available to me for numerous extended interviews at his home between April 2004 and September 2010, which often extended well into the night (in this regard, Phil always made sure that I was fed and watered). John also diligently responded to dozens of emails with detailed responses. Furthermore, he furnished me with a trove of fascinating letters, reviews, articles, journals, photographs, concert programmes and a collection of scores and CD recordings of practically every work he has written, which were all of inestimable value.

Benjamin Dwyer.

Foreword

Barra Ó Séaghdha

This large-scale study of the life and work of the Irish composer John Buckley is noteworthy in several regards. It is a significant addition to a relatively underdeveloped sector in Irish cultural criticism. It draws attention to a modest but admirably dedicated member of a generation that had to persevere in the face of public indifference. And it demonstrates how mutual respect and critical integrity can be maintained when Irish composers of different generations meet.

In the nineteenth century, Ireland missed out on the building of musical infrastructure that took place in urban Britain. Independent Ireland failed to develop the educational philosophy of, for example, Patrick Pearse and offered further generations of schoolchildren little or no outlet for their creativity. For most of the last two centuries, under both British and native rule, the welcome Irish audiences have had for opera, whether grand or light, and, to a degree, for orchestral masterworks has not been matched by a nurturing environment for the creation of new works by Irish composers. Until recently at least, those who persisted in their vocations in independent Ireland could have no great expectations: a sprinkling of first performances but almost no opportunity to hear a work again or in a different interpretation; numerous works unperformed, unrecorded and unpublished; and, where public reception was concerned, a few brief newspaper reviews, an occasional interview or feature, and perhaps an article or two.

The last twenty years or so have witnessed a significant increase in the level of activity in the field of Irish music studies, across all genres. At universities and third-level institutes, in conferences, journals and reference works, the highways and byways of Irish musical culture and history are being explored. This is not to suggest that all is well, that the tide has turned. It cannot be said that critical debate has kept pace with institutional or infrastructural growth, and huge gaps remain in our knowledge and historical understanding. More importantly from a composer's point of view, it is still extremely difficult to have a large-scale orchestral work or an opera performed.

During the economic euphoria of the Celtic Tiger years, the visual arts became a marker of ostentatious wealth and underwent their own inflationary bubble; the level of poetic creativity was routinely exaggerated well after the flowering of the 70s and early 80s. Meanwhile, as the composers of John Buckley's generation came into their prime, their substantial achievements remained largely in the shadows. Such light as there was tended to fall on the flamboyant talent and personality of Gerald Barry, while it is more often as a political activist and writer than as a composer that Raymond Deane has tended to hit the headlines.

Where public profile is concerned, the case of John Buckley is unusual in a different way: though he has done much in the field of education – in fact, for his broadcasts, lectures and selfless commitment to music education he could be called a citizen-composer – his music has graced more civic occasions than almost any other composer of his day, the full scale and variety of his achievement is not always appreciated. Organ and saxophone concertos; intimate chamber works; a chamber opera; a site-specific collaboration with artist Vivienne Roche; solo instrumental works; strikingly conceived choral works - these are only a small selection of the forms to which he has brought his particular combination of studied craft and imagination.

John Buckley is fortunate that in Benjamin Dwyer's *Constellations: The Life and Music of John Buckley*, he has found a combination of sympathetic understanding and critical distance that illuminates both individual works and the overall shape of the career. When executed with style and conviction, the study of a composer can remain a work of reference for many years. The primary audience for such a work is among performers, listeners, academics and students who wish to deepen their understanding of the composer. However, at a time when music is increasingly taking its place alongside literature and the other arts in Irish Studies, *Constellations* is also open to those with a less technical grasp of music. The book is organised in such a way that sections devoted to the broad shape of the composer's career alternate with detailed analysis and illustration of style and technique.

It is a credit to both author and composer that, despite the clear evidence of cooperation between them – letters and emails from the composer, as well as quotations from interviews – the author's assessment of the composer's work is not just honest but at times quite stringent. Happily, Dwyer sees Buckley as increasingly masterful in realising his own musical world. Thus, there is a double gain for readers: a portrait of the composer and a demonstration of a constructively critical spirit in action. The relationship between the two, obviously based on mutual respect, is intriguing from another point of view in that Benjamin Dwyer, almost twenty years younger than Buckley, is himself a composer of substance. The book is therefore a meeting of generations as well as a meeting of minds.

Benjamin Dwyer's engagement with contemporary music is intense. As a virtuoso guitarist, he has a particular insight into the interpretation of new music, while his growing reputation as a composer is founded on such works as his multi-media creation *Scenes from Crow* (arising from a deep engagement with Ted Hughes's *Crow* sequence), numerous orchestral works and an outstanding set of études for guitar. He was artistic director of the Music21 new music concert series and festival (formerly Mostly Modern) for 18 years, a founder-member of the VOX21 ensemble (which commissioned many new works by Irish and international composers), and in 2007 was the driving force behind *Remembering Ligeti,* a multi-faceted celebration and examination of the composer. In addition to his teaching activities at the Royal Irish Academy of Music, he has contributed to such publications as the *Journal of Music in Ireland* and the *Musical Times* with articles on Berg, Ligeti, Britten and other topics. Dwyer's broad expertise and extensive engagement in contemporary music in all its aspects is reflected in the energy and liveliness of his writing.

Constellations: The Life and Music of John Buckley fully deserves to take its place as a striking addition to the canon of music criticism in Ireland.

Introduction

John Buckley is regarded as one of the finest Irish composers of his generation. Along with Gerald Barry, Jerome de Bromhead, Frank Corcoran, Raymond Deane, Roger Doyle and Jane O'Leary amongst others, he emerged in the 1970s as part of a new flowering in Irish composition. This phenomenon was not marked by homogeneity or bound by a unifying aesthetic but rather comprised a disparate body of composers who sought to find their individual voices within a broader European context. However, their collective desire to embrace purely modernist ideals in place of traditional Irish folk elements unites these composers despite their stylistic differences.

Extraordinarily, Buckley rose to prominence in Irish contemporary music despite the fact that he came from a relatively poor rural background in the southwest of Ireland. Even in Ireland today, government commitment to classical music in relation to education, infrastructure, radio and television broadcasting, professional development initiatives, among other areas, leaves much to be desired in comparison with broader European contexts. Ireland in the 1950s and 1960s, when Buckley was growing up in County Limerick, was even more underdeveloped in all these areas. Furthermore, the period was dominated politically by Éamon de Valera, whose essentialist vision of the slowly developing Republic was tinged with romantic views of a self-sufficient Catholic Ireland that celebrated the more traditional aspects of Irish culture.[1]

---

[1] Éamon de Valera (1882-1975) served as Taoiseach (Prime Minister) from 1937 to 1948, 1951 to 1954 and 1957 to 1959. He was President of Ireland from 1959 to 1973. His vision of the newly established Irish Free State (founded in 1922) dominated Irish political and social life for decades. He espoused a policy of self-sufficiency in an attempt to reduce the traditional economic links Ireland had with Britain. He once said: 'If there is to be any hope of prosperity for this

Classical music, which in Ireland was historically (though not exclusively) practiced and enjoyed by the previously ruling Protestant class, was hardly an aspect of Irish culture likely to be afforded any great support from the government of this time. Buckley's emergence as a leading figure in contemporary classical music is fascinating in light of the socio-economic and socio-political conditions he faced. He tackled the problem of working as a composer of contemporary art music in a relatively unsupportive environment by conducting a parallel professional life as an educationalist. Thus, he veered towards initial studies in education rather than pure music composition, and he worked as a school teacher throughout the 1970s. Even when he decided on a freelance career as a composer in 1982, teaching remained central to his ethos, and his involvement with music education cannot be separated from any thorough study of his work as a composer. Indeed, Buckley's contribution to music education has exerted a remarkable influence over the past thirty years and continues to do so.

In the 1990s, Buckley came to the forefront of Irish music, composing a prodigious number of important large-scale compositions, many of which came about as commissions from major institutions and music ensembles in Ireland and abroad. Among the commissioners were the National Concert Hall, St Patrick's College, Maynooth (now the National University of Ireland, Maynooth), the University of Limerick, Ensemble Contrasts Wien, and the Aurelia Saxophone Quartet (Holland). These commissions marked Buckley as the preferred composer for celebrations of a national dimension and as a major representative of Irish music abroad. From this period onwards his music developed a more refined character, and his penchant for French sonority came to the fore. This new timbral sheen, allied to a technique displaying a firm control of musical materials and further enhanced by a growing interest in the virtuosic aspects of performance, characterizes Buckley's style in this period and has led to an impressive contribution to the concerto genre. The *Organ Concerto* (1992), one of his finest works, establishes him as among the leading figures in Irish music today. However, since Ireland continues to place classical music at the periphery of cultural life, Buckley remains relatively unknown inside and outside his own country. It is hoped that this monograph will go some way towards establishing his importance as a composer.

---

country it is by reversing that policy which made us simply the kitchen garden for supplying the British with cheap food.' See Nicholas Mansergh, *Britain and Ireland* (London: Longmans, Green and Co., 1942), p. 84.

1 | Beginnings (1951-1972)

Early Years and Background

John Buckley was born on 19 December 1951 on a farm overlooking the small village of Templeglantine in County Limerick. Thirty-five miles west of the city of Limerick, on the road to Tralee, Templeglantine (or *Teampall an Ghleanntáin*, meaning the church of the small glen) is little more than a chapel village, having grown up around the church that was built there in 1829 at the time of Catholic Emancipation. A typical village, it was (until the 1970s) quiet and underdeveloped. In the 1950s, there were few cars, no telephones or televisions, and electricity had just been introduced as a result of the Rural Electrification Scheme initiated by de Valera's government.[2] Indeed, it was as late as 1959 when electricity reached Templeglantine. Buckley recalls, 'One of my earliest childhood memories is of electricity poles being set into the ground on our small farm. That was a very exciting occasion indeed. I also remember the pre-electricity times: oil lamps, bread being baked over an open fire, drawing water from the well.'[3]

His mother's family, the Brosnahans, had owned the farm before her marriage, and his father, Thomas (Tommy) Buckley, who hailed from Limerick city, moved to Templeglantine in 1950 upon marrying Eileen Brosnahan. John Buckley was the eldest of four boys, the others being

---

[2] The Rural Electrification Scheme was introduced by Éamon de Valera's Government in 1946 and was further developed by the passing of the Electricity Supply Amendment Act of 1955. The Scheme became known as the 'Quiet Revolution' because of the major socio-economic changes to which it led.

[3] All quotes derive from a series of interviews undertaken by the author with John Buckley at his home between April 2004 and September 2010. Unless otherwise stated, all quotes from Buckley will be taken from these interviews.

Danny, Joseph and Patrick. Danny, two years younger than John, was born with severe disabilities and died at the age of ten. His mother had looked after him while working on the farm at a time when there were few state resources. These challenges faced by the family made already difficult conditions more testing.

The farm was a holding of about twenty acres. It was poor land, and the Buckleys had to work extremely hard to keep the small homestead productive. Life was simple, if tough; it was very much the ideal envisaged by de Valera. Buckley remembers,

> It was very poor, wet hilly land. On the other hand, however, we always had vegetables and potatoes that we grew ourselves. We killed our own pigs and had bacon all year round. We had cows and hens. To a great extent, we were in fact self-sufficient with regard to food and other necessities.

Buckley's parents worked arduously all their lives to maintain the farm. Perhaps because of this life of labour, his mother was most influential in directing her son towards a career away from the hardships of farming life.

Despite the poor quality of the land and the inherent difficulties encountered by the people of West Limerick and North Kerry, the region has for centuries been rich in traditional music and Irish-language poetry. It was also home to the prominent Bardic traditions of the sixteenth and seventeenth centuries. The Irish Bards formed a professional hereditary caste of highly trained, learned poets known in Gaelic as *Aosdána* (from *aos dána* – 'people of the arts').[4] One of the last great bards from this part of Ireland was Aogán Ó Rathaille (1670-1729) whose 'Gile na Gile' is an undisputed masterpiece of Irish-language poetry.[5]

---

[4] Aosdána is also the name given to an institution established by the Arts Council of Ireland in 1981 to honour those artists 'whose work has made an outstanding contribution to the arts in Ireland, and to encourage and assist members in devoting their energies fully to their art.' Membership of Aosdána, made by peer nomination and election, is limited to 250 living artists who have produced a distinguished body of work. Members must have been born in Ireland or have been resident there for five years, and must have produced a body of work that is original and creative. A number of members are recognized by their peers for outstanding achievement by the title of *Saoi*. No more than seven current members may be so honoured at one time. The title of *Saoi* is conferred by the President of Ireland and is held for life. Under certain conditions, members of Aosdána may avail of the *Cnuas*, a stipend that is designed to enable them to devote their energies more fully to their creative work.

[5] For a comprehensive assessment of the poet see Brendán Ó Buachalla, *Aogán Ó Rathaille* (Dublin: Field Day, 2007).

More recently, the region produced some of the leading musical and literary figures of the latter half of the twentieth century, including the composer Seán Ó Riada (1931-1971), perhaps the single most influential figure in the renaissance of traditional Irish music from the 1960s through his work with the pioneering ensemble Ceoltóirí Chualann, and his writings and broadcasts on the topic. Born in Adare, County Limerick, he was assistant director for Radio Éireann and was musical director of the Abbey Theatre in Dublin for five years.[6] His score for the film *Mise Éire* brought him national acclaim.[7] Writers from the area include the poets Brendan Kennelly (b. 1936) and Michael Hartnett (1941-1999), the playwright John B. Keane (1928-2002) and the novelist and playwright Bryan McMahon (1909-1998).

Introduction to Music

Traditional Irish music was prominent in the area where Buckley grew up, and his exposure to it came early – even his mother played the fiddle in the family home. Indeed, the *Sliabh Luachra* region is noted for its rich and distinctive style of traditional performance, which makes extensive use of the polka and the slide. *Sliabh Luachra* is an area located around the River Blackwater on the Cork and Kerry borderland. Opinions differ as to its exact location and extent, but it is generally accepted that it refers to the mountainous rush-filled upland that straddles the border areas of Cork, Kerry and Limerick.[8]

At the age of nine, Buckley started taking classes in traditional music on the button accordion with the well-known local teacher Liam Moloney, who owned the dance hall in Templeglantine and headed the Moloney Ceili Band. Throughout the centuries, traditional music has been, for the most part, transmitted orally, which made Moloney's teaching, based entirely on notation, rather unusual. His approach was, for Buckley, an unlikely introduction to written music – the first in a number of unusual coincidences and fortuitous events that would steer the young boy towards a career in classical music, a far from obvious

---

[6] Radio Éireann was the national radio station (now Radio Telefís Éireann – RTÉ).
[7] *Mise Éire* (I am Ireland) is a short documentary film made by George Morrison in 1959 that tells the story of Irish revolutionary nationalism. A clearly partisan film, with a romantic and, at times, overly sentimental score, it enjoyed iconic status for many years following its release.
[8] The name *Sliabh Luachra* means 'mountain of rushes.' However, it is not a single mountain, but a series of hills and valleys known as the 'seven glens of Sliabh Luachra' or 'seacht ngleann Sliabh Luachra'.

choice or foregone conclusion in rural Ireland in the 1950s. 'Traditional music was generally taught by ear,' Buckley comments,

> imitating the teacher and joining in the tunes. Moloney, however, taught by notation, introducing me to conventional notation in my first lesson. He wrote everything in a small music manuscript book, the first time I had ever seen one. In a way, I was receiving a type of traditional theoretical training alongside and through the medium of Irish traditional tunes. I remember the first melody I learned to play was *The Green Glens of Antrim*.

Country life at that time was isolated to a degree that is difficult to appreciate today. People rarely traveled beyond their immediate locality, and few had any experience of the wider world. 'It seemed to me,' Buckley said in describing his childhood, 'that the extent of the universe was defined more or less by the parish, and the distance that one could walk, or an occasional exotic journey to town on the horse and cart. It was quite an amazing thing to see the metropolis of Abbeyfeale or Newcastlewest' (towns near Templeglantine). And yet, for the budding musician, there was one outlet that opened up a whole new world – the radio.[9]

Until the age of twelve, the radio was the most influential medium for Buckley. It liberated and released his imagination, giving him access, for the first time, to musical worlds beyond the traditional Irish music and the Ceili bands through which he had been educated musically thus far. 'It was the most extraordinary event when the first radio arrived into our kitchen,' Buckley remembers,

> and of course it was the old type with batteries because it was still pre-electricity times. It was a source of absolutely endless fascination for me. I found that by turning the dial you could hear on the long-wave fragments of Chinese, snippets of opera, and maybe swing music from the United States. The radio really opened my imagination to the fact that there was an immense universe out there about which I knew nothing. It brought that universe into the small kitchen, and, simultaneously, it drew my imagination out into that universe.

This early experience of radio and its transcendental power was to have a lasting and profound effect on the composer. He paid homage to that influence in a score written many years later entitled *A Thin Halo of Blue* (1990-91): a radiophonic work of immense complexity for

---

[9] Radio broadcasting was launched in the Irish Free State in 1926. It was known as 2RN (this was its 'call-sign', designated by international authority). In 1937 it became known as Radio Éireann and eventually Radio Telefís Éireann (RTÉ) by which it is known today. For a detailed history of Irish radio broadcasting see Richard Pine, *Music and Broadcasting in Ireland* (Dublin: Four Courts Press, 2005).

orchestra, narrator, choir, piano and tape, the inspiration for which can be traced back to a 'wireless' in a small country kitchen three decades earlier.

School Days

Eileen Buckley was the dominant influence on her eldest son's intellectual development. She was, like most people of her generation, very religious; devotional observances, such as reciting the Rosary, were a daily routine in the household. Perhaps more significantly, she was a fervent believer in the importance of education. She was well-read, highly intelligent and a fluent Gaelic speaker, but had not been given the opportunity to pursue her academic education and, instead, became a nurse after completing her Intermediate Certificate. She was, however, a natural teacher – something which was to have a profound influence on her son later in his professional career. Absolutely convinced that education was the only way forward, she taught her son the entire sixth-class curriculum herself at home so that he could focus on the County Council Scholarship Exams for free secondary education.[10] In 1964, access to secondary education was not available to all who wanted it. Although Buckley was not awarded the scholarship (he came second and there was only one placement in the county), the education he received from his mother was excellent grounding for his eventual attendance at the secondary-level boarding school. 'My mother had a profound influence on my thinking.' Buckley comments:

> She had not had the opportunity to develop her own formal education beyond the Intermediate Certificate, but she was highly intelligent and articulate. I was greatly influenced and inspired by the importance she attached to the role of education. From an early age, I viewed education as a crucial issue for the individual and society generally. Even though my mother was by no means an intellectual, she understood and communicated the critical function of language, culture and education.

Thus, at the age of twelve Buckley was sent to a boarding school run at that time by the Salesian Order of priests in Ballinakill, County Laois, about one hundred miles from Templeglantine.[11] It was not uncommon

---

[10] It was not until 1966 that the Fianna Fáil Minister for Education, Donogh O'Malley, introduced free secondary education throughout the Republic of Ireland.
[11] The Salesians of Don Bosco (or the Salesian Society, originally known as the Society of St Francis de Sales) is a Roman Catholic religious order founded in the mid-nineteenth century by Saint John Bosco in an attempt, through works of

at this time, especially in rural areas, for one member of a family (very often the eldest boy) to enter the priesthood. The Salesian Order had an established relationship with the village of Templeglantine: a number of priests hailed from the parish and Buckley's next door neighbour, John Horan, had already gone to the college in Ballinakill and would go on to become the Provincial of the Salesian Order. Every year a representative of the Order visited Templeglantine to offer places in the school. Although no overt pressure was placed on families, it was tacitly understood by both sides that a proportion of young students would advance to the priesthood. The enticement to enter into such an arrangement was, of course, a fine secondary education.[12]

In 1941, the Salesians took possession of Heywood House, an old mansion with sunken Italian gardens created by the renowned architect and landscape designer Sir Edwin Lutyens. The grounds comprised extensive woodlands and lakes complete with architectural follies, creating an idyllic environment for the imagination of the young Buckley. 'Although it didn't strike me at the time,' Buckley remembers,

> the remarkable setting must have provided an inspirational backdrop for the development of my creative imagination. These extraordinary surroundings were a source of endless fascination for me.

The Heywood Gardens are to this day regarded as one of the finest examples of their type in western Europe.

Buckley was an excellent student and was active in many aspects of school life. He greatly enjoyed his academic work for which he had a natural flair. He was also heavily involved in sports, particularly athletics, and he held the 1968 Leinster schoolboys' record for the 880 yards track race (commonly known as the half mile race) and also competed in cross-country championships at inter-schools level. Although away from home and isolated from his family, Buckley affectionately remembers his time at Ballinakill and seems to have

---

charity, to care for the young and poor children of the industrial revolution. The Salesians' charter describes the society's mission as 'the Christian perfection of its associates obtained by the exercise of spiritual and corporal works of charity towards the young, especially the poor, and the education of boys to the priesthood' (see website: www.salesians.org). The Salesians' work in Ireland began in 1919 in Pallaskenry, Co. Limerick. The Salesian House, Ballinakill, Portlaoise, Co. Laois, where Buckley attended was formally closed in 2004, bringing its sixty-three years teaching service to an end.

[12] The College at Ballinakill asked that a donation be made, whatever the parents could afford. The school was run on grants from the Department of Education, but to a large extent, Salesian houses were run on the generosity of people who made gifts towards the running of the schools. Ballinakill was not, therefore, a fee-paying school in the sense of being an expensive establishment.

thrived there. It should be noted that the education offered by the Salesian Order was significantly broader than the average Irish education at this time. It was tremendously supportive towards endeavours of the imagination and creativity in all its forms, from arts and crafts (it offered opportunities like wood-turning, card making, and it had a printing press), through basic electronics to sports and music, alongside the standard curriculum. The Order was dedicated to intellectual development; it hosted debating societies, Irish-language societies, and the study of Latin and Greek was central to its curriculum. All these activities contributed to a remarkably erudite culture, which provided Buckley with a thoroughly rounded education. During the period in which he attended the college, music was not offered as a core subject in the Leaving Certificate. However, for a young boy with an interest in music, Ballinakill provided a unique opportunity as it boasted an orchestra (a most unusual resource in Irish educational institutions at the time).

In Ballinakill there was an expectation that boys interested in music would join the orchestra. 'Now the college had bought three new instruments,' Buckley recalls, 'a clarinet, a trumpet and a flute. As it happened, three boys had arrived who had a particular interest in music. I was the third and the clarinet and the trumpet had already been chosen, so I was put on the flute.' There were no official instrument teachers at the college, but the young musicians seemed to manage. Buckley learned by way of tutor books and assistance from non-specialist music teachers. He performed classical music for the first time in the college orchestra. Its repertoire included Schubert's *Rosamunde Overture* and arrangements of some of Haydn's minuets. This exposure was significant in terms of his musical development, but the young student had no inkling that he might one day be a professional composer. Although he found playing in the orchestra to be an enjoyable new experience, he regarded it more or less as a continuation of what he had already achieved on the button accordion.

Buckley had the further good fortune to meet a number of inspirational priests within the Order who had a considerable influence on his musical development; these included two *aficionados* of classical music, Father Al O'Carroll and Father Pat McCarr. McCarr went on to make a significant contribution to the development of music education by publishing a number of school text books designed to assist students sitting music at Leaving Certificate level. Even though they were basic (many were published as hand-written documents), it must be recognized that these books were among the first available aids in

Ireland for students studying music. One, published in 1989, was entitled *A Musical Journey – Purcell to Buckley*.[13] Although, as noted, the students at Ballinakill during Buckley's time there were not formally studying music for the Leaving Certificate, McCarr frequently played music for the interested boys. These sessions had a profound effect on him:

> I remember that within the period of about a week, he introduced us to two pieces of music. The first was Beethoven's *Eroica Symphony*. And the other piece, remarkably, because this was 1967, was Penderecki's *Threnody for the Victims of Hiroshima*, which had been composed only six years before. These pieces struck me with such force that from that moment I knew I wanted to be a composer.

Once his interest was stimulated, Buckley immersed himself in scores and recordings from the school's well-stocked library, familiarizing himself with many standard works of the classical repertoire. Shortly afterwards, he heard a live orchestra for the first time when he attended a performance of Handel's *Judas Maccabaeus* given in Carlow by the town's Choral Society. Although it might seem to be minimal by comparison with the best that is offered by the more progressive schools today, this exposure to classical music was by no means representative of the experiences of most Irish school children at that time.

The Move to Dublin

In this period, it was commonly accepted that a certain percentage of the students from the college would become priests of the Order, and Ballinakill acted as an unofficial seminary for the priesthood. Indeed it had served as a seminary in previous times. Buckley comments: 'I believe that there was some degree of expectation that I might pursue a religious vocation, because of my academic application and interest in teaching.' In those days, the Salesian Order was dedicating itself almost exclusively to education, a preoccupation closely allied to its ethos of social responsibility, which Buckley found interesting. 'I didn't feel a strong sense of priestly vocation,' he recalls, 'but I was drawn towards education and making a contribution to society, attributes deeply embedded in the ethos of the Salesian Order.'

---

[13] By 1989 John Buckley's *Sonata for Unaccompanied Violin* was a set work for the Leaving Certificate. A study of it was included in the book: Pat McCarr, *A Musical Journey – Purcell to Buckley* (Kilkenny: J & G Print, 1989).

Not surprisingly, Buckley did not consider going to university to study music. As he had not taken music as a subject for the Leaving Certificate, he would not necessarily have been offered a place on a BMus course. Buckley explains:

> Despite the great support for music in Ballinakill, it was not offered as a Leaving Certificate subject, so pursuing a university degree in music didn't seem a possibility, nor did it appear the only route to becoming a composer, my ultimate ambition. Studying at a teacher training college would offer a third-level qualification and music was available as an academic option.

Most ambitious young men and women from a rural background tended to gravitate towards secure careers in banking, the civil service and primary-school teaching. Many regarded the latter as a calling. 'You responded to what was known as the "call to training,"' Buckley remembers. 'This was your invitation to come to the Training College. It was like a clarion call that spread its sound across the country. It was spoken of as a vocation.'

A career as a school teacher would not only allow Buckley to fulfill his desire to become an educator, but would further give him access to sport and music, activities included in the primary school curriculum. In pursuit of this, he applied for a place at St Patrick's College in Drumcondra, on the northside of Dublin, to study for the National Teacher Diploma.[14] His application was successful, and in September 1969, he took the train to Dublin to embark on a new phase in his life.

As a foundation course in music was part of its curriculum, St Patrick's gave Buckley the opportunity to study music and nurture his desire to become a composer. His music teacher at St Patrick's, Seán Hayes, exerted a strong influence on him, as Fathers McCarr and O'Carroll had done. As there were few students taking the music course, Buckley was able to benefit from a substantial amount of personal attention. There were over three hundred students attending St

---

[14] St Patrick's College was established in 1875 to meet the teacher training needs of a denominational primary school system. The administration of the College was placed in the care of the Vincentian Fathers where it remained until 1999 when they withdrew from the management. Dr Pauric Travers was appointed as the first lay President of the College. In 1974, the three-year BEd degree for teachers was introduced and the College became a recognized College of the National University of Ireland (NUI). In 1993, St Patrick's College became a College of Dublin City University (DCU). Under the linkage agreement with DCU, two new joint Faculties were created: the Joint Faculty of Education and the Joint Faculty of Humanities. In the early 1990s, the College embarked on a process of growth and diversification, which culminated in the introduction of a variety of new programmes including a BA and MA in Humanities and a taught MEd, MA and PhD by research.

Patrick's, nearly all of whom were from the country. Each had been given a private room, and although small and spartan, it provided Buckley with real comfort and a new sense of independence. His exciting new life in Dublin provided him with opportunities to experience more classical music. 'Coming from the restrictions of a boarding school,' he recalls,

> I had the freedom of the city! There were symphony concerts in the St Francis Xavier Hall and in the Gaiety Theatre on Sunday nights. In the late 1960s and early 1970s the RTÉ Symphony Orchestra played an incredible range of modern music. Many concerts featured works by Irish composers, far more so than nowadays. I heard works by Victory, Boydell, Bodley, Kinsella and Wilson, all the Irish repertoire.

Irish works that made a particular impact on Buckley included the newly composed *Configurations* (1967) by Seóirse Bodley (b. 1933), the uncompromising modernity of which exposed him to a contemporary Irish music directly inspired by European models. Brian Boydell's *In Memoriam Mahatma Ghandi* (1948) also made a strong impression, as did Aloys Fleischmann's *Cornucopia* and John Kinsella's *Montage II* (both from 1970). Hearing a performance of Penderecki's *Threnody for the Victims of Hiroshima* (1961), a work Buckley knew well since his time at Ballinakill, deeply affected him. The live aspect of these orchestral events, including the chance to hear the classics, also opened up new horizons for Buckley – Beethoven inspired him as much as the contemporary composers. As a member of *Ógra Ceoil*, a youth organization run by the Music Association of Ireland, which provided inexpensive student tickets to symphony concerts, he was able to attend concerts on a weekly basis.[15]

Buckley took lessons at one of Dublin's most prominent music institutions, the Royal Irish Academy of Music.[16] Some years before, the

---

[15] Founded in 1948, the Music Association of Ireland organized music recitals, workshops in primary and secondary schools, festivals, and summer projects. It also co-ordinated the Irish auditions for the European Youth Orchestra. It published a monthly diary of musical events throughout the country, newsletters and policy statements on music in education, and it founded and organized the Dublin Festival of 20th Century Music. *Ógra Ceoil* means 'Music Youth'.

[16] In 1848, John Stanford (father of Sir Charles Villiers Stanford), R.M. Levey (the leading Dublin violinist of the time), the Rev. Charles Graves and Joseph Robinson, among others, founded an academy to 'provide systematic instruction in instrumental music.' The Academy held its first classes in the Antient Concert Rooms in what is now Pearse Street before moving to No. 18 St Stephen's Green. In 1871, the Academy moved to its present home at 36 Westland Row, acquiring the two neighboring houses of Nos. 37 and 38 in 1911. Although it became 'Royal' in 1872, it did not receive its present constitution until 1889 when, as the beneficiary of Elizabeth Strean Coulson, it received over £13,000. Together with another significant bequest from J. Ormsby Vandeleur, this enabled an Order in

Professor of Flute at the Academy, Doris Keogh, had visited Ballinakill to give a concert. On that occasion, she had met Buckley and suggested that he might like to study flute with her if he ever came to Dublin. Keogh was noted for her vast array of musical interests and her energetic approach to teaching and musical development in Ireland. She founded the Capriol Consort, a pioneering recorder group that specialized in Renaissance music, and she also had a keen interest in contemporary music. Buckley studied with her for several years and found her classes very stimulating; she further encouraged his first efforts at composition. He also participated in various chamber ensembles and played in the Academy's student orchestra, which was conducted by Colman Pearce, who subsequently became the principal conductor of the RTÉ Symphony Orchestra. This association developed into a close friendship, and Pearce later became a notable interpreter of Buckley's music.

Although Buckley had long harboured a desire to write music, his lack of technical knowledge meant that he was not able to progress beyond the opening bars of any piece. While attending the Academy for flute lessons, he also studied with A.J. Potter (1918-1980), the Professor of Composition and one of the most prominent figures in Irish musical life at the time. Potter had studied at the Royal College of Music in London with Vaughan Williams, earned his Doctorate from Trinity College Dublin, and, in the early 1950s, won a number of prominent composition competitions, including the *Festival of Britain Prize* in 1951. For many years he was a popular radio broadcaster, and his orchestrations of traditional Irish melodies made him a favourite with Irish audiences. Potter's composition classes were idiosyncratic in that, at least in Buckley's experience, they took the form of orchestration lessons rather than instruction in the rudiments of composition. Buckley remembers the excitement at being confronted for the first time with the challenge of filling in an empty manuscript:

> My first composition lessons with A.J. Potter took place in the Autumn of 1971. He prescribed two movements from Schumann's *Album for the Young*, asking me to orchestrate them for small orchestra for the following week. Potter taught by enquiry rather than by direct admonition. He also kindly supplied me with a quantity of twenty-

---

Council to be effected under the Educational Endowments (Ireland) Act of 1885, which bestowed stability and structure on the institution. More recently a major change in the Academy's constitution was the decision in the 1980s to appoint a Director. Its present Director is Deborah Kelleher. Cited from the website www.riam.ie accessed 12 January 2011. For a full history of the Royal Irish Academy of Music see Richard Pine and Charles Acton, eds. *To Talent Alone, The Royal Irish Academy of Music 1848-1998* (Dublin: Gill & Macmillan, 1998).

eight stave manuscript paper, which I had never previously encountered. I was, of course, familiar with the normal twelve-stave manuscript exercise books and had had the privilege of studying orchestral scores by Mozart and Beethoven while in Ballinakill, but this was my first encounter with the blank pages of full orchestral manuscript paper; moreover one that I was required to fill. The encounter with both Potter and the manuscript paper filled me with awe, uncertainty and anticipation. With a sense of mounting excitement, I felt I had drawn one step closer to my youthful ambition of becoming a composer.

This was the experience for which Buckley had been waiting so long. Unfortunately, Potter had to retire before the end of the academic year due to illness and Buckley's lessons with him came to an abrupt end.

2 | Early Works (1973-1976)

Following Potter's departure from the Academy, Buckley was offered a new teacher, James Wilson (1922-2005), who was to have a more lasting influence on the young composer. A Londoner, Wilson came to Ireland in the 1940s and was a prolific composer with seven operas and twelve concertos to his name. Along with his work as Professor at the Academy, he was a founder-member of Aosdána and a leading figure in the Irish music scene for over half a century. Wilson's method of teaching composition was very different from Potter's and, at the outset, Buckley was expected to produce original material. Wilson's approach was informal and congenial, and he never attempted to impose a particular style or musical ideology on his pupil but rather offered technical advice on instrumentation, form and structure. Together, they decided the type of piece Buckley should write. He recalls that, in one case, Wilson, taking a cue from Hindemith, suggested the cor anglais as a possible starting point for a new work. Wilson had completed his own substantial *Sonata for Cor Anglais and Piano* (1968) just three years previously, and thus his teaching method combined the study of the 20th-century canon with direct personal experience. Some classes were devoted to listening to music and to the analysis of scores – more often than not, those of Wilson. Most commonly, however, Buckley's initial sketches were analysed and commented upon, weaknesses and strengths were identified, and inconsistencies in development sections were highlighted and improved upon.

Buckley's initial efforts at composition were frequently little more than naïve attempts at pastiche. He recalls a comment made by Wilson during one of their sessions in which he gently pointed out the stylistic limitations of the music his pupil was writing, and intimated, in a most characteristic way, that he should have the courage to find his own voice:

> I had written something, which I thought was wonderful, and was highly pleased with myself. I showed it to Jim and he said in the politest way imaginable, 'Well, it's very nice, but wouldn't you be better off trying to write some good Buckley, rather than bad Tchaikovsky.' It was a lesson I have never forgotten.

Teacher and Composer

In 1971, Buckley graduated with a National Teacher Diploma (now a BEd degree). Teachers were in great demand in Ireland at the time, and he was immediately offered two jobs: one in his old school in Templeglantine and another in the Holy Spirit School in Ballymun. He chose the latter as he was eager to remain in Dublin and continue his musical studies. In the early 1970s (and for many years to come), Ballymun was one of the most socially deprived areas in the whole country, largely due to disastrous experiments in social housing implemented by the government in the 1960s, which imitated the high-rise monstrosities of Birmingham and outer London and which, when built, also produced similar social problems. Recalling his arrival in the school to take up his post, Buckley comments:

> On the first morning, the principal offered me a box of white chalk and ushered me into a room devoid of charts, books or resources of any kind. The room, however, did contain forty-three seven-year-old children, mainly from the adjacent high-rise flats. Ballymun in 1971 was beset with many social problems, such as the lack of any infrastructural support and high levels of unemployment. Sometimes I felt myself to be a social worker, sometimes a counselor, occasionally even a teacher. I was nineteen.

Despite the obvious difficulties faced by Buckley in his new job, his training with the Salesians and the educational ethos imbued in him by his mother led him to persist in his attempts to awaken a genuine interest in learning in the children under his care. He involved the young students in many different creative activities. Buckley recalls: 'I did basket work, I did stamp collecting, I organized a chess club, I got an athletics club going and entered the children into competitions.' Not surprisingly, he gave much of his attention to music, producing several popular musicals (including *Oklahoma* and *Joseph and His Amazing Technicoloured Dreamcoat*), teaching the children staff notation, singing and percussion instruments. He acquired tape recordings and started bringing the children to classical musical concerts. 'It got to the point', he remembers, 'where even the graffiti on the local walls appeared with staff notation above the words. And the principal would say "Buckley, your children are at it again!"' Notwithstanding the small successes he achieved in this regard, Buckley is reluctant to over-romanticize his efforts: the lack of resources and the children's underprivileged backgrounds meant that there were severe limits to what he could realistically hope to accomplish.

Although life as a teacher was difficult, it had certain benefits. The organization of the school day and the extended holidays given to teachers meant that Buckley could find time to devote to composition. Most days, after school finished, he would travel to St Patrick's College, where he had secured a room in which to compose and prepare the scores to show Wilson at the Academy. At this time, St Patrick's College also played a central role in Buckley's social life as it was here that he met his future wife Philomena McGinley.[17] Phil had a degree in geography and had been studying for a graduate diploma in education. They met in 1973 through a mutual friend and the relationship developed from there. They often socialized in *The Cat & Cage,* a well-known pub near the college. They married in Donnycarney Church in July 1976. Phil shared Buckley's interest in the arts, education and music. Before long they decided to have a family: Deirdre was born in 1978, Niamh in 1981 and Oisín in 1985.

Buckley studied with Wilson at the Academy until 1974, after which he continued to work with him privately until 1976. They had a mutually suitable informal arrangement: in return for Buckley's agreeing to do some odd jobs around his house, Wilson agreed to look at his compositions. It seems that in this transaction the young composer emerged as the net beneficiary: 'My recollection is that I always got a long composition lesson and a lovely dinner and almost never did any work around the house, and usually borrowed a book or two from Jim's extensive library as well!' In addition to benefiting from the informal compositional classes, Buckley learned a great deal of a more general nature from the older composer, who was always ready to discuss his views and elaborate on his personal perspectives on composition, as well as share his broad knowledge of music and of the arts.

Wilson's guidance influenced the first ten or so compositions in Buckley's present catalogue: 'These works', Buckley insists, 'would, to a greater or lesser extent, have some of his imprint on them.' They

---

[17] Originally an all-male institution, St Patrick's College admitted female students for the first time in 1971.

include *Three Pieces for Solo Flute, Sonata for Cor Anglais and Piano, Auburn Elegy* (satb/2fl/cl), *The Seasonable Month* (sop/fl/pf), all from 1973, *Sequence* (cl/bn/pf), *Brass Quintet No. 1* (1974), *Keoghal* (recorder quintet, 1975) and *Wind Quintet* (1976). Wilson's influence can be observed in Buckley's choice of instrumentation, use of formal design and continuity of line. An interest in pastoral music and themes that emerges in *The Seasonable Month* and *Auburn Elegy* (a setting of an extract from Oliver Goldsmith's *The Deserted Village*)[18] was clearly nurtured through Wilson's own debt to Vaughan Williams. However, the somewhat more adventurous works for flute, and the recorder quintet *Keoghal*, highlight the influence of Doris Keogh, for whom they were written.[19] The more astringent *Sequence, Quintet No. 1* and *Wind Quintet* lean in the modernist direction that Buckley was soon to take.

Contemporary Music in Ireland in the 1970s

For many reasons, art music had only been a peripheral presence in Irish cultural life until the mid-twentieth century, with the exception of opera and light opera, which flourished in many larger cities. The country had no professional orchestra until 1948; there were very few other professional working ensembles of note; no opera or ballet companies operated on a full-time basis and there were no professional chamber groups. Concert life was very restricted, and educational opportunities were similarly limited. As a result, very few professional positions were open to musicians.

However, these poor conditions did slowly change, largely because of the efforts of the generation of Irish musicians working from the 1920s and 1930s onwards, which included such eminent figures as John F. Larchet (1884-1967), Aloys Fleischmann (1910-1992) and Brian Boydell (1917-2000). Larchet was Professor of Music at both the Royal Irish Academy of Music and University College Dublin between the 1920s and the 1950s, and Director of Music at the Abbey Theatre from 1907 until 1934. Fleischmann was Professor of Music at University College Cork for over forty-five years from 1934 and founder of the Cork

---

[18] In the poem *The Deserted Village* (1770), Goldsmith (1730-1774) revisits Auburn, a village he remembers with affection, and comments on its demise brought about as a result of emigration and the influence of industry – 'wealth accumulates and men decay.'

[19] Using the surname Keogh [/kjoʊ/] as a model, the pronunciation of *Keoghal* becomes [/cʲoɪlʲ/]. In Gaelic this sounds the same as the word 'ceoil' ('music') serving as a pun on Doris Keogh's name. *Keoghal* was written for the Capriol Consort.

Symphony Orchestra and the Cork International Choral Festival. Boydell was a founder of the Music Association of Ireland and of the Dowland Consort and Professor of Music at Trinity College Dublin for twenty years from 1962. Each made significant contributions. It was through their efforts, and those of others like them, that the Irish art music scene developed positively.

From the 1950s, a new generation of composers, which included A.J. Potter, Wilson, and Gerard Victory (1921-1995), Director of Music at RTÉ from 1967 to 1982, built upon this enlivened scene and increased performance opportunities. As Buckley notes, in the 1970s the RTÉ Symphony Orchestra and other RTÉ performing groups presented a considerable amount of Irish music. Notwithstanding, Irish composers still faced difficulties: for example, they were unable to find publishers with the resources to bring out and promote new music. RTÉ was, by and large, the sole provider for professional performing musicians, and commissioning fees were generally very small, if indeed composers obtained them at all. In short, it was impossible for composers of this generation to freelance. A.J. Potter eventually did so, but only following the introduction of the 1969 Finance Act, brought in by Charles Haughey, which relieved creative artists from taxation and represented a turning point for the profession in Ireland.[20] Even so, Potter still felt the need to continue producing popular arrangements of Irish tunes in order to supplement his income. At this stage, Aosdána, the state-sponsored body for supporting creative artists, did not yet exist.

These slow developments in infrastructure and support for art music coincided with the emergence of a new generation of composers that looked to Europe rather than traditional Irish music as a source of inspiration. Although prior to the 1960s some Irish composers had experimented with modernist techniques to a degree, it was the subsequent generation that embraced more emphatically developments taking place outside Ireland. Seóirse Bodley's *Configurations*, which Buckley heard in the early 1970s, was a pivotal work in this regard. Some of the early compositions of John Kinsella, such as *Montage II*, extensively explored modern European trends. Although new Irish music was being performed relatively often by the RTÉ performing groups, the general paucity of educational resources for music and a troubled historical relationship with art music meant that the collective understanding of new music remained inhibited. Given the changes

---

[20] Charles Haughey was the fourth leader of the political party Fianna Fáil. He was Minister for Finance from 1966 to 1970, and Taoiseach (Prime Minister) three times (1979-81, 1982, and 1987-92).

Ireland was undergoing at this time (Seán Lemass's government was introducing many new social and economic initiatives), it is difficult to accurately appraise the degree to which music reflected societal change.[21] There were many conflicting influences, and aspirations towards modernity were juxtaposed with more conservative positions. Despite RTÉ's achievements, there was little awareness of modernism in music in Ireland amongst the general public.

Ó Riada was certainly the most well-known figure in Irish music by the 1960s, and although he did engage with aspects of modernism in the 1950s (*Nomos No. 1* from 1957, for example), he was largely known for his immensely popular film scores *Mise Éire* (1959), *Saoirse?* (1960) and *An Tine Bheo* (1966). These titles translate respectively as *I am Ireland*, *Freedom?* and *The Living Fire*; the nationalist impulse is clear. Other established composers, such as A.J. Potter, were also recognized predominantly for their arrangements of Irish tunes. New music, therefore, had a small audience and remained on the periphery of Irish musical life. While RTÉ programmed music by established figures, these works often received just one performance. For the most part, opportunities for the exposure of new music were lacking.

New Developments

This inadequate situation continued into the early 1970s. Buckley and the young composers of his generation still found themselves in difficult circumstances largely resulting from the very slow development of an indigenous tradition of classical music and the generally poor state of musical infrastructure in Ireland. One exception, of course, was the Dublin Festival of 20th Century Music, which was set up by the Music Association of Ireland in 1969 and continued biennially until 1984. It was, even by present standards, an audacious festival of international stature and featured the music of many renowned composers such as Witold Lutoslawski, Peter Maxwell Davies, Andrzej Panufnik, Elliott Carter, Olivier Messiaen, Iannis Xenakis, and Karlheinz Stockhausen. From its inception, the festival included a concert of music by young Irish composers that provided an extremely beneficial platform for their work. The exposure to such a vast array of new music by so many established figures of the modernist and *avant-garde* schools

---

[21] Seán Lemass (1899-1971) was Taoiseach (Prime Minister) of Ireland from 1959 to 1966. He succeeded Éamon de Valera and was central to many economic developments throughout the 1960s. He became known as the 'architect of modern Ireland'.

profoundly affected Irish composition, specifically in relation to the younger composers. That many of these renowned figures came to Dublin to participate in the Festival can only have been inspirational.

The Dublin Festival of 20th Century Music helped set the stage for the emergence of this new generation of Irish composers, which represented a unique phase in Irish composition. These young composers felt emboldened to wholeheartedly adopt developments (often from the extreme *avant-garde*) that were shaping new music throughout Europe. This trend naturally paralleled the economic and social shifts of post de Valera Ireland as it included the embracing of many European political and economic ideals (it joined the European Economic Community in 1973).[22] As a heretofore unacknowledged part of this *zeitgeist*, the young Irish composers appearing in the late 1960s and early 1970s engaged in this exciting pan-European commerce of musical ideologies and developments. Indeed, just as throughout the western world social change undermined the old order, across the island of Ireland there was a surge of political, social, and revolutionary reformism with permanent and far reaching consequences.[23]

This so-called 'group' of composers did not form a homogeneous entity in terms of a specific musical aesthetic. Indeed, Buckley suggests that they developed their own individual style and technique both in accordance with and in opposition to each other, and each went on to create his and her own individual responses to *avant-garde* trends. However, they did share a desire to openly embrace an international modernism, and none of them felt compelled to look within Irish traditional music as a basis for composition. Aware that they would face considerable challenges in having their new music performed, they formed the Association of Young Irish Composers (AYIC). 'The AYIC', Buckley recalls,

> emerged from a series of informal meetings in the early 1970s, arising from the Dublin Festival of 20th Century Music, the most significant such festival ever to take place in Ireland. As a group of young and

---

[22] The European Economic Community (EEC) was founded with the signing of the Treaty of Rome in 1957 and became the European Union (EU) with the Maastricht Treaty of 1992.

[23] Interestingly, at the same period, a similar surge in activity around contemporary poetry took place in Ulster when a new generation of young poets emerged to form what became known as the Belfast Group. This was a gathering of eclectic voices united only by the social and political times of which they were part. It included such figures as Ciaran Carson, Seamus Deane, Seamus Heaney, Michael Longley, Derek Mahon, Paul Muldoon and Frank Ormsby. For a history of this development see Heather Clarke, *The Ulster Renaissance: Poetry in Belfast, 1962-1972* (London: Oxford University Press, 2006).

aspiring composers, we set about organizing concerts of our music for a largely unsuspecting and generally indifferent public. It was not unusual, in the early years, for performing musicians to outnumber audience members. We were truly freelance composers in the sense of booking halls, begging musicians to play, and persuading friends and the general public to attend. Press reviews, as might be expected, ranged from indifference to hostility.

Raymond Deane describes the camaraderie of this group:

> We were actually a very companionable bunch of people [...] So it was very pleasant from that point of view. We performed each other's music. There was a lot of co-operation and a lot of collaboration. We did have this illusion of public interest [...] it wasn't completely an illusion, but it didn't last.[24]

Deane's comments illustrate the limited success the AYIC had. Alongside Deane and Buckley, those in the AYIC included Derek Ball (1949), Gerald Barry (1952), Brian Beckett (1950), David Byers (1947), Roger Doyle (1949), Jerome de Bromhead (1945), Jane O'Leary (1946), Phillip Hammond (1951) and Denise Kelly (1954). The AYIC promoted and presented concerts throughout the country and conducted numerous radio interviews, broadcasts and workshops. However, the organization in the early days had limited resources and consequently its effectiveness was, despite some progress, inhibited. In 1976, the AYIC was renamed the Association of Irish Composers and amalgamated with composers of all ages.

As a result of the AYIC experiment, Buckley became very active in the promotion of new music. He had been elected treasurer of the AYIC and soon became a member of the artistic committee for the Dublin Festival of 20th Century Music. Given Irish society's general lack of interest in their goals, most Irish composers had little choice but to promote their own music. Buckley was no different in this regard, and he found himself obliged to employ all his powers of persuasion in an attempt to secure performances of his music. He came to realize that his attendance at concerts also gave him an opportunity to lobby prospective performers, whom he would approach in an attempt to interest them in his work. He recalls one particular occasion, when, following a concert given by the RTÉ Singers, he approached their conductor, Hans Waldemar Rosen (1904-1994). 'I managed to get talking to him after the concert.' Buckley recalls,

> I said, 'I'm a composer,' and he said, 'Oh that's great, you must show

---

[24] Taken from an interview held in public at the Contemporary Music Centre in Dublin conducted by the present writer to mark Raymond Deane's 50th birthday. Sources: Recording in the CMC sound archives.

me something some time', and I said, 'Yes, I have it here,' and pulled a score out from inside my coat and made him take it and I could see the look of dismay on his face, but he took it, and within a year the RTÉ Singers were performing that piece [*Auburn Elegy*], and did it on quite a number of occasions in the early seventies.

Buckley was also fortunate in arousing the interest of oboist Lindsay Armstrong and pianist Gillian Smith in his *Sonata for Cor Anglais and Piano*, which they performed at the 1974 Dublin Festival of 20th Century Music, the first professional performance his music received. Unlike most of Buckley's later music, the work's traditional pastoral style pays homage to a British precedent: as noted, his first important influence is Vaughan Williams. 'Quite a number of the early pieces' Buckley states, 'have an elegiac pastoral quality to them, like the *Cor Anglais Sonata* and *Auburn Elegy*.'[25] That pastoral quality guaranteed success, and the piece has continued to find favour since. 'Mr. Buckley's cor anglais sonata is a work of real charm and delight,' *The Irish Times* critic Charles Acton commented. He added with naïvety (given the difficulties Irish composers experienced in getting published), 'I am only surprised that no wind publisher has yet taken it.'[26]

The Dublin Festival of 20th Century Music gave Buckley his first formal commission in 1977. He responded with *'Why Not?' Mr. Berio* (trombone and piano), which was premiered on 12 January the following year at the Festival by trombonist Sean Cahill and pianist Veronica McSwiney. The style of this work differs sharply from the earlier pastoral pieces and displays a decisive move into more adventurous territory. As noted, it was Doris Keogh, his flute teacher, who had a strong influence in fostering this stylistic shift. Buckley's study of Berio's *Sequenza I* with Keogh opened up a new world of compositional possibilities. Perhaps now *'Why Not?' Mr. Berio* seems an immature pun on the outburst 'Why?' that Berio wrote into his trombone *Sequenza V*, but, along with *Wind Quintet*, it does symbolize aptly the directional shift towards modernism that Buckley was taking at the time.

---

[25] Michael Dervan, 'Taking the Strain', *The Bridge* (Winter 1986).
[26] Charles Acton, *The Irish Times*, 19 September 1979.

SELECTED ANALYSIS

Three important early works, *Sonata for Cor Anglais and Piano*, *Three Pieces for Solo Flute* and *Wind Quintet*, demonstrate the broad influences on Buckley as a student. These compositions highlight his gradual shift from initial dependence on pastoral and neo-classical models to experiments with more modernist modes of expression.

Sonata for Cor Anglais and Piano

Sonata for Cor Anglais and Piano is listed as the first work in Buckley's catalogue of compositions. Written in three movements – 'Molto moderato', 'Allegro moderato' and 'Scherzando, allegro commodo' – the work clearly demonstrates Wilson's influence. This manifests itself both in its lyrical pastoralism and in its spiky neo-classicism à la Stravinsky, Hindemith and Bartók. Though sonata by name, the music does not follow the prescribed structural outline of classical sonata form, but rather develops its material through the generation of small melodic motifs. Largely constructed of triads, the work is loosely tonal. However, designating a home key is difficult as the modal meanderings of the piece often direct the music towards incongruous harmonic areas before familiar tonal regions are established.

The staccato rhythms of the piano announce the second movement's quirky neo-classicism. Despite the optimistic start, only twenty-six bars of this animated material are heard before it is halted rather suddenly. Arrested development of this type is a common shortfall in many student works. Thus, the elaboration of the musical argument has been postponed in favour of a cadenza and a return to pastoral calm, which has the unfortunate effect of diffusing the energy created at the outset. Although the composer attempts to recuperate a rhythmic verve, the movement finishes before it can be fully achieved.

Intended to serve as the development of the second movement, the third movement, a clever *moto perpetuo*, is similar enough in character to preclude significant contrast, although it does maintain a convincing rhythmic drive through to the end, which holds the listener's attention. As a student work, *Sonata for Cor Anglais and Piano* should be assessed in light of its strengths rather than its weaknesses. The work demonstrates cleverly controlled tonal ambiguity and an imaginative focus on the motivic material used to project the musical argument.

Early Works (1973-1976)   25

The first movement is perhaps the strongest of the three and a closer observation highlights strengths in Buckley's early writing. Bar 7 contains the two main melodic motifs of the movement:

[Note: All instruments are in concert pitch in all the following musical examples.]

Ex. 1: *Sonata for Cor Anglais and Piano*, movement I, bar 7 (cor anglais part)

In the second of these (motif B), the intervals that rise from the root note d',[27] alternating from a semitone to e♭' to a tone to e♮', act as further agents of ambiguity. Consequently, whenever motif B recurs, it undermines the tonal centres upon which it operates. In the right-hand piano part of bar 15, the e''' natural of motif B clashes with the E♭ harmony played by the left-hand.

Ex. 2: *Sonata for Cor Anglais and Piano*, movement I, bar 15

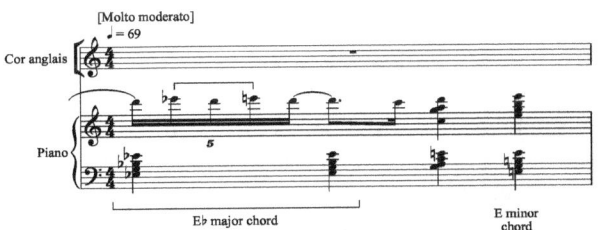

Although tonal dubiety is central to the work, it is sometimes loosely controlled and modulations occur abruptly. However, bars 12 and 13 demonstrate Buckley's efficacious handling of bi-tonal constructions. The two main motifs are knitted into the musical argument of the entire

---

[27] Helmholtz pitch notation is used here and subsequently. For example, d' indicates the note D immediately above middle C.

movement: on the third beat of bar 12, motif A (cor anglais), which is essentially a figuration on E minor, is superimposed on an E♭13 chord in the piano. On the other hand, Motif B (again, cor anglais) in the next beat, with its undulating f' and f♯' notes, continues the tonal ambiguity against the C9 chord in the piano. The following bar (13) sees the cor anglais melody finishing on a sustained e', while the piano offers an arpeggio that starts in E major, providing a suitable tonal accompaniment. However, the E tonality is immediately obfuscated when the arpeggio shifts to an E♭ major triad. Thus, the passage displays Buckley's effective control of bi-tonal harmonic complexes.

Ex. 3: *Sonata for Cor Anglais and Piano*, movement I, bars 12-13

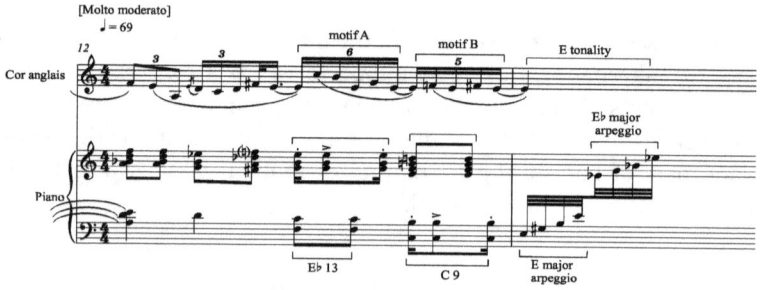

Three Pieces for Solo Flute

Three Pieces for Solo Flute dates from 1973 and represents Buckley's earliest embrace of a more contemporary style. Premiered by Derek Moore on 26 April 1974 in Trinity College Dublin, this impressive, well-crafted work is only the third listed in his catalogue of compositions and can therefore be considered quite an achievement. The work displays the influence of Buckley's flute teacher Doris Keogh, with whom he had been studying major contemporary flute works such as Berio's *Sequenza I*. Similarly, Bruno Bartolozzi's treatise on extended techniques for wind instruments, *New Sounds for Woodwind*, aided in his research.[28] Although *Three Pieces for Solo Flute* demonstrates many modernist characteristics, with its expansive dynamic range, numerous

---

[28] Bruno Bartolozzi, *New Sounds for Woodwind* (London: Oxford University Press, 1967).

wide leaps in pitch and its essentially atonal character, an inherent lyricism is never lost.

Piece I: Through-composed, the first piece demonstrates Buckley's early freedom in relation to formal structure. Despite this, its quasi-improvisatory phrases have 'question and answer' type formations and other quasi-symmetrical figurations that create subtly structured contours. Two phrases are composed over the opening five bars: the second of these answers the first in a loose retrograde shape. The first phrase extends from c" to high g♭'" (on the first crotchet of bar 3), and is answered by the second phrase starting with f' on the second beat of bar 3, which extends to the repeated d' notes of bar 5. The leap to the high g♭'" (bar 3) is answered by a corresponding descent to the low d' (bar 5), while the arc of the quintuplets of bar 2 is reversed in the demisemiquavers of bar 4.

Ex. 4: *Three Pieces for Solo Flute*, **movement I, bars 1-5**

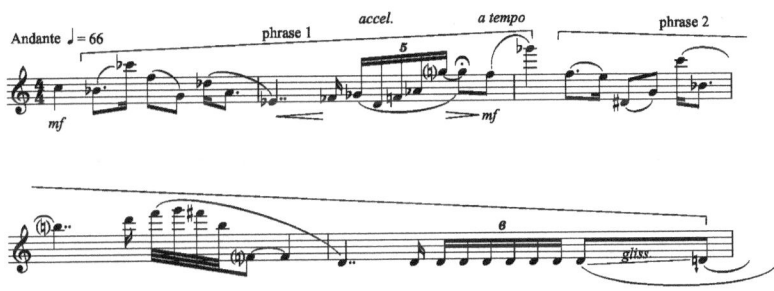

Starting on the second beat of bar 17, Buckley constructs four phrases that fall into two groups of two, each of which is delineated by a new dynamic marking. Though freely constructed (there are no exact sequences), the rhythmic consistency and relative conformity of each phrase (excepting a minor extension to the last one) creates a controlling influence. These compositional techniques demonstrate Buckley's skill in crafting subliminally regulated phrases.

Ex. 5: *Three Pieces for Solo Flute*, movement I, bars 17-21

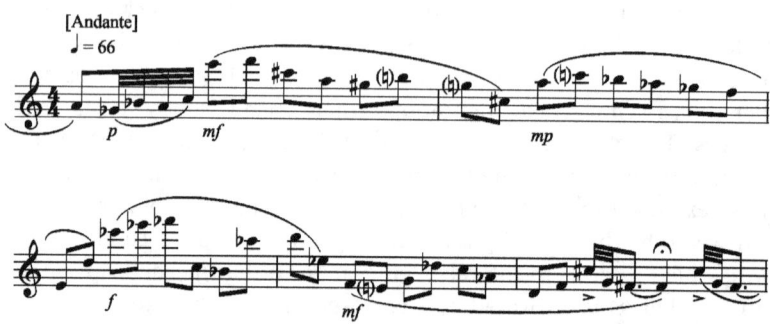

Piece II: This movement is the most adventurous of the three pieces, and for long periods explores the thin higher register of the instrument. The emphasis on wide pitch leaps, repeated *ff* notes, sustained use of staccato notes covering vast intervallic distances, use of micro-tonal techniques, and the shifting time signatures demonstrate the work's uncompromising modernist credentials, which are only occasionally betrayed by some lyrical phrases.

Ex. 6: *Three Pieces for Solo Flute*, movement II, bars 17-32

Piece III: Following the modernism of the second piece, Buckley returns to more lyrical territory in the third. The general mood of the movement invokes Debussy's *Prélude à l'Après-Midi d'un Faune* and maintains a more sustained emphasis on creating tonal centres through the reiteration of sustained pitches, typically at the end of phrases. The use of accents and dynamic markings further highlights these pitch centres. From bar 24, for example, a held c♯" is reiterated up an octave four more times over just three bars.

Ex. 7: *Three Pieces for Solo Flute*, movement III, bars 24-26

An important work in Buckley's early output, *Three Pieces for Solo Flute* tested his affiliations – a stark modernist urge is counterpoised with a lyrical pastoralism. Though its loose formal contours were, after some time, replaced by more rigorous structural schemata, the work is an important early indicator of Buckley's stance in relation to these influences: his music still insists upon a committed post-tonality inflected with nascent expressiveness.

Wind Quintet

Written in 1976 (revised in 1985), *Wind Quintet* represents the final stage of Buckley's student phase. Despite its lingering nostalgia for a tonal lyricism, it demonstrates a brave willingness to embrace many compositional techniques of the *avant-garde* in a more comprehensive way than previously attempted. Throughout the work, Buckley incorporates advanced aleatoric systems, numerous extended techniques and a use of micro-tonal procedures. However, the adoption of quasi-improvised rhythmic figurations, created by the manipulation of lip pressure and the use of alternative fingerings, establishes the work so strongly in an atonalism governed by timbral and rhythmic concerns that the appearance of more traditionally harmonic sections occasionally creates an evident stylistic unease.

Though it is not possible to analyse *Wind Quintet* in terms of defined tonality, the middle slow movement is, however, directed by tonal-based harmonic progressions. In contrast, the two outer movements are typically driven by contrapuntal devices. The central movement glances back to a pastoral world: the chorale-like harmonic phrases are inter-linked with florid solos on the flute and cor anglais, recalling *Sonata for Cor Anglais and Piano*. This traditional setting breaks off for a more experimental central section that generates three separate linear entities simultaneously pursuing distinctly different material. However, the simple A-B-A coda structure of the work returns the music to its opening pastoral material.

The cleverly humorous third movement pays tribute to the more experimental works of Charles Ives. The most successful of the three in terms of continuity, it consistently sustains a post-modernist attitude throughout. Near the end, the work quotes the tune *Yankee Doodle* – a reference to the American War of Independence, the bi-centenary of which was being celebrated in 1976 (the year *Wind Quintet* was written). Though Ives was a serial quoter, his influence can be traced to more than just the *Yankee Doodle* reference. Ives's *The Unanswered Question* was among the first works to juxtapose distinct musical textures and tempi. Furthermore, it superimposes tonal and non-tonal procedures, which provides an important precedent for Buckley.

The first movement of *Wind Quintet* falls into seven connected sections as follows:

Fig. 1: *Wind Quintet*, movement I, structural plan

> Opening flute solo (unmetred)
> Flute and oboe duologue (independent tempi)
> Rehearsal letter B (clarinet, horn and bassoon entry)
> Rehearsal letter D (tutti)
> Rehearsal letter E (multiple tempi)
> Rehearsal letter F (uniform tempo)
> Rehearsal letter G (coda)

[Note: the grouping here does not always follow the same outline as the rehearsal letters of the score, which is in concert pitch throughout.]

Section I: This section opens with a flute solo, and its quasi-improvisatory manner releases it from controlling time signatures. In the six systems of this section, the flute plays predominantly in its high register and explores micro-tonal and extended trill techniques in strongly gestural phrases dominated by expansive leaps and dissonant intervals (minor and major 2nds and their compounds and complements). These intervals (bracketed in the musical example) occur at the opening and provide the pitch characteristics for the entire movement.

Ex. 8: *Wind Quintet*, movement I, systems 2 and 3 (flute part)

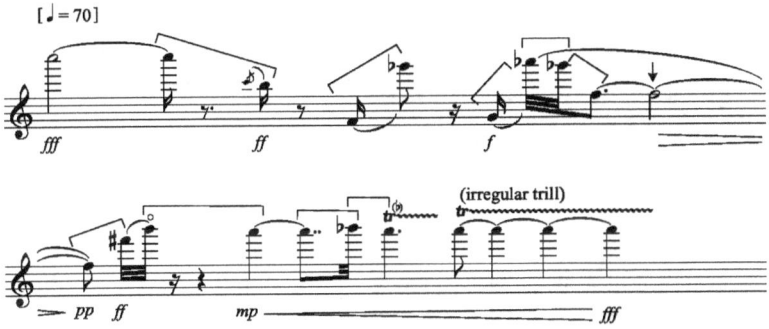

Section 2: This section introduces the oboe into the musical argument and instigates a duologue with the flute, thereby creating a character of free interplay. At rehearsal letter A, where the heading states 'Independent Tempi', Buckley explores a restricted aleatoricism with the employment of some extended techniques. Limited aleatoricism has remained a feature of his work, and he has never allowed the performer to exercise complete control over the musical materials. In this case, the flautist must replace a specifically written note (g' displaying a triangle notehead) with a succession of rapidly executed note groups that weave around the given note. The original note can be manipulated in this way by the technique of 'over-blowing' (that is, the variation of air pressure) so that different overtones of the harmonic series can be attained from the fundamental note. By employing this technique, the octave of the fundamental (g"), its twelfth (d''') and its double octave (g''') become the principle points around which the note groups are rapidly executed. Buckley constructs these overblown notes in different rhythmic combinations, resulting in a highly effective elaboration of rapid melismatic figurations. Although these passages seem to be freely

improvised, they are, in fact, highly controlled and structured by the composer.

Ex. 9: *Wind Quintet*, movement I rehearsal mark A (flute part)

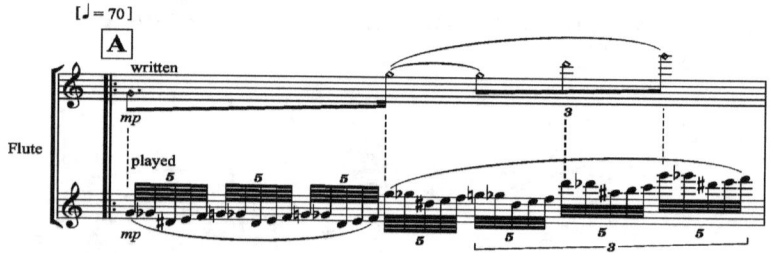

The quasi-improvisatory flute music is superimposed upon the oboe line. Though the oboe part is notated fully, it offers opportunities for extemporization in relation to its dynamics and articulation, which are governed by graphic instructions placed under the oboe's semibreve. The superimposition of distinct linear entities forms the compositional intention. The pitch relationships within the material given to each instrument remain consistent. However, as the instruction is for 'Independent Tempi', neither the amalgamation of the combined pitches nor the resultant harmony can ever be exactly determined or repeated in successive performances. The nature of Buckley's highly controlled aleatoric techniques allows for a certain level of differentiation within the work.

Section 3: This music comes as something of a surprise in terms of stylistic continuity, and is perhaps a direct result of the influence of Ives – a great exemplar in the juxtaposition of highly differentiated musical materials. In *Wind Quintet*, the music at rehearsal mark B for clarinet, horn and bassoon is chorale-like and quasi-tonal; the introduction of time signatures and bar lines for the first time further binds the music to a more traditional structural format. Emerging from the chorale-like opening, the writing develops a syncopated bounce that drives the music towards the presentation of a significant theme-motif situated on three upbeats (one bar after rehearsal mark C).

Early Works (1973-1976)   33

Ex. 10: *Wind Quintet*, movement I, one bar after rehearsal mark C (main theme motif)

Section 4: The fourth section provides a substantial amount of musical development. The quintet is divided into two linear entities: the original duet (flute and oboe) and a trio of clarinet, horn and bassoon, the latter group providing an independent support for the instruments above it. These groupings engage in a dialectical argument that provides a rhythmically intricate and powerfully energizing moment in the work. The theme-motif appears amid the improvisatory figurations of the first grouping. The second grouping plays in identically rhythmic formulations, but the intervallic relationships between clarinet and horn alter continuously from perfect fourths (to perfect fifths), to major thirds, to minor thirds, further indicating that each grouping pursues its own harmonic logic separately from the other.

Ex. 11: *Wind Quintet*, movement I, rehearsal mark D (clarinet and horn parts)

The complexity of the resultant rhythmic formulations when all the strands are heard simultaneously provides the interest in this section. Although dense in its entirety, the nature of the juxtaposition of each strand allows for the theme-motif to be heard quite clearly.

Section 5: This section realigns the instrument groupings: flute and oboe forming one pair, clarinet and bassoon another, and horn playing solo. Independent tempi are allocated to each grouping:

Fig. 2

Group 1: (flute & oboe) crotchet = 70
The flute reworks material from its solo in Section 1 while the oboe reiterates the main theme-motive.
Group 2: (clarinet & bassoon) crotchet = 66
This group provides an inter-linking ostinato line around which the other groups oscillate
Group 3: (horn) crotchet = 66–74
The horn focuses on rhythmic and pitch fragments heard previously (predominantly seconds and sevenths.)

Although the music for all the groups is fully notated, the use of restricted aleatoric techniques and the multiple temporality creates a flexible and complex interplay of parts. Given the potential for confusion, the type of material allocated to each group demonstrates Buckley's efforts to maintain consistency. Although the entities are just distinct enough to allow three separate arguments to be heard, elements of confusion inevitably do arise. As if to compensate for this potential confusion, the music suddenly ceases and all five instruments return to an identical rhythmic grouping (one bar after rehearsal mark F) outlining the syncopated main theme motif heard earlier, thus restoring order, if just for a while.

Ex. 12: *Wind Quintet*, **movement I, rehearsal mark F**

Section 6: Following the brief solidarity of Ex. 12, the music in Section 6 (lasting just seven bars) dissipates into fragmented figurations: the theme motif spreads across all instruments of the quintet, using the technique of *Klangfarbenmelodie* resulting in a new timbral colouration.

Section 7: This section provides the coda for the movement. Against a series of chorale-like chords, the oboe and bassoon melodically outline the characteristic intervals of the minor second and the major seventh. The resultant interplay closes the movement in acquiescent beauty. The minor second acts as a central feature: the entire movement opens and closes using this interval. The final two notes heard together (F♯ on the flute and F on the bassoon) further indicate the predominance of the interval as a unifying element.

Wind Quintet represents an audacious move forward for the young composer, directing him toward the first of his mature modernist works. Although it continues to display traits of traditional quasi-tonal writing, *Wind Quintet* betrays no hint of the overt use of traditional

Irish materials suggested in some earlier works such as *Keoghal*. The superimposition of distinct linear entities is boldly achieved. However, unlike Ives's *The Unanswered Question*, which clearly distinguishes separate elements not only texturally (brass, strings and woodwind) but also spatially, *Wind Quintet* makes these delineations less successfully, not having the benefit of distinct instrumental categories or spatial positioning. Furthermore, the conscious development of harmonic formulations takes second place to the results gleaned from the superimposition of separate contrapuntal and timbral entities. The work remains significant, however, in that it clearly inaugurates a new phase for Buckley.

3 | Between the Celtic and the Avant-garde (1977-1987)

PART 1: TOWARDS IRELAND

Recognition

In 1976, Buckley submitted his recently composed *Wind Quintet* for the prestigious Varming Prize: a competition for young composers organized by the Music Association of Ireland. Written for a composer workshop at the Project Arts Centre in Dublin, the aleatoric nature of the work and its novel sounds prompted one critic to describe it as an exploration of '*recherché* sonorities'.[29] *Wind Quintet* was awarded the Prize, which included a performance by the internationally renowned Danish Wind Quintet at the 1978 Dublin Festival of 20th Century Music. A subsequent performance took place in Copenhagen. As noted, it marks the moment Buckley's personal voice emerges. Following *Wind Quintet*, Wilson felt that he could no longer help the young experimentalist who wanted to break new ground (particularly in the area of timbre and aleatoricism) and recommended he seek inspiration from abroad.

Buckley's success with the Varming Prize was followed by another major development. In 1978, he was awarded the prestigious Macaulay Fellowship.[30] Buckley submitted six scores with his application, which

---

[29] Douglas Sealy, *The Irish Times*, 14 October 1997.
[30] The Macaulay Foundation was established in 1958 by William J.B. Macaulay in honour of a former President of Ireland, Seán Tomás Ó Ceallaigh (1882-1966). The Fellowship, administered by the Arts Council of Ireland, is designed to

was sent to the English composer Richard Rodney Bennett for independent assessment. The report was very positive: 'Mr. Buckley shows a remarkable gift of writing a well-poised score [...] His brass quintet is especially outstanding regarding inventiveness and form control.' Bennett's only adverse criticism was of a 'symphony' that Buckley had included in the portfolio. This work, he said, 'showed a facet of his talents which I do not like: too much of everything. I hope this is a sign of his evolution.'[31] Nevertheless, despite these reservations, he recommended that the young composer should go abroad and study with György Ligeti, Ton de Leeuw or Klaus Huber.

Studies at Cardiff

The Fellowship award, which had a value of about £3,000 (quite a substantial amount of money at the time), presented Buckley with a number of opportunities. Many of his colleagues from the Association of Young Irish Composers had already gone abroad – Gerald Barry and Raymond Deane had moved to Germany. With a wife and young child to consider (his daughter Deirdre was born in 1978), it was considerably more difficult for Buckley to pack his bags and head to Europe than it was for Deane and Barry. Furthermore, the Department of Education offered no opportunities for taking extended leave, and Buckley would have lost his job had he left for even six months. The music critic Fanny Feehan publicly addressed the absurd situation of one statutory body supporting a young artist while another foils him: 'But if Mr. Buckley were to go away as previous [Macaulay Fellowship] winners did, Ó Duinn to Antal Doratia (sic.), Bodley to Egon Wellesz,' she wrote, 'the unfortunate man would lose his job because he is employed by the Department of Education as a teacher [...]. The Minister for Education, Mr. John Wilson [...] may not know it, but unlike writers, composers are very thin on the ground.'[32]

Buckley had, at this time, written to a number of composers whose music interested him, including the English composer and pianist John McCabe. Eventually, on the recommendation of Colman Pearce, he decided to study on a part-time basis with Alun Hoddinott, who was

---

further the liberal education of the recipient. It is offered on a rotating basis based upon previously completed work by artists from all disciplines.

[31] From an appraisal written by Richard Rodney Bennett for the awarding of the Macaulay Fellowship, administered by the Arts Council of Ireland. Source: photocopy in possession of John Buckley.

[32] Fanny Feehan, 'Shortsightedness is the only word', *Irish Independent*, 1978. The correct spelling is: Antal Doráti.

then Professor of Music at the University of Cardiff. Hoddinott was one of the foremost British composers of his generation. Born in Bargoed, Glamorganshire, in 1929, he graduated from University College Cardiff and subsequently studied with the Australian composer and pianist Arthur Benjamin. He was awarded the Walford Davies prize when he was twenty-four, and achieved national success a year later when his *Clarinet Concerto* was given its first performance at the Cheltenham Festival by Gervase de Peyer and the Hallé Orchestra, under Sir John Barbirolli. In 1951, he was appointed lecturer in music at the Welsh College of Music and Drama; he later became lecturer at University College Cardiff and was made Professor and Head of Department there in 1967.

While his Irish contemporaries such as Barry, Corcoran and Deane went to Germany to embrace the new trends, Buckley's trips to Wales provided the engagement with modernism he sought.[33] If the piano work *Oileáin* epitomized Hoddinott's Celtic influence on Buckley, the starkly modernist *Sonata for Unaccompanied Violin* of 1983 emerged as a direct result of Hoddinott's influence in organizing structure. 'Your paragraphs are far too short,' Buckley remembers being advised, 'you are taking short breaths, try to breathe in longer paragraphs. Imagine broader architectural outlines.' Motivic development, particularly within the paradigm of non-tonal harmonic canvasses, was also a major point of discussion. Hoddinott explained the linear development and expansion of small motifs into broader shapes and paragraphs, how those paragraphs are shaped into longer sectional divisions and, in turn, how they are shaped into movements and from movements into complete works.

Commentators have been quick to identify in Hoddinott's music certain qualities suggesting a Celtic resonance. Basil Deane, for example, writing in 1978, remarks on the

> dominant characteristics in Hoddinott's music that betray a Celtic rather than an Anglo-Saxon temperament: obsessive drive, sombre brooding, rhetorical lyricism, fiery outbursts, and, embracing all these, a love of language itself, a delight in virtuosic manipulation of the means of communication.[34]

Characterized by its delicate use of timbre, his orchestral writing employs dramatic percussion colouring and sumptuous textures

---

33 Frank Corcoran initially went to Berlin in 1980. He now lives and teaches in Hamburg.
34 Basil Deane, ed. Roy Bohana, *Alun Hoddinott – Composers of Wales 2* (Cardiff: University of Wales Press, 1978).

wrought from multi-divided strings – sonorities which profoundly influenced Buckley. Furthermore, Hoddinott was strongly inspired by visual imagery, particularly in relation to light, as the titles of several of his later works attest: *The Sun, the Great Luminary of the Universe* (1970), *Landscapes* (1975), *The Heaventree of Stars* (1980) and *Lanterne des morts* (1981). These traits would in time form a central aspect of Buckley's compositional concerns. 'I suppose I enjoyed his sheer ability to handle instrumental forces', he stated in an interview from 1986. 'Even still, when I listen to works like his *Third Symphony* or *The Sun, The Great Luminary of the Universe*, I'm very struck by his orchestral ability.'[35] The young composer studied with Hoddinott in a private capacity, taking classes at the composer's home. He found these sessions most productive and the two quickly established a rapport, which may well have been nurtured by their shared Celtic background: Hoddinott would often refer to 'our common Celtic heritage'.

Myth and Modernism

Buckley's position vis-à-vis Celticism is of particular interest considering his personal background. Despite an early introduction to traditional Irish music, he never felt compelled to use folk materials as a source of inspiration for his work, believing that this reclamation had been achieved largely by previous composers. He states,

> By the 1970s, the expressive potential of Irish folk music had been fully exhausted by composers such as Potter [1918-1980], John F. Larchet [1884-1967], Arthur Duff [1889-1956] and Hamilton Harty [1879-1941], and through innumerable arrangements of traditional Irish tunes by Carl Hardebeck [1869-1945], Éamonn Ó Gallchobhair [1900-1982], Walter Beckett [1914-1996] and others, and so didn't seem to offer any potential for further development along the lines I wished to pursue. Folk music didn't lend itself to the musical imagination and ambitions I had then.

Although later composers like Bodley did attempt to subsume traditional Irish materials into a broader atonal canvas, Buckley felt he could not take this route. Describing the choices available to his generation, he states: 'Many of those composers studied abroad, and those who didn't study abroad full-time like myself, drew our influences from the models of the European *avant-garde*. And of that generation very few, if any, were drawn towards traditional or Celtic models.'

---

[35] Michael Dervan, 'Taking the Strain', *The Bridge* (Winter 1986).

However, this reluctance to use traditional or folk music precedents did not prevent Buckley from leaning heavily on Gaelic mythology as a source of inspiration for his own post-tonal harmonies, as *Taller than Roman Spears* (1977, rev. 1986), *Oileáin* (1979), *Boireann* (1983) and *I Am Wind on Sea* (1987) aptly demonstrate. *Taller than Roman Spears* and *Oileáin*, in particular, followed on from earlier Irish composers who had made use of mythological sagas, such as Brian Boydell, in his incidental music to Pádraic Fallon's play *The Wooing of Étaín* (1954) and in his *Megalithic Ritual Dances* (1956), and James Wilson, in his 1970 monodrama *The Táin*. In this sense, Buckley followed a trajectory for which there was, at least, some precedent. While these works were not without some modernist characteristics, Buckley extended these procedures to a much greater degree. That he mined his Celtic heritage for inspiration while circumventing both classical tonality and traditional Irish music remains one of the most interesting facets of his work from this period.

Buckley felt that the neutrality of post-tonality and modernist processes offered the only adequate musical medium to reflect an ancient Irish past. Most of the nineteenth- and early twentieth-century musical styles carry political baggage because of their close association with the nationalist cause. In contrast, Buckley's modernist approach allows for access to the Celtic past without romanticizing it or using this access for political purposes. Buckley still rejects as misconceived any unexamined assumption that nineteenth- or early twentieth-century folk-inspired music is the ideal vehicle for cultural renovation. In his use of post-tonal music and Irish mythology, Buckley shares common ground with fellow-Irish composer Frank Corcoran (though each worked independently). Corcoran explains:

> I have, mostly, avoided the trap of using traditional Irish material in my work – quotation, parody, etc., have all had their day. But from very early on in my career as a composer, I have wanted to tap into the Irish psychic well. My *Medieval Irish Epigrams* [1973] were written nearly twenty-five years before I tackled *Mad Sweeney* in Seamus Heaney's English version, yet it, too, is fascinated by the fascinating and mysterious hundred years (roughly) of sixth-century Ireland with its saints and druids and schizophrenic interfacing of Christianity and a late Iron Age heroism. All the *Sweeney*-triggered works, and my more recent *Quasi* series, are a result of a filtering irony that continues to handle what comes up from that psychic well.[36]

Thus, in the hands of both Buckley and Corcoran, ancient Celtic mythology found a new expression through contemporary musical

---

36 Frank Corcoran, e-mail message to author, 11 February 2008.

language that rejected the narrative, social and political ramifications of traditional forms as heretofore used in Ireland. Buckley's music from this period has a cold abstraction, but also displays a jagged roughness that is 'immediately pungent and barbaric'.[37] It paints an epic barrenness of angular soundscapes as unforgiving as any Irish landscape. Most pertinently, it largely circumvents recent Irish traditional music and European classical tonality in an attempt to tap into trace memories of what Corcoran notably terms an 'Irish dream-landscape.'[38]

Where Buckley's music very occasionally suggests Irish folk elements (as in the second movement of *Taller than Roman Spears*, for example), those materials are subsumed and transformed into a totally modernist idiom. This process is not an arrangement or juxtaposition of folk elements, but acts as a sublimation of cultural influences. Stravinsky's *Le Sacre du Printemps,* with its incorporation of Russian folk material into a modernist context, exemplifies this method, as does Picasso's revolutionary *Demoiselles d'Avignon,* which forges a direct link to an ancient African primordialism. All these works cite or suggest elements they seek to purge. It should also be remembered that by the 1970s, most vestiges of nationalism or folk-inspired developments in international contemporary art music had all but vanished.

This search for a new post-tonal language in Ireland (which emanated from Europe) coincided with traditional Irish music's renaissance at the hands of Seán Ó Riada. However, it is noteworthy that Ó Riada, by far the most widely-known composer in Ireland, exerted no influence whatsoever on Buckley, or his peers, despite an abundance of published commentary citing his central position in Irish music circles. Buckley states on the subject:

> Ó Riada's influence as a composer on my own work was negligible, though I did follow with great interest the developments he was forging in the field of Irish traditional music. It was on this and film scores that his reputation rested at that period. As a composer, my inspiration and influence were drawn from the models of European modernity.

---

[37] Pat O'Kelly, *Irish Press*, 27 July 1978.
[38] Frank Corcoran: Introduction to his web site www.frankcorcoran.com (cited 23 August 2006).

SELECTED ANALYSIS

Taller Than Roman Spears

Bennett's report for the Macaulay Fellowship refers to a 'symphony', which was Buckley's first large-scale orchestral work and, in fact, entitled *Taller than Roman Spears*. The work received its premiere with the RTÉ Symphony Orchestra, conducted by Colman Pearce in the St Francis Xavier Hall on 26 July 1977. It is cast in four movements, each of which evokes one of the major rituals in the ancient Celtic calendar. Its title is taken from *The Celts*, a poem by the Irish nationalist writer Thomas D'Arcy Magee (1825-1868). The first stanza begins:

> Long, long ago, beyond the misty space
> Of twice a thousand years,
> In Erin old there dwelt a mighty race,
> Taller than Roman spears ...

The poem, which tells the stories of many Celtic figures, such as Fionn mac Cumhaill and Manannán mac Lir, set the ancient Irish context and offered Buckley a resonant image for a work inspired by ancient Celtic rituals. He only added the title after the work had been completed, and so it was used merely to evoke a Celtic past. The work re-envisages the four major Celtic rituals of the year – *Samhain, Imbolg, Bealtaine* and *Lughnasadh*.

The Celtic year is divided into two seasons: the light and the dark, at *Bealtaine* on 1 May and *Samhain* on 1 November. It is likely that *Samhain* was the more important festival, marking the beginning of a whole new cycle. The most potent time of the festival was November Eve, the night of 31 October, known today as Halloween. *Samhain* literally means 'summer's end.' *Imbolg* translates as 'ewe's milk', because the ewes at this time of the year are pregnant and start lactating. Known as a time for ritual purification, it is the halfway point between winter and spring, a time when animals are stirring from hibernation and plants are budding, even if much of the earth is still under a blanket of snow. It therefore represents awakening.

Bealtaine is celebrated around 1 May and the word still signifies the month of May in the Irish language. The astronomical date for this midpoint is slightly later, around 5 May, depending on the year. The festival marked the beginning of the pastoral summer season when the herds of livestock were driven out to summer pastures and grazing lands. The lighting of bonfires on mountains and hills on *Oíche Bhealtaine* (the eve of *Bealtaine*) was of ritual and political significance and may have been symbolic of the increasing power of the summer sun.

Lú was one of the chief gods of the *Tuatha Dé Danann* (people of the Goddess Danu) and was represented in mythological texts as a hero and High King. He was known for his skill with a sling and his prowess in many arts. The Celtic harvest ritual on 1 August took its name from *Lú*, giving us *Lughnasadh*, the Irish word for the month of August.

At this period of his creative output, the mythologies of the Celtic tradition offered Buckley a significant source of inspiration. However, *Taller than Roman Spears* is not an overtly programmatic work; instead, Celtic mythology provided him with an entry into a version of ancient Irish identity, which he explored through abstract musical deliberation.

'Samhain': A closer look at this movement will highlight some of the ways Buckley constructed his musical material orchestrally. The movement, lasting approximately six minutes, covers seventy-two bars and can be divided into fourteen parts. Although these sections do not outline the formal structure of the movement, they do show the relatively simple block complexes of orchestration Buckley uses.

Fig. 3: Formal Structure of 'Samhain'

1:	Bars 1–8	woodwind
2:	Bars 9–14	tuned percussion/bassoons
3:	Bars 15–16	woodwind
4:	Bars 17–20	percussion/horns
5:	Bars 21–25	woodwind/horns
6:	Bars 26–31.	woodwind/brass/strings
7:	Bars 31–33	bassoons/trumpets/trombones
8:	Bars 34–38	tutti
9:	Bars 38–47	strings
10:	Bars 48–49	percussion/strings
11:	Bars 50–53	woodwind/percussion/strings
12:	Bars 53–55	brass/percussion
13:	Bars 56–60	tutti
14:	Bars 60–72:	various instrumental groupings

This chart also demonstrates Buckley's control of climaxes and their juxtaposition against less intensely charged sections. For example, the expansion of instrumental groupings towards the extremity of the first tutti at section 8 is reduced immediately to the lyrical strings at section 9. He approaches formal construction both simply and effectively. Each section has a distinct sonic identity. The multiple combinations of these groups provide a variety of timbral possibilities to striking effect when fully amalgamated.

'Samhain' has two central rhythmic motifs. Rhythmic motif A is presented at the very beginning of the work and is heard as a series of accented chords on the oboes and clarinets.

Ex. 13: *Taller than Roman Spears*, movement I, bars 1-3 (oboes and clarinets)

This motif is played against the flutes using rhythmic notation identical to the opening of *Wind Quintet*. The resulting combination is strikingly similar to the orchestral sounds heard in Stravinsky's *Le Sacre du Printemps* ('Les augures printaniers'). The resemblance is even greater from bar 4 onwards when the rhythmic motif A is completed and the oboes and clarinets begin to play swirling semiquaver figurations. As both works take their thematic inspiration from mythological ritual, it should not be too surprising that Stravinky's *Rite* influenced the young Irish composer.

Rhythmic motif B is first heard on the xylophone in bar 12 and becomes the central punctuating force throughout the movement, occurring in its entirety twenty-seven times. The motif is also subjected to contrapuntal treatment in section 13 where it is distributed amongst the percussion and brass.

Ex. 14: *Taller than Roman Spears*, movement I, bar 12 (xylophone part)

The movement also uses micro-tonality in the strings. Starting at bar 26, Buckley subdivides first violins into twelve parts, second violins into ten, violas and cellos each into eight, and the basses into six. Each player is allocated a given note, resulting in a dense micro-tonal cluster.

Ex. 15: *Taller than Roman Spears*, movement I, bar 26

Having separately developed these three significant entities – rhythmic motif A, rhythmic motif B, and the micro-tonal string clusters – Buckley brings them together for the first tutti at section 8. Previously autonomous musical ideas are now juxtaposed in a moment of contrapuntal brilliance.

Ex. 16: *Taller than Roman Spears*, movement I, bar 34

Without dispensing with the movement's established sound entities, Buckley develops his material by altering the rhythmic ideas in ever more complex ways. At the second tutti (section 14: bars 56-60), the autonomy of each orchestral grouping has been established, but now the musical material within each grouping emerges more sophisticatedly, as exemplified in the interplay of material in the different sections. From bar 60 to the end of the movement (as outlined in Fig. 3), Buckley disintegrates the autonomous groupings in favour of a more complex, dispersed orchestration. The audacious control of musical material within a well-structured unit marks this movement as the most successful of the work.

The second movement 'Imbolg', dominated by the strings, is the most traditional of the four. Following introductory passages that share material between the strings and various woodwind instruments, the core of the movement starts at bar 19. With this movement, Buckley comes closest in his orchestral output to writing music inspired by traditional Irish music. While there are no direct quotes, the music conjures an atmosphere of traditional music with the appropriation of common rhythmic and melodic patterns typical of it, and with the incorporation of turns and grace notes reminiscent of traditional fiddle playing.

Ex. 17: *Taller than Roman Spears*, movement II, bar 19-23 (cello part)

Identifiable aspects of Irish music are consciously sublimated into a dense modernist texture. Indeed, the amalgamation of these labyrinthine melismas with the considerable rhythmic complexity of the accompaniment in the other string parts renders the resultant harmony obscure. The extreme level of harmonic density and rhythmic intricacy in the string writing verges on the counterproductive. The danger implicit in such elaborately wrought melodic combinations is that the individual characteristics of the lines remain undifferentiated and their interrelationships border on the arbitrary. However, there is also a distinct freshness here, an attempt not only to recognize the Irish elements of the theme but also to 're-cognize' an ancient Celtic identity through a modern European aesthetic.

The third movement, 'Bealtaine', is the most progressive and experimental of the entire work. The opening reintroduces micro-tonal string writing that acts as a backdrop to more accented punctuations on woodwind. Later in the score, these punctuations are reinforced by all the instruments stabbing furiously at the percussion solos, which, again, invite comparison with *Le Sacre*, this time with the last movement of the First Part, 'Danse de la terre'.

Between bars 8 and 11, Buckley creates a special notation for the strings: while rhythms are accurately notated, a number of graphic note-heads correlating to specific instructions are attached to the note-stems. These instructions include playing as high as possible, hitting the body of the instrument, playing arpeggios behind the bridge and tremolo on one string behind the bridge, and executing pizzicato and Bartók pizzicato techniques. The woodwind and brass employ numerous extended techniques to similar effect. This semi-aleatoric approach creates a chaotic and savage sound that conjures up the explosive fires lit during the festival of *Bealtaine*. The sheer aggression of these processes drives the music ferociously towards the centre of the movement, which is of a completely different character. Lasting three minutes approximately, it is co-ordinated entirely by a graphic chart.

Fig. 4: Conductor's Chart, central section of movement III

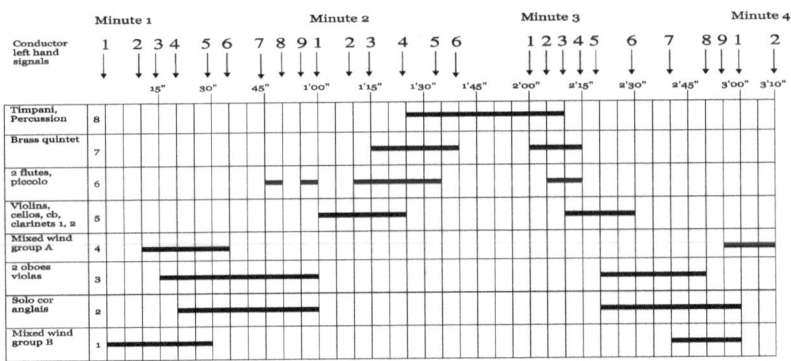

The orchestra is divided into eight distinct groups, each of which is given a fragment of musical material to be performed at the command of the conductor. This approach to aleatoric processes is Buckley's most advanced engagement in *avant-garde* techniques and, significantly, these experiments pre-date the composer's specific study of Lutoslawski and his aleatoric procedures that were to consciously inform the *Concerto for Chamber Orchestra* of 1981. Most significant is the type of musical material allocated to the groups and the timing of their entry and exit. Buckley gives groups 2, 3 and 4 material of a clearly tonal nature, while groups 1, 5, 6, 7 and 8 have decidedly atonal aggregates. This procedure sets up a mechanism through which, over a period of three minutes, the listener is taken from a tonal arena to a more distant, chaotic, atonal sphere (perhaps reminiscent of a cacophonous tribal assembly) and slowly back again. It further suggests a journey from the figurative to the abstract and vice versa, and imaginatively forces the listener to reassess accepted impressions and identifications of tonality. Following this section, the movement returns to the opening raucous Stravinskian punctuations, including the staccato chords that fade out to a *ppp* finish.

The short fourth movement, 'Lughnasadh' summarizes the three previous movements, a preoccupation that substantially reduces its ability to establish a distinct and separate identity. The rhythmic motif B at the core of *Samhain* reappears at bar 11, whilst the 'Irish' melody of 'Imbolg' returns in bar 28. A third melody drawn from the cor anglais solo of the third movement is further woven into the contrapuntal fabric. The reintroduction of the aggressive accented chords of 'Bealtaine' brings the work to a decisive, if rather abrupt, close. As an early work, *Taller than Roman Spears* is, despite its blemishes, a brave and fine achievement and represents Buckley's final direct connection to traditional Irish music as a potential source of inspiration.

Oileáin

Hoddinott's concern with the Celtic past resonated with Buckley, and the former's epic broodiness was reflected in the Irish composer's works from this period, such as *Oileáin* and *Boireann*.[39] The genesis of the former composition, in fact, lay in numerous discussions between the two about Celtic mythology. Many of the ideas they shared were outlined in a book owned by both composers called *Celtic Heritage – Ancient Tradition in Ireland and Wales*.[40] More than any other piece, *Oileáin* (islands) represents an alignment of their views and interests in Celticism as a source of inspiration for composition. Apart from offering advice on the subject matter, Hoddinott suggested a broader landscape for the work. The second movement's expansion of the musical argument across five staves illustrates this amplification. The work's breadth is matched by a visceral and aggressive ruggedness, and although Buckley generally will not be drawn into specific political arguments, this percussive and violent 'Celtic' music was a direct

---

[39] *Boireann* literally means 'rocky country', but refers to the area known as the Burren in north County Clare.
[40] Alwyn Rees and Brinley Rees, *Celtic Heritage – Ancient Tradition in Ireland and Wales* (London: Thames and Hudson, 1961).

response to the harrowing political situation of the Northern Troubles in those years. As one critic put it:

> The most striking aspect of Buckley's music is its extraordinary violence, all the piano music, with the exception of the straightforward *Lullabies for Deirdre*, make their point by attacking rather than by attracting, and the rawness of the emotion rarely allows time for quieter episodes. *Oileáin* (1979), written against the background of the conflict in the North, was as brutal as the times it mirrored.[41]

Oileáin is Buckley's first piece for solo piano. Its four movements come to approximately fifteen minutes and are so expansive in their construction and emotional conception that the work has the stature of a modern sonata. Thus, it represents a quantum leap in Buckley's control of structural schemata and his developing musical imagination. Written in 1979 under commission from Cardiff University, the work was premiered there on 3 May by one of Britain's leading pianists, Martin Jones.

More specifically, *Oileáin* signals Buckley's initial exploration and integration of a distinctly French style of piano writing. His attempts to absorb the techniques of Messiaen as a central influence (invoked in both spirit and method) into a broader, dissonant and more abrasive tableau are not always entirely successful. However, the work displays a newfound confidence in his ability to devise ample structural forms. Regarding nomenclature, the essentially programmatic aspects of *Oileáin* finally prevent us from applying the term sonata. This work belongs to a series of compositions Buckley wrote between 1979 and 1987 in which he attempted to conflate a Celtic inspiration with his developing contemporary voice. Not every work of this period falls into this category – the majority are, in a true sense, abstract modern compositions. However, he was drawn repeatedly towards the exploration of ancient Celtic mythology as a conduit for his contemporary European-influenced musical constructions, and a number of compositions written in these years reflect this interest.

Oileáin derives its inspiration from the famous Celtic saga of *The Voyage of Maeldúin*. Celtic mythology is awash with tales of voyages to islands. The voyage in the Celtic tradition is one of dimension, of transcending boundaries. The surviving legends of the *Immrama* (wonder voyages) offer the most graphic and detailed descriptions of journeys made to these imaginary islands. *The Voyage of Maeldúin's Boat* (*Immram Curaig Mhaeldúin*) was probably first composed in the eighth century, but is preserved in an eleventh-century manuscript

---

[41] Douglas Sealy, *The Irish Times*, 22 November 1995.

called the *Book of the Dun Cow* (*Lebor na hUidre*). Though only the middle section of the tale is extant, the full legend can be found in the *Yellow Book of Lecan* (*Leabhar Buídhe Lecaín*), dating from the fourteenth-century. The narrative tells how, after seeing his father's slayer on an island but being unable to land there, Maeldúin and his party are blown out to sea where they visit a great number of islands and have many strange adventures. The tale becomes a rich collection of stories and incidents in which Celtic and pre-Christian *peregrinatio* (pilgrimage stories) find resonance with Homeric tales of exploration. Although over thirty islands are visited in total, Buckley chose only four as a basis for *Oileáin*.

1) An Island of Beasts like Horses
This island was full of great beasts resembling horses that continually tore pieces of flesh from each other's sides. The island ran with blood. The adventurers rowed hastily away and were disheartened because they were lost.

2) An Island of Black Mourners
This island was full of black mourners constantly weeping and lamenting. One of Maeldúin's remaining foster-brothers landed there and immediately turned black and began weeping like the rest. Two men were sent to fetch him and they were struck by the same fate. Four more went with their heads wrapped in cloths so that they could not see the land or breathe the air. They seized two of the transformed men and carried them away by force, leaving behind the foster-brother.

3) An Island of Black and White
This island had a strong fence dividing it, with a flock of black sheep on one side and white sheep on the other. Between them was a man who tended the flocks. Sometimes he put a white sheep among the black, which became black at once, or a black sheep among the white, whereupon it immediately turned white (the same phenomenon is recorded as being witnessed by Peredur in the Welsh tale of that name in the *Mabinogion*). As an experiment, Maeldúin flung a white stick on the side where the black sheep were grazing. It turned black immediately and the adventurers fled in terror without ever landing on the island.

4) An Island whose People Shout 'It is they!'
When the voyagers arrived here they found the water splashing the high cliffs around the island and a crowd of people who screamed at them, 'It is they, it is they!' till they were out of breath. A woman came who pelted them with large nuts, which they gathered and took with them. As they went they heard the people crying to each other, 'Where are they now? They are gone away.' The islanders had a premonition of the adventurers and feared their arrival.

As in *Taller than Roman Spears*, the extent to which *Oileáin* tells the story of each island is open to debate. The opening low-register chords and the grotesque high dissonances of 'An Island of Beasts like Horses' might provide convincing imagery of savage brutishness. The stark repeated chords of 'An Island of Black Mourners' suggest a funeral cortège, while the use of 'white' notes against 'black' notes on the piano invokes 'An Island of Black and White'. The central section of 'An Island whose People Shout "It is they!"', where we are told that the sea was splashing the high cliffs, does provide a strong image of water, reminiscent of Debussy's 'Reflets dans l'eau' from *Images*. Movement I of *Oileáin* exemplifies many of the defining characteristics appearing throughout the complete work.

Despite the apparent extravagance of movement I, the compositional approach is relatively straightforward. The composer has written florid improvisatory commentaries around two prominent motifs, the first rhythmic and the second harmonic (of which there are two versions).

1) The rhythmic motif:

Ex. 18: *Oileáin*, movement I, bars 58-60

This rhythm is typically represented by chords built upon the diminished octave or the minor ninth, which are filled in with perfect and augmented fourths and fifths.

2) The harmonic motif in two versions: a) a broken chord figuration outlining a C centre (Ex. 19), and b) a similar broken chord figuration outlining an F centre (Ex. 20).

Ex. 19: *Oileáin*, movement I, bars 26-28

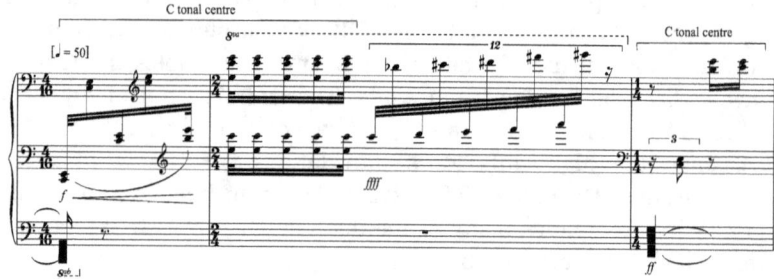

Ex. 20: *Oileáin*, movement I, bars 79-80

The first movement falls into three sections:

Fig. 5: Outlining structure of 'An Island of Beasts like Horses'

1) Introduction comprising ever-decreasing rhythmic units (bars 1-7).
2) Main section centred upon the rhythmic motif (Ex. 18) and establishing a tonal centre around C (bars 8-73)

3) Final (coda-like) section reiterating an F tonal centre interlaced with floating commentaries from distant tonal strata (bars 73-100).

The introductory section is constructed within a series of decreasing rhythmic gestures, giving the impression of exponential accumulation of the material. The section provides the opportunity for Buckley to bring together various characteristic features later subjected to development as outlined in figure 6.

Fig. 6: Characteristic features of material in bars 1-7

1) The opening C♯ in the bass, the basis of many of the low cluster chords
2) Cluster chords occurring sporadically throughout the work
3) Fast and widely dispersed chords and clusters striving to form the main rhythmic motif
4) C/E dyad tonal colouration pre-empting the later emergence of tonal focal points on C

1) Introduction (bars 1-7)
These four types of musical material are placed within rhythmic units and reduce from $8/16^{ths}$ (that is, eight semiquaver units) to $2/16^{ths}$.

Fig. 7: Rhythmic units of bars 1-7

Bar	1	2	3	4	5	6	7
Units	$8/16^{th}$	$8/16^{th}$	$6/16^{th}$	$8/16^{th}$	$8/16^{th}$	$3/16^{th}$	$2/16^{th}$

Within this narrowing metric field, the musical material must formulate itself into ever more rational harmonic and rhythmic entities. The music begins with low-register chord clusters that defy any sense of harmonic identity and regular pulse. Very quickly, however, more distinct fragments germinate, and by bar 8, the main rhythmic motif has crystallized in a manner similar to that shown in Ex. 18 above.

2) Main Section (bars 8-73)
The rhythmic motif formed for the first time at bar 8 repeats (and occasionally overlaps) no less than twelve times (bars 8-10; 15-17; 19-21; 21-23; 38-40; 41-43; 44-45; 58-60; 61/62; 67-69; 69-71 and finally 71-73). This repetition provides motivic stability to a movement of a generally extemporized nature. Between these rhythmic anchors,

Buckley counterpoises cluster chords, cascades of falling arpeggios and prolonged variants of the rhythmic motif providing the most aggressive and rhythmically intense moments. Typical of Buckley's early compositions inspired by mythology, *Oileáin* displays a relatively relaxed approach to formal structure, driven more by the primordial savagery of the Celtic-inspired subject matter. This movement shows a proclivity for sudden shifts of mood, with numerous tempo changes, many *accelerandi* and abrupt juxtapositions of contrasting musical material. The final appearance of the rhythmic motif marks a sudden modulation in mood and acts as a segue for the third, coda-like section.

3) Final Section (bar 73-100)

The music fluctuates around the tonal centre of F. This tonal anchor (see Ex: 20), repeated ten times in one form or another, intertwines with a florid lace of tonally incongruous notes, echoing Messiaen's similar use of polytonal techniques, notably in his *Vingt Regards sur l'Enfant Jésus*. Furthermore, Buckley adds reminiscences of the C/E dyad and the C♯ that initiated the whole movement. The music closes in a mood of unsettled calm. Dissonance in *Oileáin* plays a strongly independent role, as it is not heard as harmonic deviation from a given tonal centre, but rather as a non-consonant formulation enjoying a status distinct from any specific harmonic anchor. This particularly modernist French characteristic allows sound and pure timbre equal status with, and autonomy from, controlling factors such as voice leading and traditional harmonic theory. It also allows Buckley to interface thick chord clusters with tonal triads – a juxtaposition which correlates aptly with his chosen position of counterpoising the ancient (Celtic mythology) with the modern (European aesthetics).

Oileáin illustrates Buckley's attempts to reconcile his received tonal training with a developing post-tonal language, and Messiaen's piano music acts as a model for this symbiosis. Buckley's debt to the French master is exposed in the opening of 'An Island of Black Mourners': its repeated chords bound by a common note and governed by an enclosed geometry show the influence of Messiaen's 'Regard du Père' perhaps too directly.

Despite some minor concerns, the work shows Buckley's discovery of the piano and his joyously indulgent exploration of timbre, indicating a direction he would take in his later piano works. *Oileáin* displays a barbaric splendour and a percussive rawness (prominent in many of his Celtic-inspired compositions) that contradicts the refinement inherent in the French influence. This unique incongruity makes for strangely hybrid music and a disturbingly powerful ambiguity.

I Am Wind on Sea

An examination of Buckley's scores from the late 1980s reveals his increasing concern with devising unusual sonorities and his sensuous explorations of instrumental timbre. In this respect, a vocal work from 1987, *I Am Wind on Sea*, inaugurates a new phase in the composer's development – though it is, to date, the last of his scores to draw on the remote Celtic past for inspiration. He sets *The Song of Amhergín* in his own translation from the Old Irish. Amhergín, the legendary poet of the Milesians, is said to have spoken these words as he first set his right foot upon the soil of Ireland when he and his invading kinsmen defeated the Tuatha Dé Danann. In the words of Alwyn and Brinley Rees, the poems of Amhergín are 'in the nature of creation incantations' and embody 'the primeval unity of all things'.[42] Buckley set this mystical utterance for mezzo-soprano voice, unaccompanied except for the crotales and woodblocks the singer plays. The highly embellished vocal line combined with the sounds of the percussion instruments creates an exotic-sounding work of extreme primitivism, which 'makes the text seem a cipher for ancient ideas', as one critic pointed out.[43] The strangeness of the effects prompted another critic to suggest that the performer 'could have been a visitor from Outer Mongolia.'[44] *I Am Wind on Sea* received its premiere with the Irish-American mezzo-soprano Aylish Kerrigan (for whom it was written) in Madrid on 4 October 1987 under the auspices of the Centro para la Difusión de la Música Contemporánea at the Círculo de Belles Artes.

> I am wind on sea,
> I am the mighty wave,
> I am sound of ocean,
> I am stag of seven fights,
> I am hawk on cliff,
> I am the sun's beam,
> I am boar ready for combat,
> I am a salmon in pool,
> I am lake on plain,
> I am word of poetry,
> I am point of spear pouring forth combat,

---

42 Alwyn Rees and Brinley Rees, *Celtic Heritage – Ancient Tradition in Ireland and Wales* (London: Thames and Hudson, 1961), p. 99.
43 Martin Adams, *The Irish Times*, 16 February 1998.
44 Douglas Sealy, *The Irish Times*, 30 November 2000.

I am the giver of inspiration.
Who can make smooth the rock mountain?
I am wind on sea,
Who can tell the seasons of the moon?
I am wind on sea,
Who can tell where the sun sets?
I am wind on sea.

(Translation by John Buckley)

Dedicated to his daughter Niamh, *I Am Wind on Sea* is Buckley's most explicit exploration of Irish mythology. He has avoided any obvious reference to Irish music, apart from an elaborate use of vocal embellishment and ornamentation that may have some correlation with *sean-nós* singing. In *Traditional Music in Ireland,* Tomás Ó Canainn defines *sean nós* in the following manner:

> [It is] a rather complex way of singing in Gaelic, confined mainly to some areas in the west and south of the country. It is unaccompanied and has a highly ornamented melodic line [...] not all areas have the same type of ornamentation – one finds a very florid line in Connacht, contrasting with a somewhat less decorated one in the south, and, by comparison, a stark simplicity in the northern songs.[45]

Buckley clearly explores this ancient text through a 20th-century vocal technique, which, though reminiscent of *sean-nós* style, would be inconceivable before Berio. He has been careful, however, to avoid any blatant imitation of the Italian master. His approach allows an ingenious retention of his affection for a vocal lyricism, while simultaneously employing a battery of contemporary extended vocal techniques to very effective musical purpose.

In a masterful stratagem, the innovative use of percussion instruments invokes a ritualistic and paganistic world correlating to the pre-Christian declamatory nature of the text. The performance of this 'song' becomes a rite, in the essential meaning of the term and imbues the work with a ceremonial formality and an objective distance of stark liturgical solemnity. This reserve further enhances Buckley's translation of the text, which reflects a nascent ritualism rather than the rhetorical grandiloquence of the versions emerging in the late Victorian era. A comparison with the translation by Douglas Hyde (1860-1949) will demonstrate Buckley's preferences:

> I am the wind which breathes upon the sea,
> I am the wave of the ocean,
> I am the murmur of the billows,

---

[45] Tomás Ó Canainn, *Traditional Music in Ireland* (London: Routledge and Kegan Paul, 1978), p. 49.

I am the ox of the seven combats,
I am the vulture upon the rocks,
I am a beam of the sun,
I am the fairest of plants.
I am a wild boar in valour,
I am a salmon in the water,
I am a lake in the plain,
I am a word of science,
I am the point of a lance in battle,
I am the God who created in the head the fire.
Who is it who throws light into the meeting on the mountain
Who announces the ages of the moon?
Who teaches the place where couches the sun?
(If not I)

(Translated by Douglas Hyde)

In stark contrast to Hyde's version, Buckley minimizes the language, avoiding any rhetorical exuberance. The objective simplicity and economic terseness of his translation emphasizes instead the poetry's meaning. Stravinsky achieved a similar starkness when choosing Latin texts for his *Symphony of Psalms* (see Psalm 38, verses 13, 14; Psalm 39, verses 2, 3 and 4; and Psalm 150) and his *Oedipus Rex*.[46]

In addition to the translation, Buckley's approach to word setting further distances the language by employing two techniques to great effect: the deconstruction of words into elongated syllables and the extended use of onomatopoeia (the formation or use of words that imitate the sounds associated with the objects or actions to which they refer; Buckley's onomatopoeic technique is applied to syllables). These two techniques reflect a postmodern artistic disposition towards fragmentation and deconstruction. The context for Buckley's musical-textual deconstructions is observable in an example from Derek Walcott's epic poem, *Omeros* (1990), which demonstrates how postmodern fragmentary techniques may yield superlative artistic results:

I said, 'Omeros,'
and *O* was the conch-shell's invocation, *mer* was
both mother and sea in our Antillean patois,
os, a grey bone, and the white surf as it crashes
and spreads its sibilant collar on a lace shore.

---

[46] In an article on Stravinsky's *Oedipus Rex*, written by the composer's one-time assistant Arthur Lourié, Latin is described as '... the dead, desiccated language of chemists and lawyers.' 'Oedipus Rex', *La Revue musicale*, 8 (1927), p. 240-253, cited in Stephen Walsh, *Stravinsky: Oedipus Rex* (Cambridge: Cambridge University Press, 1993).

> Omeros was the crunch of dry leaves, and the washes
> that echoed from a cave-mouth when the tide has ebbed.[47]

From the three syllables of the word Omeros, Walcott excavates a seemingly endless array of latent meanings – the sound of a conch-shell's call, an idea of sea, a vision of mother, a grey bone. The poet delves deeper and discovers that Omeros (the Greek name for Homer) contains within its roots, constructions, rhythms and cadences, the sounds of 'the white surf as it crashes'. The onomatopoeic quality of the word 'crashes' and the alliterative line 'spreads it sibilant collar on the lace shore' are particularly effective. The alliteration literally sounds the images of the words. Walcott remarkably extracts the literal meanings of words in order to yield the incommensurable connotations they possess. Through its linguistic fragmentation, he finds the words' deeper and alternative meanings, as well as more subtle resonances. He has exceeded the normal semantic, utilitarian usage of words and has uncovered substrata of latent significations verging on the transcendental.

In *I Am Wind on Sea*, Buckley has independently attempted to achieve something similar in the way he elongates chosen syllables, reiterates consonances and vowels, and transforms word fragments into fundamental sound descriptions. The employment of this technique in conjunction with its application to vocal and instrumental music offers an experience different from the Walcott poem. However, the result, though more abstract, remains similar by offering new ways of saying, singing and hearing a word. In *I Am Wind on Sea*, Buckley extensively subjects various phonetic characteristics of selected words and syllables to this treatment, and, consequently, transforms their distinguishing features beyond recognition. However, the rhythmic and metrical components, the onomatopoeic characteristics extracted from the chosen words or phonemes, result in a new, inexhaustible semantic potential. As the literal surface of language is transcended and subtle meanings of the sounds latent within the words are exposed – text itself becomes music.

For example, in the opening five staves of the score the word 'I' is expressed through an endless variety of phonetic vocal variants, rhythmic and timbral modulations and ornamentations. Music from the second half of system 8 sets the word 'wave'. Through rhythmic repetition, dynamic control of volume, and vocal and rhythmic modulation, the word is excavated not only for its latent phonetic

---

[47] Derek Walcott, *Omeros* (London: Faber & Faber, 1990), p. 14.

variants, but also for a sonic description of a wave: first, of its rhythmic undulating energy, and second, of its dissipation after it has crashed. This passage could very well be a musical equivalent of Walcott's 'white surf as it crashes/ and spreads its sibilant collar on a lace shore.'

Ex. 21: *I Am Wind on Sea*, section of systems 8-9

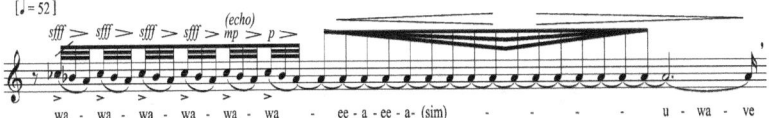

There are numerous effective examples of the use of onomatopoeia. At system 10, with the words 'I am sound of ocean', the singer must create the sound 'sshhh' at the pertinent time when singing 'ocean'. Again, this technique parallels Walcott's textual 'crashes' and 'washes'. The voice plunges from the note E down to the low B♭, strongly suggesting the depth of the ocean.

Ex. 22: *I Am Wind on Sea*, systems 10-11

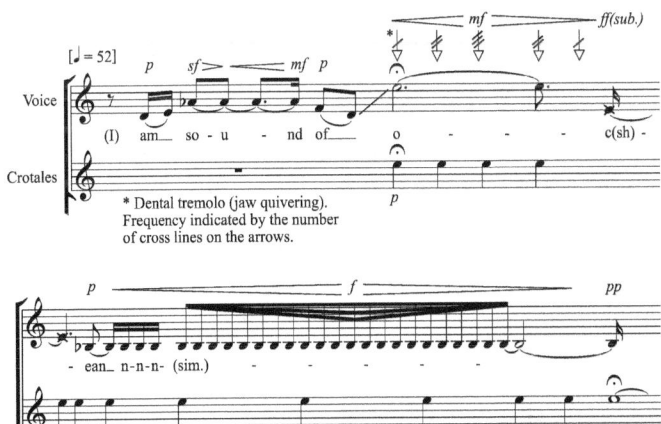

The use of the percussion instruments provides, both musically and theatrically, a sense of ritual. The crotales act as extensions to the voice: at the opening, the voice and crotales resonate at the same pitch. The percussion instrument integrates itself completely into the sound of the voice, creating a unique timbre. Elsewhere the crotales act as sonic foils against which the voice resonates. Both crotales and woodblocks maintain the flow of the music when the voice stops for breath. They perform a descriptive function when they paint the scenario offered in the text – for example, the use of woodblocks for the first time to powerful and surprising effect.

Ex. 23: *I Am Wind on Sea*, system 13

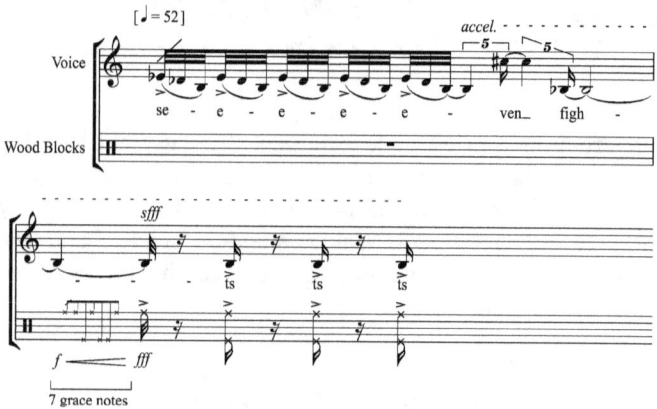

On the word 'fights', the woodblocks enter with a violent clash and three powerful *fff* accentuations on the consonants 'ts' conjure up the clashes of antlers. The seven grace notes on the woodblocks (before the first 'ts') rhythmically represent the 'seven fights' of the stag. The woodblocks continue as war instruments at systems 21/22 when they coincide with the vocal lines declaring, 'I am boar ready for combat'. The vocal rolling of the 'r' of 'boar' demonstrates that the voice also participates in the sound painting of imagery. This use is most evident in the vocal stabs and thrusts at systems 28/9 where the text reads, 'I am point of spear pouring forth combat'. Buckley resorts to a graphic notation to describe visually and vocally the puncturing of spears and the sheer violence of combat.

A work of great originality, *I Am Wind on Sea* is Buckley's last significant investigation into Irish mythology to date; from this point onwards, his modernism becomes more abstract, and where he sets texts they emanate from such diverse literary sources as Yeats's esoteric plays, the poetry of Clemens Brentano and Joseph von Eichendorff, and the documented journals of astronauts. Unique in the context of Irish music, *I Am Wind on Sea* is a highly original transformation of archaic Celtic mythology that makes this tradition vital to contemporary Irish consciousness.

PART 2: TOWARDS EUROPE

Early Successes

From the late 1970s through the 1980s, Hoddinott directly influenced many of Buckley's works, including a setting of Horace for mixed voice chorus and piano, *Pulvis et Umbra*, *Five Epigrams* (flute and oboe) from 1980, the more adventurous *Concerto for Chamber Orchestra* of 1981, and *Time Piece* of 1982. However, Hoddinott felt these works were moving in a different direction from the Celtic-inspired pieces. In his view, they had shifted away from Buckley's previous, more instinctive approach to composition and were showing aspects of a constructivism foreign to Hoddinott's aesthetic. Despite this new trajectory and his teacher's misgivings, Buckley remembers that Hoddinott always offered his support and guidance, and this encouragement was beginning to bear fruit beyond the compositional classes themselves. As a result of Hoddinott's endorsement, Buckley was reviewed in Britain for the first time, and Cardiff University undertook publication of some of his works.[48] Given that Britain has never been the most fertile ground for the nurturing and celebration of Irish composition, his minor successes are substantial and even groundbreaking. International exposure had already begun when his *Brass Quintet No. 1* was featured on the 1978 International Rostrum of Composers, an annual forum founded in 1954 and organized by UNESCO's International Music Council offering broadcasting representatives the opportunity to exchange and publicize contemporary music. Buckley was represented subsequently on four further occasions with *Pulvis et Umbra* in 1980, *Boireann* in 1984, *And Wake the Purple Year* in 1987 and *Concerto for Organ and Orchestra* in 1993. As noted, *Oileáin* was premiered in 1979 by the eminent pianist Martin Jones and the *Sonata for Unaccompanied Violin*, commissioned by Cardiff University, was premiered by James Barton in Wales in 1983.

Hoddinott also provided Buckley with valuable career guidance in education, encouraging him to teach at third-level rather than primary-

---

[48] *Oileáin* was published by Cardiff University Press. By this time, however, Thatcherism was making its presence felt in Britain and all ancillary support for universities was withdrawn, thereby greatly restricting any future publishing activities Cardiff University Press may have wanted to pursue. Thus, Buckley would have to wait another twenty years before he secured a publication contract.

level. To this end, Buckley undertook a Master's Degree at University College Cork, under Professor Aloys Fleischmann. Buckley's involvement with Fleischmann was elucidatory for the young composer. 'He was a marvellously incisive music analyst and critic,' Buckley wrote,

> his seminars on the newly commissioned works each year for the Cork International Choral Festival being a particular revelation. He would frequently demonstrate points of harmonic or structural significance, much to the surprise and delight of the composer, who might often be unaware of such detail.[49]

Buckley's classes in Wales continued for four years (between 1979 and 1982 approximately), and so his additional engagement with Cork coincided with his ongoing sessions with Hoddinott. The long-term plan was to lecture at third level, which would provide a nurturing environment for his compositional work and his aspirations as an educationalist. The decision to take the Master's Degree in Cork (as opposed to Cardiff) was based entirely on financial and logistical practicalities. Cardiff University required all its full-time MA students to be resident in the country and, with a young family in Dublin, Buckley could not undertake this option. Attending University College Cork meant he did not have to uproot from Ireland, and the degree was undertaken by independent research. In any event, at this stage, Buckley was working at a much more advanced level than a Master's Degree would require, and therefore it was agreed that a portfolio of compositions was to be submitted for assessment. Buckley included in his submission a number of recently completed works such as *Brass Quintet No. 1, Taller than Roman Spears, Oileáin, Pulvis et Umbra*, and other pieces. The portfolio was duly sent to Raymond Warren in Britain for appraisal and subsequently a First-Class Honours Master's Degree was conferred in 1980.

Buckley had further plans regarding his education and commenced a PhD at Cardiff. The thesis in support of his original compositions was entitled *Aspects of Notation in Aleatoric Music*, and was supervised by Stephen Walsh, the well-known critic and musicologist, who has written numerous books on composers, most notably Stravinsky. Buckley's in-depth study of this aspect of notation was connected intimately with the pieces he was composing at the time. Amongst the works analysed were Stockhausen's *Refrain* (1959), Lutoslawski's *String Quartet* (1964) and Berio's *Circles* (1966). From these scores he

---

[49] Ruth Fleischmann, ed. *Aloys Fleischmann – A Life for Music in Ireland Remembered by Contemporaries* (Cork: Mercier Press, 2000).

absorbed many technical resources into his own music, further refining his personal approach to aleatoric procedures.

Buckley did not complete this doctorate for a number of reasons. By 1982, he was earning a living as a freelance composer (he had retired from teaching at Ballymun) and was inundated suddenly with commissions. Furthermore, he aspired to becoming a member of Aosdána, which would offer some financial assistance to him, and he envisaged this possibility in the near future. A perusal of Buckley's composition catalogue for this period demonstrates the development of his freelance career. His sudden success negated the necessity of a doctorate. The fulfillment of these commissions also deprived him of the time to work on the thesis, despite the obvious progress he was making in his academic research. Quite simply, the lure of being a composer-in-demand took precedence.

Fleischmann's support proved critical in securing important commissions, including one for the 1981 Seminar on Contemporary Choral Music, held as part of the Cork International Choral Festival that Fleischmann directed. For this occasion, Buckley wrote *Scel lem Duíb* (My Story for You), a setting of an Irish poem from the ninth or tenth century. More significantly, Fleischmann arranged for a commission for a new score for the country's only professional ballet company, the Irish National Ballet, based in Cork.[50]

The centenary of the birth of Patrick Pearse, the Irish poet and revolutionary, was celebrated nationally in 1979.[51] Several composers were invited to write new works commemorating aspects of Pearse's career: RTÉ commissioned Fleischmann's *Ómós don Phiarsach* (Homage to Pearse, 1979), John Kinsella wrote *Wayfarer* (1979) for the Ulster Orchestra, while Seóirse Bodley composed his *Symphony No. 2 – I Have Loved the Lands of Ireland* (1980). The Department of the

---

[50] Founded in 1973 by Joan Denise Moriarty, the Irish Ballet Company was later renamed Irish National Ballet in 1983. The withdrawal of its Arts Council subsidy forced its closure in 1989.

[51] Patrick Pearse was born in 1879. He was educated by the Christian Brothers in Westland Row, Dublin, and completed a degree in Arts and Law at the Royal University in 1901. His interest in the Irish language led him to join the Gaelic League, and he became editor of its paper – *An Claidheamh Soluis* (The Sword of Light). Initially in his political career, he was a moderate and supported the Home Rule movement, but he later believed that independence would only be achieved by force and sacrifice. Pearse was recruited into the Irish Republican Brotherhood in 1912 and became a member of its Military Council. He was president of the Provisional Government and was stationed in the General Post Office during the Easter Rising. He was executed in Kilmainham Gaol on 3 May 1916.

Taoiseach (Prime Minister) invited Joan Denise Moriarty, founder and artistic director of Irish National Ballet and a longtime collaborator of Fleischmann's, to create a ballet relating to Pearse's poem *Fornocht do Chonnac Thú* (literally, 'naked I saw thee', but known in English as *Renunciation*, the title that Pearse gave to his own translation). Moriarty invited Buckley to write the score for the ballet. The poem is charged with eroticism, as indeed was the great lyric poem on which it is based, *Gile na Gile* by Aogán Ó Rathaille. It portrays Pearse's rejection of sexual desire for his loved one in favour of his irrepressible love of country and the ultimate sacrifice that this love demanded.

Renunciation

Naked I saw thee,
O beauty of beauty!
And I blinded my eyes
For fear I should flinch.

I heard thy music,
O sweetness of sweetness!
And I shut my ears
For fear I should fail.

I kissed thy lips
O sweetness of sweetness!
And I hardened my heart
For fear of my ruin.

I blinded my eyes
And my ears I shut,
I hardened my heart
And my love I quenched.

I turned my back
On the dream I had shaped,
And to this road before me
My face I turned.

I set my face
To the road here before me,
To the work that I see,
To the death that I shall meet.

(Patrick Pearse, 1914, from the Irish)

The score was dedicated to Moriarty. Though it was completed in 1980 under the title *Fornocht do Chonnac Thú*, the ballet was not produced until June 1983 when it was presented under the title *Diúltú* ('Renunciation'), in the Abbey Theatre as part of the Irish National Ballet's Dublin season. It was danced to a recording of the score made by the RTÉ Symphony Orchestra under Colman Pearce, and the delayed premiere was due to problems with recording and performance rights. It was presented again the following year at the Cork Opera House for the tenth-anniversary season of Irish National Ballet.

Fornocht do Chonnac Thú was first heard, however, as a concert work when it premiered at Saint Francis Xavier Hall in Dublin with the RTÉ Symphony Orchestra and Colman Pearce on 29 July 1981.[52] Although Hoddinott admired the work for its creative use of the orchestra and its broad architectural shapes, it provoked a mixed critical response. One commentator pronounced that the 'music stands well without choreography ... [it] indicates a firm grasp of orchestral colour and the musical argument is clear and coherent.'[53] A subsequent performance, however, drew a less enthusiastic response: 'However well the music may work in the context for which it was conceived, as a concert piece it does not appear to hold together and it must rank among this composer's less successful works.'[54] Critical reaction to the staged ballet was equally ambivalent. The critic of the *Sunday Press* had a number of misgivings: 'The trouble with the piece is that it gives the distinct impression that Pearse was never very keen on "The Loved One" and so was really not renouncing much. [...] That may be historically accurate, but it doesn't make for great drama or dance.'[55] In spite of this somewhat mixed reception, the Irish National Ballet subsequently took the work on tour, and it received some thirty-five performances. This exposure and Buckley's association with the renowned choreographer helped secure him a respected position in Irish cultural life.

Connecting with Cage and Lutoslawski

In 1981, Buckley had the opportunity to work with distinguished choreographer Merce Cunningham when he was invited by the Arts Council to participate in a two-week Summer School in Guildford, Surrey. The purpose of this event was to explore ways in which creative collaborations between choreographers and composers might be fruitfully developed. As these workshop sessions were directed by John

---

[52] This turned out to be the final concert for the RTÉ Symphony Orchestra at Saint Francis Xavier Hall prior to its move to the National Concert Hall in the following September.
[53] Pat O'Kelly, *Evening Press*, 30 July 1981.
[54] Michael Dervan, *The Irish Times*, 7 October 1987.
[55] Ginnie Kennealy, *Sunday Press*, 12 June 1983.

Cage and Cunningham, Buckley had close contact with the famous American composer and his idiosyncratic theories relating to composition and performance. In keeping with his aesthetic of chance operations, Cage suggested that newly composed works should be randomly matched with newly choreographed dances. Different scores sometimes were performed simultaneously, regardless of the resulting confusion. Thus, Buckley spent an entire day writing a rather intricate piece for solo flute. Its performance, however, took place simultaneously with that of a work for five gongs, which was very loud from start to finish and naturally obliterated any sound the flute made. Buckley remembers:

> The performance ended with the last note of my piece for solo flute emerging from the final gong stroke. I approached Cage about this, complaining that I had spent considerable time and effort in composing the piece, but that none of it could be heard, apart from the final note. His response was: 'But wasn't that last note beautiful when it did emerge. Many of nature's beauties are hidden; we can't see the microscopic details in plants.' I had already drawn on aleatoric procedures as early as the *Wind Quintet* of 1976, but in a much more controlled and limited manner. Cage's applications of chance operations were too extreme for me, but the concept of permitting free elements to enter the composition did appeal despite the recent altercation with the five gongs.

Though discouraging on the surface, this episode was, in fact, revelatory for Buckley. Perhaps it was similar to Lutoslawski's experience following *his* confrontation with Cage. Charles Bodman Ray points out that Lutoslawski's shift in rhythmic technique occurred suddenly:

> The catalyst for change came in 1960, when he heard a radio broadcast of the *Concert for Piano and Orchestra* by John Cage, which gave him the idea of using 'chance' procedures (he later expressed his gratitude to Cage by presenting him with the autographed score of *Jeux vénitiens*).[56]

What Cage was able to communicate in concept and theory, Lutoslawski utilized in application, though in a more controlled environment. Buckley similarly absorbed Cage's ideas by embracing Cage's notions of space, chance and the broader definitions of what actually constituted sound and pitch, and applied them to his own needs within a much tighter and determined system. Improvisatory techniques, textural matrices, aleatoric configurations, spatial webs –

---

[56] Charles Bodman Rae, *The Music of Lutoslawski* (London: Faber & Faber, 1999), p. 75.

fundamental aspects promoted by Cage as central to a new way of hearing music – were all adopted by Buckley. Though added to his armoury, he always utilized them under a strict regime of control. This assimilation brought him into close kinship with Lutoslawski, who would henceforth profoundly influence Buckley. In this context, Cage's importance for Buckley extends to the act of bringing him closer to Lutoslawski.

SELECTED ANALYSIS

Concerto for Chamber Orchestra

Following the encounter with Cage, Buckley composed his *Concerto for Chamber Orchestra* – a work that incorporates a substantial use of aleatoric procedures. 'At the time I was writing the *Chamber Concerto* I had come in contact with the music of Lutoslawski and it was his approach (rather than Cage's) that was to have a far greater influence on the technicalities of the music I was to write throughout the 1980s.' This development validated an approach to composition where short static sound blocks, largely derived from aleatoric procedures, were juxtaposed in a manner focusing almost exclusively on their individual timbral and textural qualities. The *Five Epigrams for Flute and Oboe* of 1980 signalled Buckley's move towards an uncompromising modernism, and the 1980s saw him embrace a European *avant-garde* aesthetic more completely. *Concerto for Chamber Orchestra* was commissioned in 1981 by the New Irish Chamber Orchestra (now known as the Irish Chamber Orchestra) and premiered in January 1982 at the Dublin Festival of 20th Century Music with Seóirse Bodley conducting.

A series of extended techniques, including flutter tonguing, multiphonics and key-clicks, highlights the concerto's modernist pedigree. In addition to Lutoslawski, György Ligeti can be cited as a precursor for Buckley. The Hungarian composer's *Chamber Concerto* of 1969/70 supremely exemplifies the manipulation of layers of sound and the formation of timbral webs that exercised an influence on Buckley.

Although the orchestral concerto genre is a familiar form, Buckley curiously chose to insert into his concerto a number of complex and virtuosic solos, duos and trios requiring specialized skills from individual orchestra members. Consequently, the emphasis is diverted from the orchestral body to these performers, thus creating within the *Concerto for Chamber Orchestra* a host of mini-concertos for one, two and three instrumentalists. Furthermore, as Buckley is preoccupied primarily with aleatoricism as a method of layering strata of sounds, he has largely abandoned any opportunities to construct more sophisticated rhythmic and timbral aggregates (complex combinations formed by intermixing instrumental groupings) in favour of relatively simple blocks of sound typically constructed from homogeneous groupings. On the other hand, his increased control over aleatoric processes combined with the use of extended instrumental techniques has resulted occasionally in some remarkable orchestral effects. For example, the sub-divided violins establish a flurry of shimmering textures in the first movement at Rehearsal Mark C (page 4).

Fig. 8 below demonstrates the first movement's formal construction. There is no design of harmonic development in any traditional sense as Buckley's main concern is the compilation of blocks of sound and the addition of these to smaller combinations of other instruments or with other dissimilar aleatoric constructs. He emphasizes timbre and the accumulation of distinct timbral blocks to create new, more complex aggregates of sound. The solos and duos, which predominantly explore highly virtuosic extended techniques, act as link passages between the larger sections. They also provide individual commentaries whose directional qualities counterpoise the essentially static nature of the aleatoric masses of sound.

Fig. 8: *Concerto for Chamber Orchestra*, movement I

Opening:	horn duo
Rehearsal Mark A:	horn duo + bassoons/cellos pedal on D♭
Rehearsal Mark C:	1st aleatoric block in strings + violas/cellos duos double bass solo
Rehearsal Mark G:	2nd aleatoric block in strings + horn duos cello/bassoon
Rehearsal Mark J:	3rd aleatoric block in woodwind/horns
Rehearsal Mark K:	1st layering of two aleatoric blocks woodwind/horns and strings, oboes and cellos
Rehearsal Mark P:	non-aleatoric section: strings/horns/woodwind
Rehearsal Mark S:	2nd layering of two aleatoric blocks wind and strings
Rehearsal Mark T:	horn duo
Rehearsal Mark V:	bassoons + non-aleatoric music to end.

The employment of the pedal is a salient feature in the *Concerto for Chamber Orchestra*. In the second movement, the sustaining cello pedal on C, which supports a flute solo, abruptly introduces a tonal centre. Indeed, the movement shifts from an acceptance of relatively traditional tonal centres to the most extreme explorations of pure atonal sound webs undermining stylistic reconciliation. An interesting feature of this movement (though not exclusive to it) is Buckley's manipulation of chronological time. The superimposition of two oboe solos, one accelerating and the other decelerating, effectively distorts and confuses the sense of forward movement.

Ex. 24: *Concerto for Chamber Orchestra*, movement II, rehearsal mark B (oboes)

The opening of the third movement, fully notated and built into highly constructed rhythmic units, comes as a further stylistic surprise. Written for strings only, and in a style reminiscent of neo-classicism, the piece may be modelled on Tippett's *Concerto for Double String Orchestra*. It certainly has a rhythmic and harmonic buoyancy reminiscent of the English composer's early work. Non-tonal solo figurations (a series of tightly-knit repetitive fragments that emanate from the cellos and violas) act as a link to the main central section (at H, page 36). A process of addition and cumulation (a steady construction of fragment upon fragment rising through the *divisi* strings) creates a seven-part repetitive mechanism invoking the automated constructs of Steve Reich. As a pedal E in the bass underpins the whole section, the music is harmonically static even though Buckley introduces a number of altered melodic constructs above it at J (page 40). A cello solo is utilized to escape from the mechanical roundabout. However, repetition remains a feature to the end, and a series of superimposed and repeated static chords of varying rhythmic identities exposes a complex aggregate of metric patterns (see 2 and 3 bars after O, page 48). As the 'neo-classical' music of the opening does not make another appearance, the work might be seen as an exercise in disintegrating structures.

The fourth movement is dominated by the woodwind and horns, apart from a single string cluster emerging from the diminishing textures near the end of the movement at H. The strings create a powerful crescendo only to dissolve again into the woodwind and horn sonority. This Ivesian moment may well derive from Buckley's surreal experience at John Cage's summer school the previous month, when the final note of his flute piece eventually emerged from the diminishing sound of the gongs. The movement forms complexes of rhythmic patterns framed by a relatively conservative setting of sustained horns supporting melodic lines on the flutes and oboes. After eight bars, this music gives way to automated fragments (similar to those used in the previous movement) that self-construct over an A♭ tonal centre. Harmonically static, the interest here is rhythmic, with the creation of groupings that increase and decrease in complexity depending on the entrance and exit of instruments. Rehearsal Mark D returns to the opening material and another duo, this time on bassoons. The free nature of this 'linking' duo emerges as a stylistic opposite to the mechanical structures set up in the previous section.

For its consistency alone, the fifth movement is the most successful. It concentrates solely on the layering of separate sound blocks.

Fig. 9: *Concerto for Chamber Orchestra*, movement V

Opening:	trills on woodwind and strings
Rehearsal Mark A:	cello duo
Rehearsal Mark B:	trills and tremolos on strings + flutes
Rehearsal Mark D:	double bass solo
Rehearsal Mark E:	violins and violas + commentaries on double bass, cellos/woodwind and horns
Rehearsal Mark F:	juxtaposition of woodwind blocks with string blocks
Rehearsal Mark H:	tutti of aleatoric blocks
Rehearsal Mark J:	opening trilled music on strings
Rehearsal Mark K:	double bass solo
Rehearsal Mark L:	trills accumulating throughout orchestra to finish *fffff*

Figure 9 demonstrates the movement's construction, which uses simple blocks of identifiable sound entities. The two solos given to the double bass, though interesting in themselves, tend to dissipate the energy created by the larger forces. The climax of the work at H displays Buckley's most effective use of aleatoric practices, and his sharpened timing in relation to the sudden entrances and exits of sound blocks yields exciting shifts of tone colour.

Ex. 25: *Concerto for Chamber Orchestra*, movement V, rehearsal mark H

Despite moments of genuine interest, *Concerto for Chamber Orchestra* remains a problematic work. The constant shifting from tutti forces to smaller groupings provides effective contrast, but it also tends to arrest development – the musical arguments rarely move beyond short essays in tone-painting. More significantly, Buckley has incorporated an extensive amount of heterogeneous material into his musical canvas – the aleatoric and notated constructions of separate atonal sound entities, the partially-tonal mechanical complexes of movements III and IV, the tonal-based (over pedal points) lyrical flute music of movement II, the atonal timbral-centred 'improvisations' for smaller forces (solos, duos and trios, etc.) and the unadulterated tonal 'neo-classical' contours of movement III. All of these materials, which emanate from disparate musical practices, attempt to integrate tonal and timbral devises that are functionally incongruent and point to a weakening of discipline in relation to style and structural formation. The problem at the heart of the work is Buckley's reluctance to fully embrace the modernist processes he so effectively uses elsewhere. Rather than entering completely into the stylistic and structural distinction of aleatoricism, he attempts to integrate these modernist processes into the Procrustean bed of his own more conservative technical and musical armory. The result is a stylistic incongruence that all too often causes friction, and the work consequently struggles to reconcile itself.

Time Piece

A commission from the University of Cardiff, *Time Piece* was premiered there on 26 November 1982 by Kathryn Lucas (flute), Edward Pillanger (clarinet), Justin Pearson (cello) and Oliver Knussen directing from the piano. The work focuses on concepts of time (both chronological and musical) using various processes of aleatoricism. Buckley maintains strict control over the harmonic canvas, thereby avoiding the problems of stylistic incongruity in some of his previous works. The employment of a number of specific aleatoric techniques allied to explorations of multiple temporal entities might suggest that *Time Piece* lacks formal structure. On the contrary, the work falls into three highly organized sections, each designed to investigate aspects of temporality, microtonality and the construction of timbral aggregates.

Fig. 10: *Time Piece*, structural layout

SECTION I

Opening:	Episode I on a G unison
Rehearsal Mark C:	Episode II on a C unison
Rehearsal Mark F:	Episode III on a F unison
Rehearsal Mark H:	Episode IV on a B♭ unison
Rehearsal Mark L:	Extended cello solo

SECTION II

Rehearsal Mark M:	Section for fl/cl/cello over repeated piano chords
Rehearsal Mark N:	Development of Episodes I, II and III exploring small chromatic webs around the given pitch centres of each episode

SECTION III

Rehearsal Mark R:	1st paragraph: aleatoric duet (fl and cl) after accented piano chord
Rehearsal Mark S:	2nd paragraph: aleatoric cello solo after accented piano chord
Rehearsal Mark T:	3rd paragraph: aleatoric duet (fl and cl) after accented piano chord
Rehearsal Mark U:	4th paragraph: aleatoric cello solo after accented piano chord
Rehearsal Mark V:	5th paragraph: aleatoric duet (fl and cl) after accented piano chord
Rehearsal Mark W:	6th paragraph: very short paragraph of cello figuration
Rehearsal Mark X:	7th paragraph: very short paragraph of flute, clarinet and cello figuration
Rehearsal Mark Y:	8th paragraph: Tutti paragraph of aleatoric music
Rehearsal Mark Z:	Coda of rising scales tapering on fading cello

SECTION I

Section I constructs four episodes based on four pitch centres assembled in a cycle of fourths: [G-C-F-B♭]. It is framed by opening piano octaves and closed by a series of piano chords, each time altered harmonically but always with the same rhythmic motif. Within these framing chords, the flute, clarinet and cello develop the musical material in various ways.

[Note: In the musical examples, the clarinet in B♭ is written in concert pitch. In the full score, however, the clarinet is notated in B♭, sounding a tone lower than written.]

Ex. 26: *Time Piece*, section 1 structural plan

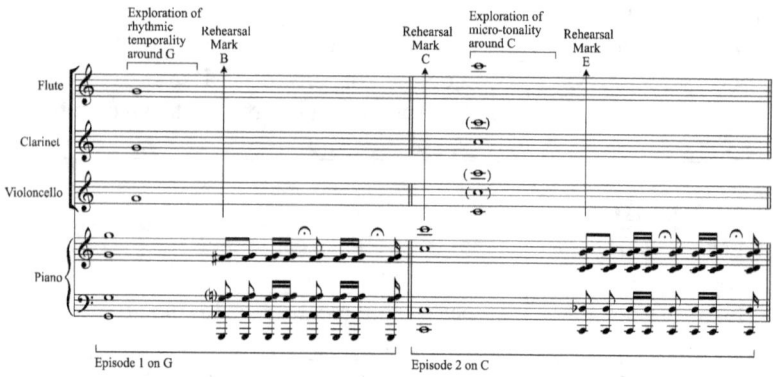

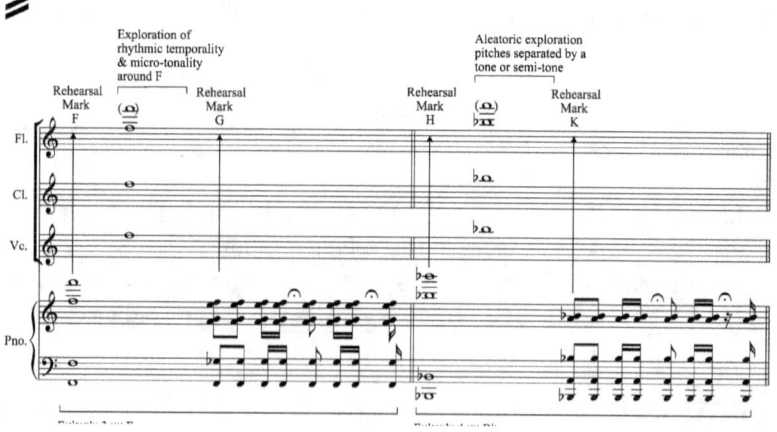

Episode 1: In the first episode, based on the pitch g', the flute, clarinet and cello each construct rhythmic units of increasing and decreasing values (see systems 2 and 3, page 1 of score): the flute and cello start with note lengths of .75 seconds, which then accelerate. The clarinet enters on staccato notes initially separated by rests of one-second duration that also accelerate before settling on a flutter-tongue. Buckley creates a complex combination of three separate strands of music, each of which has an autonomous temporality independently modulating in speed.

Episode 2: This episode shifts attention from the play of temporal entities to the exploration of micro-tonality around the central pitch c''' (and octaves) and the sonic exploitation of the clashes of upper partials, bringing to mind Ligeti's *Ten Pieces for Wind Quintet* (1968). Buckley employs a free tempo, allowing the musicians to explore readily the timbral complexes resulting from the close proximity of the notes (see rehearsal mark D, page 4).

Episode 3: Centred around the pitch f''' (and octaves), this music continues the processes from the previous episode before introducing repeated trills and glissandi that are subjected to multiple modulating tempi while their dynamics are altered continuously, making for an aleatoric section of great elasticity.

Episode 4: Based on the pitch centre of b♭'' (and octaves), this episode also utilizes repeated figurations, superimposing different, choppy rhythmic units (see Rehearsal Mark H, page 8 and J, page 9) of grace notes and rests. These sound aggregates suddenly halt at the entrance of the piano at J.

SECTION II

Following an extended cello solo (a linking technique carried on from the *Concerto for Chamber Orchestra*), Buckley divides Section II into two parts separated by a very short piano solo. The first part of Section II (which starts at M, page 11) builds upon repeated piano chords on which Buckley superimposes a distorted canon in three parts for flute, clarinet and cello. The flute and clarinet explore high *sff* trills punctuated by Bartók pizzicati on the cello. Example 27 shows two sample staves from this passage. Here, all rhythmic values are approximate. Consequently, the placing of notes in vertical alignment does not imply simultaneity. The relationship of the three canonic voices constantly shifts due to the insertion of rests of varying durations and pause marks. The trills are meticulously notated – a major second trill in the flute is answered by a minor second in the clarinet and vice versa.

Ex. 27: *Time Piece*, rehearsal mark M (two sample systems: flute, clarinet and cello parts)

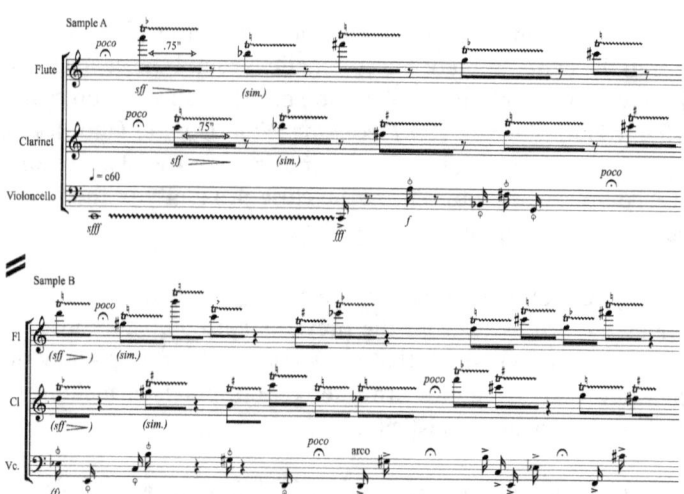

The second part of Section II (beginning at rehearsal mark N) is structurally akin to Section I as it divides into three episodes built upon a cycle of fourths [G-C-F]. A small chromatic web weaves around each of these three central pitches, creating a blurred tonal field. The piano trills and tremolos provide the support for these episodes. The first episode features a duo for clarinet and cello, the second, a duo for flute and clarinet, while the third culminating episode features all three. The sense of culmination is further accentuated by the increasing level of activity and dynamic range.

SECTION III

Section III of *Time Piece* (at rehearsal mark R) is carefully constructed around a series of eight aggressive, accented *fff* piano chords. The duration of the gaps between the chords gradually diminishes as follows: 15", 12", 10", 7", 5", 3", 2", 1". This play with time enforces an ever-increasing sense of apprehension, which drives the music towards the final gestures of Y (page 18).

Buckley has placed a number of wind duets between these chords (at rehearsal marks R, T, V and X) and cello solos (at rehearsal marks S, U, W and X). He holds back the tutti until the end to guarantee a climax to the entire work. That point (Y) is built on the aleatoric repeated *fff* fragments played by all instruments, which raises the work to a new level of intensity. Within this aggregate, the piano continues to distort time by altering the tempo of its tremolo material. Through a series of reductive measures, Buckley depletes the energy of the music and a series of freely rising scales draws the section to a peaceful coda.

Time Piece best represents Buckley's avant-garde phase. The rigorously controlled structure holds in check the potentially loosening effect of aleatoric processes. As one of Buckley's few forays into conceptual art, *Time Piece* is also unusual. Though not strictly conceptual, it effectively and meaningfully plays with psychological perceptions of time and distance. Its uncompromising and consistent atonality renders it more successful than its larger precursor, the *Concerto for Chamber Orchestra*. *Time Piece* most persuasively opens up spatial and temporal precincts within its musical structures.

4 | Educational and Peripheral Works (1982-1988)

From the early 1980s, Buckley's professional career became increasingly diversified. In addition to his work as a full-time teacher and as a composer, he became involved in a range of educational initiatives of considerable significance to Irish musical life. In 1982, he started lecturing on music appreciation at the People's College, an activity he continues to the present day.[57] His educational activities expanded to include third-level teaching when he was invited to give courses in 20th-century music and composition in 1985 at St Patrick's College, Maynooth (now the National University of Ireland, Maynooth). This association lasted fifteen years and, along with fellow-composer and lecturer Martin O'Leary, Buckley was instrumental in developing an MA programme in composition there. He also devised, scripted and presented a series of thirty-six educational programmes aimed at primary-school children called *A B C Sharp* for RTÉ *lyric* fm radio. They were very successful in introducing young people to classical music through a narrative format. RTÉ also published an information booklet connected to each series that was sent to every primary school in Ireland. The programmes were broadcast between 2000 and 2003. In 2001, a CD comprising a selection of eight of the programmes was made commercially available nationwide.

---

[57] Founded in 1948 in Dublin, the People's College is an independently run institute affiliated to the Congress of Trade Unions and supported by the Department of Education and Science.

Ennis Composition Summer School

By far the most significant of Buckley's educational initiatives was the establishment of the Ennis Composition Summer School, in July 1983. In 1982, Mid-West Arts, an organization funded jointly by the Arts Council of Ireland and relevant County Councils, invited Buckley to County Clare to explore the potential for contemporary composers to contribute to the musical life of the region. Buckley accepted the offer and subsequently met with local musicians, performing groups and politicians. He put together a series of proposals, one of which was for a summer school in composition with the goal of achieving a national profile. Buckley's vision was influenced to a considerable extent by his experiences at the workshops run by John Cage and Merce Cunningham he had attended in Guildford the previous year.

The Arts Council provided financial support for the project, and the first course took place in Ennis, the principal town in County Clare. It lasted for one week, opening with a series of compositional workshops devised by Buckley and concluding with concerts of the students' works, which on this occasion were performed by Buckley and the students themselves. That first year all eight students were local to Ennis. From modest beginnings, the standard of the course progressed year by year. The students were expected to write very short musical exercises in different 20th-century styles such as minimalism, serialism and neo-classicism, and they were encouraged to devise harmonic and melodic sequences and explore structural formulae. Within a few years, students of the calibre of Michael Alcorn, Rhona Clarke, Marion Ingoldsby and Gráinne Mulvey were being attracted to the school. In other words, it nurtured many of today's professional composers. As Clarke recalls:

> I heard about the Ennis School and I attended that for a few years consecutively [...] I found that a very wonderful kick-start really [...] Although I had already started composing, I needed a lot of help and found it with John; it was most, most helpful.[58]

Buckley believes that the study of composition is potentially beneficial to all musicians, even if they do not envisage themselves as composers: 'I would invite students to participate in the mysterious act of creation,' he said. 'Not all would become composers, but the study of the creative act leads to better performers, teachers, students, musicologists and critics.'[59] Buckley describes how his personal

---

[58] Tina Kinsella, interview transcripts for M.Phil thesis: 'Aosdána and the Female Visual Artist', September 2008. Interview with Rhona Clarke, p.115.
[59] Brendan Glacken, 'Culture, sex and lobsters', *The Irish Times* (4 May 1995).

approach to teaching composition owes much to the example of his former mentor, James Wilson:

> Wilson's approach to the teaching of composition is a model towards which I aspire. In essence it focuses on the student and the student's work, enabling him or her to begin to develop a personal voice, without seeking to impose one's own style or aesthetic. In my teaching, I lay greater emphasis on technical considerations, but without losing sight of the end goal.

One of the most important forums for the nurturing of new music in Ireland emerged from these small beginnings. There were few places in the country where young composers could receive this kind of concentrated tuition, and the Ennis Composition Summer School thus fulfilled a genuine need. It was not long before Buckley realized that the modest week-long course needed to be extended to two weeks and that more tutors would be required. Given his affinity with Wilson's teaching methods, Buckley naturally thought of inviting the older composer to assist him, feeling that his long experience would be very valuable in developing the scope of the enterprise. Wilson accepted the invitation and remained involved with the Summer School for many years. From 1986, Michael Alcorn's involvement as Director led to further significant development, especially in the area of music technology and electro-acoustic composition.

In time, as the scope of the students' compositions became more ambitious, it was apparent that the restricted facilities of the Summer School were hampering the imaginations of the young participants. In the early years, the organizers relied on amateur performers to play through the students' work, but Buckley was anxious to engage professional musicians to ensure adequate performances. The involvement of professionals meant that additional expert advice on writing for their various instruments also would be available to the students. This proposed expansion entailed a necessary increase in funding, and the money readily forthcoming from both the Arts Council and local sources testifies to the confidence inspired by Buckley's organizational abilities and his skills as an educationalist. The Summer School subsequently developed a significant international dimension when well-known composers accepted invitations to participate as guest lecturers. Amongst these were Peter Michael Hamel from Germany, Karl Aage Rasmussen and Poul Ruders from Denmark, Timo-Juhani Kyllönen from Finland, Arne Mellnäs from Sweden, and Paul Paterson, Judith Weir, John Casken, Simon Bainbridge and Michael Finnissy from Britain. The philosophy of Buckley's ten years as director can be summed up in his own words: 'We were determined that, even if the summer school took place in a small parish, our vision wouldn't be parochial.' The school, now known as the Irish Composition Summer School, continues to flourish under the direction of Martin O'Leary and with the ongoing involvement of Nicola LeFanu.

Educational Works

By 1982, Buckley had spent eleven years teaching in Ballymun. Encouraged by the recent award of an Arts Council bursary and the commissions received through his association with Aloys Fleischmann, he decided to resign from his teaching post in September 1982 and risk the precarious existence of a freelance composer. As noted, he also aspired to elected membership of Aosdána. To earn a living, he was compelled to undertake a variety of commissions, including writing simple pieces for local brass bands, for example, or for children's choirs. He did not disdain these modest assignments, however. On the contrary, apart from the income they generated, he saw many of these smaller commissions as an opportunity to develop the educational aspect of the composer's social role. He welcomed this role, and he considered these unpretentious activities as valid as more important commissions:

> I have composed a number of works for young performers and also for a variety of non-professional groups such as brass bands and choirs. I have always enjoyed the challenge of this work but by no means found it easy. The technical limitations of the performers demand a high level of inventiveness if the works are to be of any value. I attach great importance to music making in the community at large and am pleased to have had an opportunity to contribute to it.

The works he produced in the 1980s are a mixture of educational scores, community-based commissions and film projects, together with compositions of a weightier nature. However, it should be recognized that these smaller, more functional pieces in no way impeded his aesthetic trajectory throughout the 1980s. Even in 1984, which according to the catalogue of Buckley's compositions would indicate a focus on peripheral and functional scores, he was steadily working on his *Symphony No. 1*. Buckley also found the time to compose several major works. In 1983 alone, he produced the *Suite for Harpsichord*, the *Sonata for Unaccompanied Violin* and *Boireann*.

The most significant of the peripheral works include the score for the film *The Woman Who Married Clark Gable*, which was directed by

Thaddeus O'Sullivan and starred Bob Hoskins and Brenda Fricker. Based on a short story by Seán O'Faoláin, this film met with great success on its release in 1985, and on the strength of the positive exposure Buckley received an invitation the following year to write a score for the British Channel Four television drama *A Summer Ghost*.

Buckley's financial concerns were alleviated to some extent in 1984 when he was elected to Aosdána. The Aosdána initiative, which was introduced in 1981 by the Arts Council, produced a significant improvement in the financial security of many freelance artists, as individual members who depended solely on their creative work to earn a living could apply for a *cnuas* (or stipend) to supplement their earnings. Aloys Fleischmann and Michael Hartnett nominated Buckley for membership, and he was subsequently successful in his application for a *cnuas*, which guaranteed him a moderate annual income. The formation of Aosdána coincided with the Arts Council's decision to introduce for the very first time a scheme whereby performers or groups could commission new works from composers. This development ushered in a new phase of advantageous collaborations between composer and performer. Buckley's first work commissioned under this new initiative, *Five Epigrams for Flute and Oboe*, was commissioned by Jane O'Leary's new music ensemble, Concorde. Buckley's election to Aosdána inaugurated a phase of significant growth in his career, and he was asked increasingly to undertake a number of very substantial projects.

Buckley's busy routine of creativity was interrupted in 1986 when he was involved in a serious car accident – in fact, he was lucky not to have been killed. One of the projects delayed by the accident was launched eventually in late 1987. Under the auspices of the Arts Council's scheme *The Artist in the Classroom*, Buckley devised a major educational project specifically for the Holy Spirit Girls' National School in Ballymun. It was highly successful and went on to become the subject of a prize-winning radio documentary. Despite his resignation in 1982 as a primary-school teacher, Buckley maintained his interest in education. Apart from his ongoing connection with the People's College and his involvement with the Ennis Summer School, he accepted numerous engagements as a speaker and guest lecturer.

Sonata for Unaccompanied Violin provides a good example. This was a set work for the Leaving Certificate music course, which resulted in Buckley giving introductory talks on the piece, as well as on other more general musical topics, in over sixty schools and art centres. Other workshops were organized by the Music Association of Ireland or the

National Concert Hall's Education and Outreach Programme. The latter programme led to the development of *In Tune*, a scheme launched in July 1998. The project arranged for members of the National Symphony Orchestra of Ireland (as the RTÉ Symphony Orchestra had become in 1990) to visit primary schools around Ireland, introducing children to their various instruments and to the music that had been written for them. More significantly, it introduced the children to composition – developing their potential for creative endeavour and performing the subsequent musical works in their schools and later at the National Concert Hall and other public venues. The project was presented on a national scale and was introduced to many peripheral regions. It is clear that Buckley never relinquished his role as a teacher, and used his unique status as a composer to develop music education across Ireland.

Figure 1: The Buckley family home, Templeglantine

Figure 2: Eileen Buckley (left) playing the fiddle with a friend in Templeglantine, 1939.

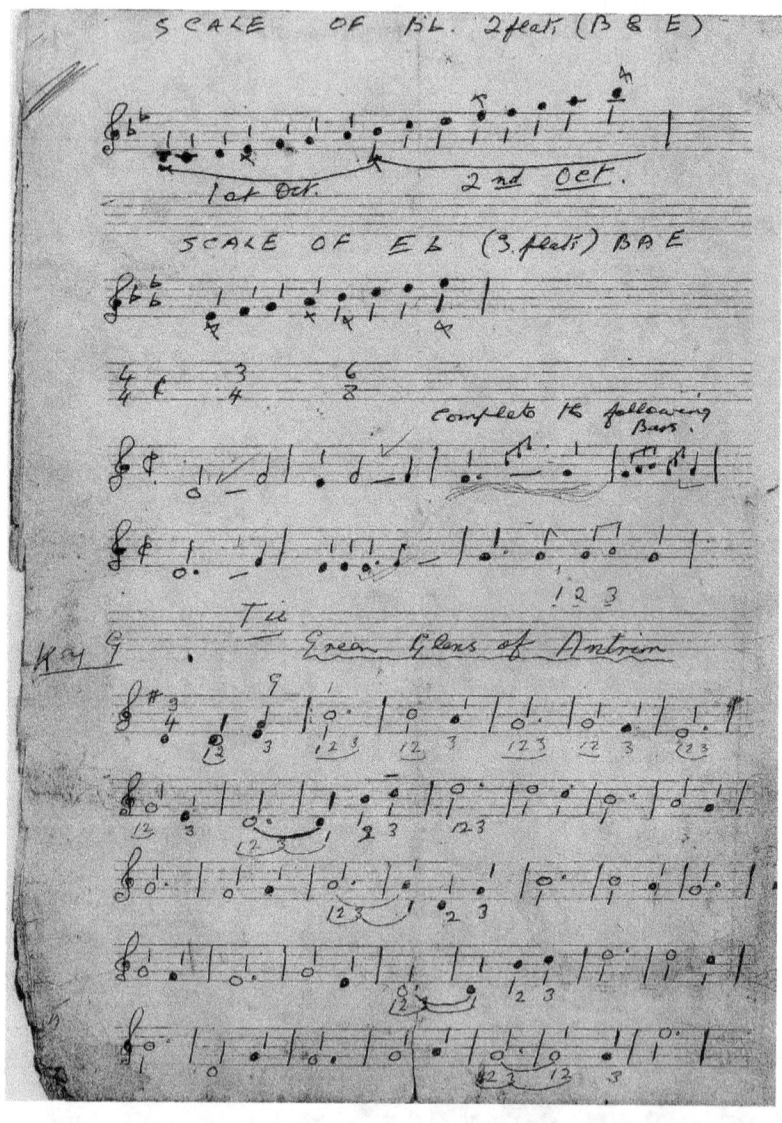

Figure 3: Original manuscript of Buckley's early music lessons in the handwriting of his first teacher, Liam Moloney. Note the transcription of *The Green Glens of Antrim*, the first song Buckley learned to play on the accordion.

Figure 4: John Buckley (on the bicycle) with his mother and brothers outside the family home in Templeglantine, 1963.

Figure 5: Buckley in 1963 at boarding school (run by the Salesian Order) in Ballinakill, Co, Laois.

Figure 6: The Royal Irish Academy of Music, where Buckley studied with A.J. Potter, James Wilson and Doris Keogh

Figure 7: Teaching at St. Patrick's College, Drumcondra

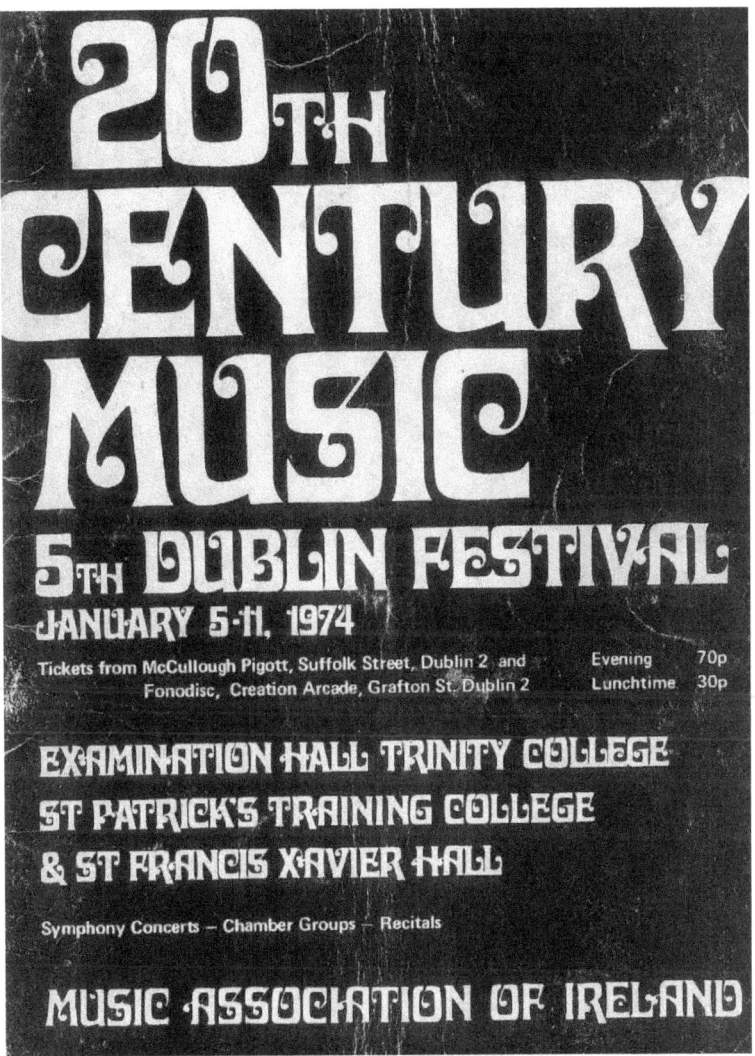

Figure 8: Programme cover for the 5th Dublin Festival of 20th Century Music (1974)

Figure 9: 'Young Composers' – members of the Association of Young Irish Composers, from the programme for the 6th Dublin Festival of 20th Century Music (1975)

5 | Consolidation (1988-1996)

Expanding Horizons

Throughout the 1980s, Buckley's music received wider international attention, largely as a result of advocacy by a number of international composers. In 1984, he was introduced by Brian Boydell to the German composer Peter Michael Hamel, who became a close friend. Born in 1947, Hamel, since 1997, has been the successor to György Ligeti as Composition Professor at the Hochschule für Musik und Theater, Hamburg. A leading German composer, he engaged with many diverse cultures, most notably India's. As a founder of the *Freies Musikzentrum München* – an institute for musical education and therapy, he is an advocate for the therapeutic value of music. 'Even though our styles are somewhat different,' Buckley explains, 'we share an interest in writing large-scale colourful works. We both regard music as a form of communication, rather than a series of sonic experiments.' Hamel also shared Buckley's interest in Irish mythology and even set the latter's translation of *The Song of Amhergín* from the Old Irish (*I Am Wind on Sea*) for choir. An earlier work of Hamel's, *Dona Nobis Pacem*, was commissioned by and premiered at the Cork International Choral Festival in 1985.

Hamel had a cottage in Cloongee, County Mayo, in the west of Ireland, where Buckley would often visit him. They enjoyed their lively discussions about music and the problems of composing, from which both men derived much benefit and stimulus. Furthermore, they helped one another to arrange performances of their work: Buckley invited Hamel to teach at the Ennis Composition Summer School and suggested to Fleischmann that he be commissioned for the Seminar on Contemporary Choral Music; Hamel in turn promoted Buckley's music in Germany, where it was performed for the first time in 1987 in a concert at the Hochschule für Musik und Theater in Munich where *Sonata for Unaccompanied Violin*, *Five Epigrams for Flute and Oboe* and *Boireann* were performed. One critic recognized a particularly Irish quality to these post-tonal works:

> Although art music in Ireland is young, it is not new to German ears [...] [The flute and piano work] really depicts the brash landscape of the Boireann – you can feel the landscape in his music.[60]

This event was followed by further concerts and radio broadcasts, including an hour-long composer portrait commissioned by Bayerischer Rundfunk. Appreciative articles on his work also began to appear in German magazines and journals such as *MusikTexte*.[61] Buckley found very refreshing the open-minded attitudes of German musicians and audiences, particularly their willingness to engage with the work of an Irish composer: 'I found Germany very open to the concept of an Irish composer, unlike Britain, which I must say for me has remained very much a closed shop.'

1985 was a major year in the European music calendar as the tercentenary of the births of Johann Sebastian Bach, George Frederick Handel and Domenico Scarlatti. It was designated European Music Year by the European Community. Ireland fully engaged with this international initiative and organized many innovative musical projects. The first ever commercial recordings of the works of Buckley and fellow-composer Raymond Deane were launched. Buckley's *Wind Quintet*, *Five Epigrams for Flute and Oboe*, *Boireann* and *Sonata for Unaccompanied Violin* were released on a commercial cassette by a small Irish independent label, Goasco. Numerous music organizations and groups were also established, including the Irish Youth Wind Ensemble, and many concerts were organized nationally and internationally.

Cultural exchange programmes were structured so that pairs of European member states were linked for musical collaboration. Ireland was paired with Sweden. Buckley, along with Jane O'Leary and Brian Boydell, was chosen by a committee from the Irish Composers' Centre (a predecessor to the Contemporary Music Centre) in conjunction with the Arts Council as the Irish representatives in Sweden. Buckley met the Swedish composer Arne Mellnäs, who would also become a valued

---

[60] Karl Robert Brachtel, 'Einfallsreiche Dialoge', *Münchner Merkur* (10 March 1987).

[61] Peter Michael Hamel, 'Der irische Komponist John Buckley: Fantasia No. 2 für Altblockflöte', *MusikTexte 20* (July/August 1987).

friend and supporter. The music of Mellnäs in particular resonated strongly with Buckley, revealing a very similar concern for timbre and sonority: 'I was immediately struck by the stylistic similarities between his work, in particular *Transparence* for orchestra, and my own compositions of that period.'[62]

Mellnäs was almost twenty years older than Buckley. Born in Stockholm in 1933, he studied at the State College of Music, Stockholm, and privately with Max Deutsch in Paris and György Ligeti in Vienna. By the time Buckley met him, he had become one of the most prominent figures in Swedish music as a member since 1984 of both the Swedish Composers' Society and the Royal Academy of Music. From 1996 until his death in 2002 he would serve as President of the International Society for Contemporary Music (ISCM).[63] Mellnäs and Buckley felt an immediate rapport, and a warm professional and personal relationship developed between them. They continued to correspond and exchange scores for many years, and Buckley often visited Mellnäs in Sweden. Mellnäs readily helped promote his friend's music in his native country: Buckley's *Wind Quintet* was performed by the Falun Blåsarkvintett in November 1985, and *I Am Wind on Sea* received its Swedish premiere on 6 October 1994 at the World Music Days organized by the ISCM in the Stockholm Cultural Centre, when it was performed by the celebrated mezzo-soprano Paula Hoffman. His work was also broadcast on Sveriges Radio, for which he gave a number of interviews. Other works of Buckley's featured in the World Music Days include *Oileáin* (Amsterdam, 1985), *Concerto for Alto Saxophone and String Orchestra* (Cluj, Romania, 1999), *Saxophone Quartet* (Luxembourg, 2000) and *Concerto for Bassoon and Orchestra* (Zagreb, 2005). In 1998, as a result of Mellnäs' advocacy, he was invited to act as a juror for the ISCM, the first Irish composer to do so. Buckley recommended that Mellnäs be commissioned by the Cork International Choral Festival, for which he wrote a new work in 1995 entitled *Spring*.

Buckley continued to compose prolifically throughout the late 1980s and early 1990s. He was increasingly offered commissions of a more rewarding nature and was able to concentrate on writing music that reflected his central artistic concerns, rather than having to fulfill more routine tasks. By this point, he had established himself as one of the

---

[62] Arne Mellnäs, *Transparence* (for orchestra: instrumentation:4444 4440 03 1 str, cel) (Stockholm: Phono Suecia, 1972)

[63] Founded in 1922, the International Society for Contemporary Music (ISCM) is a major platform for the promotion and dissemination of contemporary music. Its major annual festival – World Music Days – is held in a different member country each year.

most significant composers working in Ireland, and was called upon frequently to provide music for important official or celebratory occasions. As a result, he was offered virtually every major commission available in Ireland during this period.

The Scene in Ireland

Buckley acknowledges that considerable progress has been made and that he has personally benefitted from many of these infrastructural developments. However, he feels that progress is often offset by retrograde steps: 'The diminution in support for contemporary music by the Arts Council is a case in point.'[64] Although he contends that Irish composers have produced work that compares favourably with the music of their contemporaries in other countries, their contribution to Irish cultural life, in his view, is still marginalized and undervalued in their native country. Much music is written, often with considerable publicity surrounding the first performances, but most of it is allowed to languish in complete neglect thereafter. Buckley comments ironically that 'achievements which are noted with fanfares in the media die rather suddenly, not to be resurrected for another twenty years, if at all.' He insists that this neglect has nothing to do with the quality of the music itself or with any lack of ability on the part of Irish composers. Classical music in general, and contemporary music in particular, are simply not seen as central to the cultural life of the country. In the current climate, where so much music of so many different kinds is constantly contending for the attention of broadcasters, journalists and promoters, it is becoming increasingly difficult, he feels, for contemporary composers to make their presence felt.

Buckley is very critical of the press coverage of Irish composers, which, in his opinion, is generally minimal and inadequate:

> Unlike literary works, new compositions get almost no press coverage whatsoever. While a new novel will typically be given large-scale coverage in our leading newspapers, a new symphony may get a few column inches, deeply buried in some review, lest it call undue attention to itself. General books on Ireland invariably discuss the great writers: when Irish music is discussed it is almost always in terms of traditional music, rock or pop. Composers are hardly given a passing mention.

---

[64] John Buckley, in discussion with author, 19 September 2010. These comments refer to funding decisions made by the Arts Council of Ireland, which came into effect from around 2008.

Buckley is not the only critic of the generally poor conditions for Irish composers. Jane O'Leary, in a paper written for *Irish Musical Studies* in 1995, gave a largely positive overview of developments in the preceding twenty years or so, but nonetheless concluded the following:

> Audiences are still starved of frequent exposure to new music of all kinds and suffer from a lack of suitable venues; performers need to extend their repertoire and become more proficient in contemporary techniques. As Ireland takes its place in Europe, its composers too will have to be sufficiently well prepared to compete in the international marketplace.[65]

According to Raymond Deane, the international marketplace is the very source of the problem:

> The difficulties faced by the arts in Ireland today reflect those they face world-wide in an age in which human values are increasingly defined in terms of the marketplace.[66]

In a now famous paper for the Irish Musical Studies series, Deane, in his assessment of the Irish music environment, directs his fiercest criticism towards the conservatism of the opera companies and festivals. The Wexford Opera Festival, he says,

> concentrates on eighteenth- and nineteenth-century operas that have (often with very good reason) dropped out of the repertoire and may be expected to disappear again after the Festival [...] As for the Dublin Grand Opera Society [now Opera Ireland] few would dispute that its appeal is confined to a particular segment of the affluent Dublin bourgeoisie [...] neither of these institutions has ever betrayed much interest in presenting operas by living Irish composers.[67]

Deane exposes the strange paradox of the Irish composer: even though some are honoured officially as members of Aosdána, any such recognition rings false due to the unfortunate reality of their professional lives as composers without an audience: 'However substantial their output, its existence is virtual until it is given access to a listenership. In a very real sense, composers are being honoured for not existing.'[68]

---

[65] Jane O'Leary, 'Contemporary Music in Ireland: Developments in the Past Twenty Years' in *Irish Musical Studies (4) - The Maynooth International Musicological Conference 1995 (Selected Proceedings: Part One)* edited by Patrick F. Devine and Harry White (Dublin: Four Courts Press, 1996), p. 295.
[66] Raymond Deane: 'The Honour of non-Existence - Classical Composers in Irish Society', *Irish Musical Studies (3) - Music and Irish Cultural History*, edited by Gerard Gillen and Harry White (Dublin: Irish Academic Press, 1995), p. 199.
[67] Ibid. p. 200.
[68] Ibid. p. 205.

It is generally acknowledged that growth in Irish musical life has been slow due to various complex historical factors. Contemporary composers in England can now build securely on the achievements of Vaughan Williams, Holst and their contemporaries, and on the subsequent work of composers like Britten and Tippett. A similar situation exists in most other European countries. However, circumstances in Ireland at the turn of the twentieth century were not conducive to the vigorous growth of musical life or of the infrastructures that would sustain it. Buckley comments:

> Beginning in the early part of the twentieth century and extending to the 1960s, many composers such as Hamilton Harty, John F. Larchet, Arthur Duff, Eamonn Ó Gallchobhair and A.J. Potter made extensive use of folk material in their original compositions. RTÉ commissioned numerous orchestral arrangements of traditional music for such programmes as *Music of the Nation*. This approach to composition was seen by some to represent a type of nationalism and to represent the musical expression of the emerging nation. Curiously, during the greater part of this period, traditional music itself was languishing in a state of severe decline, only to be revived during the 1960s due to the efforts of Ó Riada and others. The more modernist leanings of Boydell, May and others stand in stark contrast to this tradition, causing some commentators such as Harry White to refer to a 'divided imagination'. This historical divide is the inheritance of contemporary Irish composers pursuing a modernist aesthetic. Unlike our counterparts in many European countries, the contemporary Irish composer does not have a long lineage on which to lean.

In spite of these adverse historical circumstances, Buckley maintains that Irish composers achieved a great deal. He is scornful of the clichéd question about why there has never been an 'Irish Bartók', contending that it is an unhelpful distraction from the fact that very fine Irish composers did exist and wrote much great music. When asked about the whereabouts of putative 'Irish Bartóks', he believes that the only possible answer is that they have been ignored – not that they have never existed. 'We may not have had a Bartók, but we have had a Fleischmann, a May, a Boydell, and their work is almost entirely unknown.' As far as Buckley is concerned, all that the composer can do in the face of indifference is to continue to write music to the best of his or her ability.

> I want my music to reach the widest possible audience, as with most composers. The composer's primary responsibility and function, however, is to compose, even if the potential audience is small or indifferent. In a sense, once the music is written and performed, it assumes a life of its own; the composer no longer owns or controls it.

The Late 1980s and Early 1990s

During the late 1980s and early 1990s, Buckley composed a number of large-scale works that displayed a shift in compositional perspective. *Winter Music* (1988) demonstrates Buckley's concern with achieving an increased refinement of sound. Composed for Dublin pianist Anthony Byrne, who gave the first performance at his debut recital in the Purcell Room in London on 16 March 1988, it consists of one movement lasting ten minutes. *Winter Music* displays a textural subtlety in marked contrast to the more robust sonorities exploited in Buckley's earlier keyboard works. Importantly, the piece makes a significant move towards a French refinement of sound and an elevation of timbre as central characteristics. The work certainly shares Debussy's interest in textural subtlety and demonstrates Buckley's concerted engagement with French piano music, evident as early as *Oileáin* from 1979. Furthermore, the idiosyncratic quality of *Winter Music* points to Buckley's keen absorption of the instrument's inherent characteristics. Indeed, the piece is written as though Buckley were a pianist himself.

The works that follow *Winter Music* continue to exhibit this new stylistic characteristic. *Abendlied*, for soprano and piano, is a setting of three poems. Buckley uses the first stanza of *Abendständchen* by Clemens Brentano and two poems by Eichendorff – *Der Abend* and *Mondnacht*.[69] The latter text is also found in *Liederkreis*, Op. 39 by Schumann, and Buckley's use of it indicates a growing self-assurance on his part as a composer. In setting this text ('I was very conscious of Schumann's song while composing *Abendlied*'), he was certainly not intimidated by any possible future comparisons. The work is notable for its florid vocal writing, and this concern for embellishment may have prompted the comment that the work, 'rather oddly to my ears, ran the whole gamut of *Sturm und Drang* before settling where it promised, in "the shimmering quiet of evening."'[70] Perhaps this opinion is somewhat exaggerated as only three of the ten minutes of the work could be considered outwardly dramatic. As the renowned soprano Jane Manning has observed, '[the poems] complement each other perfectly in their subtly contrasting musical treatment. The first half of the piece (the Brentano setting) is full of dramatic tension, and the second poem is, in general, set more simply and gently.'[71] Another critic found that the 'virtuoso piano part, independent yet supportive, sowed the

---

[69] See Appendix II for words and translations.
[70] Richard Pine, *The Irish Times*, 21 July 1989.
[71] Jane Manning, *New Vocal Repertory 2* (London: Oxford University Press, 1998), p. 276.

influence of Messiaen's bird song and Bartók's night music.'[72] *Abendlied* was premiered by Penelope Price Jones and Philip Martin at the Royal Irish Academy of Music in Dublin on 14 June 1989.

The *Guitar Sonata No. 1* explores the tonal and textural possibilities of the instrument in the extreme.[73] The first movement is the most complex and developed, juxtaposing rapid flourishes (scales, arpeggios, continuous strumming) with softer meditative statements. Its climax reaches an extreme frenzy and demands an unusual degree of stamina and physical prowess from the guitarist. In stark contrast, the second movement exposes Buckley's lyricism, displaying poignancy beyond his usual emotional restraint. In the third movement, Buckley invokes the Latin-American aspect of the instrument, incorporating a specific type of percussive strumming prevalent in South American popular genres like Samba and Milonga. It is as much a homage to the rhythmic and percussive music of the Argentinian composer Alberto Ginastera (1916-1983) as it is to the indigenous musics he appropriated. Throughout the work, percussive strumming is interspersed with innovative techniques such as pitch bending, glissandi used simultaneously with rasguado (flamenco) strumming, and Bartók pizzicati (also combined with glissandi). Together, these extra-musical applications, allied to a large-scale structural canvas outlined over three strongly developed movements, create an idiomatic work of considerable virtuosity and stature, which must surely be counted amongst the most adventurous in the recent repertoire. It was premiered by the author at the Guitar Institute in New York on 5 August 1989.

Given his consistent preoccupation with the sheer sonority and texture of music, surprisingly, Buckley has not been tempted to explore the possibilities offered by electronic media. His position is clear: he admits that electro-acoustic does not interest him. The sound of traditional instruments, the virtuosic components of performance, and the modern orchestra remain central points of interest for him.

> Electro-acoustic music has never particularly appealed to me as a medium. I am drawn more to standard instruments and to the endless kaleidoscope of possibilities offered by the modern orchestra. This is where I have concentrated my creative energies and attempted to forge an individual musical voice.

Buckley's interest in electro-acoustic media, such as it is, lies in the interaction between live performers and electro-acoustic sonorities:

> As a listener, the aspect of electro-acoustic music that most interests

---

[72] Pat O'Kelly, *Evening Press*, 17 July 1989.
[73] Written for the author of this book.

me is the live interaction between performer and technology. Pieces for tape alone, during which one sits in an auditorium watching two speakers, are of no interest to me. The experience misses the essential element of human communication, when the performer brings new life to the work each time it is performed. Electro-acoustic music has rarely communicated to me or moved me in any way. For these reasons I have not been drawn to it. My inspiration lies elsewhere.

Buckley's impressive rate of productivity continued unabated, and in 1993 he completed two substantial new pieces: *De Profundis*, a twenty-five minute cantata for soprano and alto soloists, mixed-voice chorus, optional boys' choir and orchestra (commissioned by the Tallaght Choral Society in Dublin) and *Rivers of Paradise*. *De Profundis* brought Buckley into uncharacteristically dark territory. The work interweaves two psalms, *De Profundis* (Psalm CXXIX omitting the last verse) and *Domine, non est exaltatum cor meum* (Psalm CXXX), the former set for the main choir and the latter set for the boys' choir. The subdued mood of these texts, coupled with the natural technical restraints demanded by the amateur choirs for which the work was written, may also have restricted Buckley's normally liberal expressive canvas. Instead, another influence shone through. Buckley explains: 'The untypically dark nature of the work represents a personal and artistic response to the catastrophic Balkan wars of the early 1990s.'

Rivers of Paradise, on the other hand, is free from any such restraints. This was commissioned by the University of Limerick to celebrate the official opening of its new Concert Hall and was first performed there on 18 September 1993. Buckley had to respond to the most exacting commission of his career: the University specifically requested that concepts of knowledge, learning, the university, science, and other related issues form the core of the work. It further insisted upon a spoken text. Thus, the work is written for large symphony orchestra and two narrators. The title derives from the conjunction of two metaphors central to the metaphysical poet John Donne (1572-1631): 'the University as Paradise' and 'Knowledge, flowing as in a river.' The piece, therefore, celebrates and reflects upon the university and on intellectual and imaginative life as manifested in science and the arts.

The text draws upon the writings of ten different authors: John Donne; John Henry Newman (1801-1890); an anonymous Irish seventeenth-century poet; Albert Einstein (1879-1955); Galileo Galilei (1564-1642); Johannes Kepler (1571-1630); William Shakespeare (1564-1616); William Carlos Williams (1883-1963); Christopher Marlowe

(1564-1593) and T.S. Eliot (1888-1965).[74] In its sumptuous mix of text and swirling orchestration, *Rivers of Paradise* appears to be following in the footsteps of his highly successful *A Thin Halo of Blue* (1990). That Buckley would want to continue on the success of its predecessor is understandable. Whether he matched its achievement is arguable. There is something of the punctuation, the chopped rhythmic pulse and the logical rationale of narrated text that acts in direct contravention to the flow, the sense of open space and nuanced timbre of music as a non-denotative form. It might very well be this essential friction of incompatibility that gives the lied, the choral work, the aria their unique place in composition. In *Rivers of Paradise*, however, the opposing forces of spoken, explicative text and the busy swirling, abstract music are perhaps a little at odds with each other. Regardless of this possible incongruity, Buckley's infectiously celebratory *Rivers of Paradise* certainly displays both his skill and enjoyment in creating large canvasses of glistening colour and fireworks.

If Buckley failed to complete any new work in 1994 it was because he had been preoccupied with a composition designed for the largest array of forces he had yet employed. This undertaking was in fulfillment of yet another prestigious commission. St Patrick's College, Maynooth, was celebrating its bicentenary in 1995, and to mark the occasion the College invited Buckley to compose a setting of the *Te Deum*, the traditional canticle of celebration in the Roman liturgy (see Appendix V for full text). This imposing piece, of about half an hour's duration, demanded a comprehensive line-up of instrumentalists and vocalists: four soloists, soprano (Regina Nathan), alto (Colette McGahon), tenor (Emmanuel Lawler) and bass (Eugene Griffin); male-voice choir (Maynooth Seminary Choir); mixed-voice chamber choir (Maynooth College Chamber Choir); large mixed-voice choir (Maynooth University Choral Society); organ (Gerard Gillen); and orchestra (National Symphony Orchestra conducted by Colman Pearce). Two performances of the work took place at the National Concert Hall in Dublin – the first, on 16 November 1995, for private dignitaries and invited guests; the second, on the following night, for the public.

In general terms, the music for the large chorus (movements 1, 2, 4, 6 and 8) is direct in style, employing either block chords or, alternatively, fugal-type textures. The male voice choir (movement 7) has a gently flowing chromatic movement, whose origin lies in plainchant. The music for the chamber choir (movements 3 and 7) uses

---

[74] See Appendix III for complete text.

a more complex harmonic and textural approach while the four soloists have long, elaborate melodic lines, frequently in counterpoint with each other or with the choirs. In writing the piece, Buckley attempted to capture something of the sonorous majesty of the text, which ranges from celebratory declamations to passages of intimate supplication. Of its eight movements, 2 and 3 are performed without a break, as are movements 6 and 7. While the writing for the choirs is generally conservative (block tonal chords, vocal lines in unison and octaves, etc.), Buckley confined his typically more dramatic compositional techniques (chord clusters, aleatoric devices, wide intervallic leaps, etc.) to the orchestra so that a strange dichotomy is created within the work, which presents some stylistic incongruity. It remains, nonetheless, an extraordinarily impressive achievement.

From the beginning of the 1990s, a concern with achieving a greater degree of formal unity becomes more evident in Buckley's work, perhaps as a partial reaction against his previous overriding absorption with timbre for its own sake. Buckley confirms that he had been in pursuit of this structural concentration for some time, but was anxious to achieve it without sacrificing the characteristic exuberance of his earlier work. His preoccupation with instrumental colour remained very intense and as the titles of several works from these years attest – *In Lines of Dazzling Light* (1995, rev. 1998), *A Mirror Into the Light* (1999), *In Winter Light* (2004) – he was increasingly drawn to the exploration of analogies between sound and light, a preoccupation which, as has been suggested, may have been influenced by his exposure to the orchestral works of Alun Hoddinott. These somewhat impressionistic titles cannot be taken to imply any diffuseness of formal design: they merely serve to indicate the atmospheric sound-world of the music. With regard to this increasingly important source of inspiration, Buckley remarks:

> The daily cycle of life and work in the countryside is to a great extent determined by the rise and fall of light. Country people are constantly aware of light, and to this day, after almost forty years living in the city, I can tell the time accurately without a watch during daylight hours. This feeling for light plays a major role in my compositions – instrumentation, texture, timbre and gesture acting as musical parallels.

In addition to this visual stimulus, a further source of inspiration for several of Buckley's works during this period derived from his association with specific performers. He has collaborated with some of the foremost exponents of contemporary music in Ireland. These works have been coloured by the characteristic performance styles of these individual musicians. This approach is well exemplified by *Arabesque,* a five-minute piece for unaccompanied alto saxophone which he wrote in 1990 for renowned Irish saxophonist Kenneth Edge. This work exhibits Buckley's quest for greater formal rigour through the manipulation of complex lineal groupings.

The arabesque is an elaborate Islamic art developed through a stylized rendering of complex, ornate designs of intertwined floral, foliate and geometric figures. Just as the arabesque embodies many visual and literary associations, it also provides a useful function in musical composition where it characterizes a wide range and diversity of techniques. The arabesque assumed a specific identity for Schumann (*Arabeske*, Op. 18 for piano) and Debussy (*Deux Arabesques* for piano). The style can also be observed in the highly elaborate ornamentation of such works as Ravel's *Daphnis et Chloé*. Schumann's treatment of arabesque emerges from his idiosyncratic piano technique, with its intertwined embroidery of melodic line and ornament. The style is evoked in the French composers' simulation at the *début du siècle* of Art Nouveau's intricate and fluid designs through melodic gestures that emphasize irregular rhythms and fluctuating metres. These composers promoted the arabesque's expressive capacity and challenged preconceptions of ornament as marginal and superfluous. In Buckley's *Arabesque*, the very concept of embellishment acts as the basis for the form. The ornaments and quasi-improvisatory figurations that normally decorate a given musical line become the very substance of that musical line. The piece can be considered an extended embellishment where ornamentation acquires a formal, organizing function. The result is a succession of complex melodic ideas, evolving in a continuous stream that scarcely allows the performer time to breathe.

Buckley also nurtured the skills of performers from outside Ireland. In 1988, he met the winner of the Dublin International Organ Festival, Andreas Liebig. His association with Liebig proved to be profound and long-lasting. In 1985, Buckley had already written a major organ work, *At the Round Earths Imagin'd Corners,* for the Irish organist Gerard Gillen (for the Ballina Arts Festival). The title is taken from the opening lines of *Holy Sonnet No. VII* by the metaphysical poet John Donne.

> At the round earths imagin'd corners, blow
> Your trumpets, Angells, and arise, arise
> From death, you numberlesse infinities
> Of soules, and to your scattred bodies goe,
> All whom the flood did, and fire shall o'erthrow,
> All whom warre, dearth, age, agues, tyrannies,

> Despaire, law, chance, hath slaine, and you whose eyes,
> Shall behold God, and never tast deaths woe.
> But let them sleepe, Lord, and mee mourne a space,
> For, if above all these, my sinnes abound,
> 'Tis late to aske abundance of thy grace,
> When wee are there; here on this lowly ground,
> Teach mee how to repent; for that's as good
> As if thou'hadst seal'd my pardon, with thy blood.

Buckley's composition, *At the Round Earths Imagin'd Corners*, draws its inspiration and formal design from Donne's majestic sonnet without attempting a paraphrase. He states in an article, 'I have tried to capture something of the powerfully evocative imagery and sonorous language of the poem.'[75] That striking imagery is matched in the music, whose 'reassuring bird calls which contrast the previous jabbing fanfares, violent trills, stabbing chords and jarring clusters, seem to imply nature returning to normality in the wake of some catastrophic disorder.'[76] *At the Round Earths Imagin'd Corners* resonates with Liebig's philosophical and spiritual temperament, and his interpretations have been particularly penetrative. In a review for the *Evening Press*, Pat Kelly states:

> The quality of Buckley's writing [...] obviously touched the interpretative genius of Herr Liebig. The result brought a stunning account of this intensely dramatic piece of music contrast where the gentlest of motifs could have a counterbalancing and disturbing vehemence. The range and scope of the short work brought exceptional brilliance and excitement in performance.[77]

Liebig's affinity with the work has led him to perform it worldwide on no fewer than twenty occasions. The relationship between composer and organist developed personally when Buckley was asked to become godfather to Liebig's son Johannes, and professionally, when he was invited by Liebig to lecture in Ærø (an island off the coast of Denmark) where a number of his works were also performed.

Buckley spent more time in Scandinavia in 1995, when he was invited by Finnish composer Timo-Juhani Kyllönen to deliver a series of lectures on contemporary Irish music in the Sibelius Academy in Helsinki. The two composers had met in 1992, when their music was featured as part of the St Petersburg Spring Festival. Buckley invited Kyllönen to be a guest lecturer at the Ennis Composition Summer School and further proposed him for commission at the Cork

---

[75] Michael Dervan, 'Thinning Out the Textures', *Irish Times*, 26 June 1986.
[76] Pat O'Kelly, *Evening Press*, 30 October 1992.
[77] Pat O'Kelly, 'Festival winner returns to city', *Evening Press*, 22 January 1990.

International Choral Festival, for which he composed *Innisfree*, op. 33. Buckley's three lectures at the Sibelius Academy historically situated new music in Ireland and focused on music, modernity, and on his own compositions. His music also was performed in association with the lecture series. The concert included *And Wake the Purple Year*, *Sonata for Unaccompanied Violin*, *Abendlied*, *Five Epigrams for Flute and Oboe*, *Sonata for Solo Horn*, *Boireann* and *The Silver Apples of the Moon, The Golden Apples of the Sun*.

Two chamber works, *In Lines of Dazzling Light* (1995) (for clarinet, bassoon, horn, violin and piano), and the *Saxophone Quartet* (1996) show Buckley's preoccupation at the time with strict formal arrangements of abstract sound. The title of the first of these works suggests a paradoxical attempt to find sonic images that convey a certain type of light; this light is not calm and diffuse as suggested by *In Winter Light*, but rather explodes in violent, blinding flashes of sunlight. The score was the result of a commission from Ensemble Contrasts, who gave the first performance in Vienna on 22 February 1995. The following year Buckley heard a live saxophone quartet for the first time when the Aurelia Saxophone Quartet from Holland gave a concert in Dundalk. Buckley was impressed immediately by the fresh compositional possibilities offered by a quartet of saxophones and lost little time in commencing a work for the Dutch ensemble. The *Saxophone Quartet*, which is written in a vein not dissimilar to *In Lines of Dazzling Light*, remains one of the composer's favourites. It was first performed on 14 April 1998 in the Concertgebouw de Doelen in Rotterdam.

SELECTED ANALYSIS

Symphony No. 1

Due to Buckley's enduring interest in the colouristic possibilities of the modern symphony orchestra, it was inevitable that he would compose further large-scale works for the medium. Following the ballet score of 1980, his next orchestral work was a symphony. *Symphony No. 1* was completed early in 1988 and first performed in June of that year in the National Concert Hall, Dublin, by the RTÉ Symphony Orchestra under Albert Rosen. This substantial thirty-five minute work in many ways represents a culmination of the diverse approaches to composition of Buckley's work up to this point.

Despite his modernist pedigree, Buckley was both very familiar with and attracted to the symphonic canon. He always considered his earlier orchestral essays – *Taller than Roman Spears* and *Fornocht do Chonnac Thú* – as works of symphonic aspiration. Though the symphony as a form presented Buckley with a vast historical canon and a lasting emblem of tradition in western art music, by 1988 he felt that he was ready to incorporate a new sophistication of colour and form into his work within a much broader and more projected structure. With a major orchestral work entitled *Symphony No. 1*, he certainly undertook a conscious and focused engagement with that tradition. Indeed, it demonstrated his willingness to create a direct association with a long-established canon, thus distinguishing himself from other Irish composers like Raymond Deane and Gerald Barry, who considered such a challenge to be unimportant. From the mid-1980s, however, Lutoslawski had been a central influential presence for Buckley. The former's *Symphony No. 2*, in particular, demonstrated most convincingly how procedures such as aleatoricism could be integrated into the larger structures of symphonic form, which paved the way for Buckley to attempt something similar. Although the post-war *avant-garde* had largely dismissed the symphony, by the 1980s the genre had re-established its place in the musical arena, as the symphonies of Henze, Lutoslawski, Dutilleux, Maxwell-Davies and Tippett aptly demonstrate. Buckley referenced these composers in the years surrounding the preparation and writing of his own symphony. Furthermore, at this time many of Buckley's international colleagues were also engaged with the genre – Peter Michael Hamel wrote

Symphony in Three Parts in 1988 while Arne Mellnäs wrote *Ikaros, Symphony 1* in 1986.

Drafts of Buckley's *Symphony No. 1* reach as far back as 1982, when he received a substantial bursary from the Arts Council designed to assist the composer to pursue study on a large-scale project. The work, therefore, did not result from a specific commission but rather arose from long-term deliberation. *Symphony No. 1*, dedicated to James Wilson, has two movements, each of which is further divided into two sections, resulting in a four-'movement' structure that aligns the piece with the classical ideal of symphonic form.

Movement I

Section 1

Symphony No. 1 is dominated by the exploration of colouristic and timbral characteristics, and the manipulation and juxtaposition of various blocks of timbral entities provides the shape of each section within the movements. As in *Taller than Roman Spears* and *Concerto for Chamber Orchestra*, these elements are often linked by numerous duos, trios or double duos. Fig. 11 below demonstrates how Buckley constructs his material into different sub-sections. These divisions do not represent a definitive structural plan, but merely expose the interplay of various sound blocks. These sound blocks instigate changes in tempi alongside a gradual tendency towards acceleration and culmination.

Fig. 11: Arrangement of sound blocks of Movement I, section I

1	Opening	Introduction (adagio) on E and E♭ (41 bars)[78]
2	Page 12	*con fuoco*: percussion interspersed with groupings of wind/brass/strings (9 bars)
3	Page 16	*più mosso*: string section (later with interconnected wind and brass) (37 bars)
4	Page 22	*Accel.*: dominated by groupings of wind/brass/strings interspersed with a series of trios (bassoon/cello/bass)

---

[78] Please note that certain aleatoric processes used in *Symphony No. 1* function outside the structure of given bars. I will consider a page of free aleatoric writing as a bar. Buckley has not used bar numbers in the score and so my use of bar numbers will offer an idea of the relative length of a given section.

		and percussion (34 bars)
5	Page 28:	*largamente:* slower link section on unison strings (11 bars)
6	Page 30:	*con fuoco*: groupings of wind/brass/strings interspersed by violent percussion and numerous ascending textures through the groups' register (51 bars)
7	Page 42:	*con moto:* wind/percussion and strings juxtaposed to create *chinoiserie* style (14 bars)
8	Page 45:	[*con fuoco* tempo]: extended aleatoric section as climax ending on chord based on E moving slow second section (12 bars)

Although Buckley had made significant advancements in his control over aleatoric processes and structural architecture since *Taller than Roman Spears* (1977), he altered little of his formal approach to orchestration. In *Symphony No. 1*, he divides the orchestra into its traditional sections – wind/brass/non-pitched percussion/pitched percussion/strings. These delineated orchestral sections are often heard separately or in various combinations, but their fundamental identities are rarely altered and little use is made of the opportunity to intermix instrumental groupings. Strongly characteristic of a particularly French school of orchestration, the preservation of orchestral sections encapsulates Buckley's general approach to orchestration, and his central concern remains the pursuit of timbral complexes by way of the juxtaposition of distinct sound webs. For example, starting from section 8, page 45 at rehearsal mark T, he writes an aleatoric block of wind music. He adds a block of brass at page 46 and superimposes both over a block of tutti percussion to create a three-part texture.

Buckley's use of the pitched percussion as pivots around which sound webs are transformed features prominently in this movement. This technique can be seen at C (page 8) where a block of wind sound is modulated effectively through the pitched percussion into a block of string sound. Elsewhere, the non-pitched percussion is used to propel the music from aggressive woodwind and brass towards frenetic strings, and vice versa (see section 6: page 30 from M onwards).

Section 2
The second section of the first movement effectively displays Buckley's full control of timbral constructs. The dominance of various solos, duos and trios give the music a more intimate ambiance. Buckley often composes elusive tonal meshes over sustained strings where the pitched

percussion of glockenspiel, crotales and vibraphone (along with the harp and sleigh bells) play a particularly distinctive role in setting up static sound moments of extreme delicacy and evanescence. The discrete accumulation of these sound webs suggests more complex combinations, bringing to mind the French-orientated sound palette of Takemitsu. Section EE on page 70, for example, demonstrates Buckley's complete control of timbral transparency. Aleatoric processes are used scantily, but are all the more effective for that, particularly near the end of the movement (at FF+7 on page 74) where *ff staccatissimo* wind punctuations fade out into *pp* strings. At the very end of the movement, similar repetitive figures in the wind over sustained strings (at II, page 78) built on F in the double basses represent one of the most beautiful passages of the entire work and give it a transcendental quality of arrival.

Ex. 28: *Symphony No. 1*, movement I, one bar before rehearsal mark II

There are three aspects of particular interest in the first movement. First, the work ends with music comprising two harmonic entities: lower strings (basses, cellos and violas) based on an F major chord, and hovering violins, harp and tuned percussion offering E-centred harmonies above. As the 'introduction' (opening) to the symphony is built on a sustained E, the entire movement (Sections I and II) is framed by the pitch centres E and F.

Fig. 12: *Symphony No. 1*, **movement I, structural plan**

Movement I: Section 1	Movement I: Section 2
E	(E) F

This long-term harmonic structure from E to F centres is encapsulated in the melodic fragments heard in the Introduction on the crotales (bar 1), the second flute (bar 2), the second clarinet (bar 3), and on the first horn (bar 4). As the second movement also finishes on a sustained F pedal, it could be argued that this E-F relationship governs the entire movement.

Ex. 29: *Symphony No. 1*, **movement I, bars 1-4 (flute 2, clarinet 2, horn 1, crotales)**

Second, a repeated melodic motif threads itself throughout the entire movement. Though it appears in various altered guises, it plays around the interlocking intervals of a minor third, a tone and a semitone, the latter echoing the semi-tone relationship between E and F mentioned above. The three examples below outline the different contours the motif assumes.

Ex. 30: *Symphony No. 1*, movement I, 3 bars before rehearsal mark X (1st flute part)

Ex. 31: *Symphony No. 1*, movement I, four bars before rehearsal mark Z (violin I)

Ex. 32: *Symphony No. 1*, movement I, rehearsal mark BB+6 (violin I, violin II and viola parts)

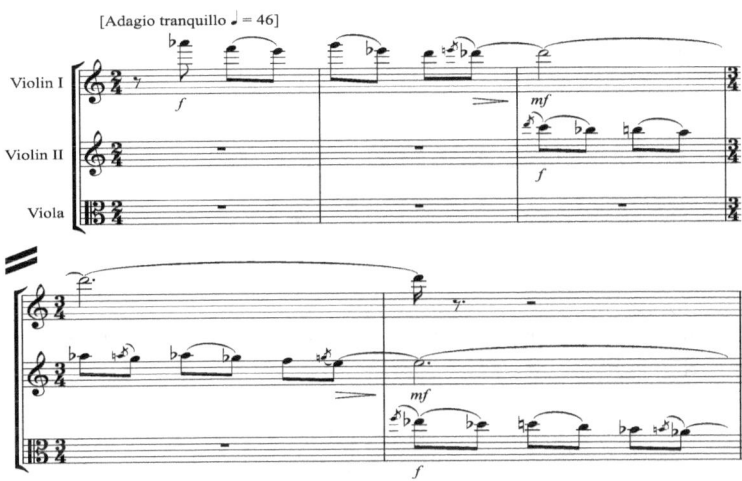

Third, at the end of this movement, a reference is made to the chamber work *Time Piece* (1982). Although *Time Piece* pre-dates *Symphony No. 1* by six years, certain aspects of it may have been absorbed into early sketches of the larger work. At five bars after HH on page 77, Buckley uses a series of rising scales in the strings. Written without a time signature, the strings are divided into three groups – 1st violins, 2nd violins and violas. The violas are given a separate tempo marking (crotchet = 66) from the violins (crotchet = 60) so that the rising scales not only blur tonally, but also rhythmically; any sense of rhythmic pulse has been smudged by the aleatoric process. A replica of this manipulation of rising scales closes *Time Piece* (see rehearsal mark Z page 19 of *Time Piece* score).

Movement II

Structurally, the second movement is more complex than the first. In the programme notes to the Marco Polo recoding, Buckley writes that each movement falls into two large-scale sections.[79] Although this is

---

[79] John Buckley, 'Organ Concerto/Symphony No. 1', *Irish Composers Series* (Marco Polo–8.223876).

perfectly clear for the first movement, the contours are not so well delineated for the second. It is difficult for the listener to formally grasp this movement as two distinct sections. The overall shape appears as follows:

Fig. 13: *Symphony No. 1*, movement II

Section 1
Introduction – Scherzo 1 – Trio – Scherzo 2

Section 2
Finale

As Buckley utilizes similar features in both sections, their delineation is somewhat undermined. The four-crotchet-beat timpani motif of the first section, for example, appears twice in the *finale*. Although the headings – *Introduction – Scherzo 1*, etc., are given in the programme notes as an aid, Buckley has not included such designations in the score and even the enthusiastic score reader might find the second movement rather intractable.

Aloys Fleischmann's critique that the emphasis on 'colour and filigree-work' detracts from the 'architectural structure' suggests that the large-scale application of musical arguments solely comprising timbral and textural soundscapes may not have sufficient anchoring strength to maintain formal coherence.[80] This potential weakness may have prompted Buckley to employ repeated sustained pedal notes, pitched percussion motifs and timpani motifs to help ground the work harmonically and structurally and offer points of orientation. Furthermore, despite the continuing emphasis on timbral figurations and colouristic elements, from this point onwards Buckley is more concerned with developing musical content from the harmony rather than harmony from the musical content.

As in *Concerto for Chamber Orchestra*, Buckley absorbs *avant-garde* processes into his own conceit of symphonic form, incorporating many of his musical gestures that predominantly take their cue from late 19th-century and early 20th-century models. The first movement of *Symphony No. 1* manages to avoid most of the ensuing stylistic clashes,

---

[80] Letter from Aloys Fleischmann to John Buckley, 10 September 1988. Letter in possession of John Buckley.

as it more successfully reconciles Buckley's innate lyricism with a modernist context. However, the bombastic timpani beats over unison pedals (at A page 81 and elsewhere) and the surprising brass 'theme' at R+3 (page 113), which fervently recalls Sibelius, raise questions over how successfully Buckley has synthesized the two worlds into a single, cohesive formal unit. These two examples bring with them an exceptional amount of extra-musical connotation from the past, which is hard to reconcile within the complex sound webs Buckley has woven around them.

Critical response to *Symphony No. 1* was mixed. One commentator observed that it 'proved an engrossing work, notable in particular for that now rare symphonic virtue, a clear and logical progression of musical thought. Admirably shaped in a kind of intellectual ellipsis, it has ideas and develops them with imagination.'[81] In *The Irish Times*, however, the use of aleatoricism itself as a compositional device came under attack:

> [the work] seemed more diffuse than the composer's obvious concern at integrating his material would have led one to expect. The work [...] still harks back to mannerisms that were once regarded as *avant-garde*. The Lutoslawskian aleatoricism of this work sounds every bit as thorough a padding generator as the nineteenth-century sequences of the works which followed it.[82]

On the other hand, Fleischmann, in a letter to Buckley, was highly complimentary about the symphony, though he did have some reservations regarding formal design:

> How very kind of you to send me the score and tape of your symphony! I really do appreciate this. Having played the work through twice, with increasing enthusiasm, I feel certain that technically your work is the most sophisticated and accomplished which has ever been produced here. The finesse of the sound-webs you have conceived, and their manipulation, is quite incredible. Rhythmically, as well, the score is a feast for the eye and the ear. Above all, I love the intensely lyrical unison lines, when they occur. Your whole language is entirely personal, novel, and wholly consistent. The performance, too, seems to me almost miraculous. Albert Rosen must have gone to endless trouble, and the players rise to heights which I think must be beyond any ever achieved before, in the performance of a new work.
>
> It does strike me that you paint consistently almost to the extent that the score seems as static as Scriabin's *Prometheus* or Debussy's *Iberia* – in this sense that colour and filigree work are the prominent

---

[81] Mary MacGoris, *Irish Independent*, 4 June 1988.
[82] Michael Dervan, *The Irish Times*, 4 June 1988. The works that followed Buckley's *Symphony No. 1* were the *Piano Concerto No. 2* by Saint-Saëns and Tchaikovsky's *Francesca da Rimini*.

elements. This to a certain extent takes from the architectural structure, for having heard the work now three times in all, I am not yet at all clear as to its outlines. With so much complexity most of the time, it is hard to separate in the mind's eye the contents of the first movement from that of the second. I may not be making myself at all clear, but I would say that if you were to adopt bolder, possibly simpler statements, with longer arches and more differentiated planes, what a towering masterpiece you could create!

However, I don't think it is in order to make suggestions to a composer of your stature now. One can only develop according to one's own internal proclivities. But you are certainly on the road to big things.[83]

A Thin Halo of Blue

In 1991, Buckley won the Marten Toonder Award. Made possible through the generosity of Dutch artist Marten Toonder and administered by the Arts Council of Ireland, the award honours established artists working in music, literature and visual arts, and is offered in rotation. Other Toonder award winners have included the writers Anthony Cronin and Paula Meehan, visual artist Dorothy Cross, and composers Kevin Volans, Seóirse Bodley and Roger Doyle. For Buckley, this represented an acknowledgement of his substantial contribution to contemporary Irish culture.

That acknowledgement is reflected in the six principal works that Buckley composed between 1990 and 1995, all of which owe their existence to prestigious commissions. In Buckley's view, the acceptance of commissions even for 'occasional' pieces can act as an imaginative stimulus. It certainly does not involve any compromise of his artistic vision, nor, in his view, does it necessarily mean that the resultant works are so dependent on the circumstances of their first performance that they have little chance of an independent future. 'I see all the music I've written as having a life beyond the occasion,' he insists.

This perspective is certainly true of *A Thin Halo of Blue* (1990), which was originally commissioned by RTÉ to represent Ireland at the Prix Italia 1991. Established in 1948 by RAI (then Radio Italiana), the Prix Italia is an international competition for radio programmes, held in various Italian cities. It has many categories, including radiophonic (music) works, documentaries and social affairs. Other entries from Ireland have included Raymond Deane's *Krespel's Concerto*, Roger

---

[83] Letter from Aloys Fleischmann to John Buckley, 10 September 1988. Letter in possession of John Buckley.

Doyle's *These Unsolved Mysteries,* Eric Sweeney's *Auguries of Innocence,* and a music programme entitled *Tunes of the Munster Pipers.*

Although Buckley did not win the competition, *A Thin Halo of Blue* remains one of his most original works, as a unique radiophonic montage of abstract vocal, orchestral, textual and documentary sources. A revised version suitable for concert performance was subsequently commissioned by the Department of the Environment for the opening ceremony of the United Nations Conference on Water and the Environment, which took place at the National Concert Hall in Dublin on 26 January 1992. Scored for narrator, mixed-voice choir, orchestra and a tape of sound-archive material, it is constructed around extracts from the journals of various astronauts in which they recorded their reflections while observing the planet earth from outer space. 'I wanted to create a sort of mystery, wonder and spaciousness,' Buckley has said of the piece, and his sophisticated sense of orchestral colour and ability to fashion delicate webs of sound equipped him perfectly to respond to the unusual subject matter.[84] Indeed, this highly programmatic work, which glistens with what was fast becoming Buckley's highly polished penchant for French-orientated sounds webs and colours, also betrays what one critic described as his 'eclectic ear [...] implying the influences of Messiaen's open air *Et Expecto Resurrectionem Mortuorum* in the dazzling use of percussion.'[85] Buckley states:

> A central fact of human experience is an exigency for journeying and voyaging towards discovery. Our great achievements in the arts and sciences spring from this inner necessity to explore the realms of our mental and physical worlds. In our century, one of the brightest manifestations of this desire has been the exploration and discovery of space [...] The exploration of space has opened new horizons to our understanding of and feeling for our own planet. Space photography has shown pattern and order hitherto unrevealed. Astronauts' comments constantly refer to the mystery, beauty, fragility and wholeness of our planet [...] A thin halo of blue is the first visible sign of the Earth as it rises over the moon's horizon [...] *A Thin Halo of Blue* is a musical and poetic response to our desire for voyage and our consequent view of home ...

These excerpts taken from the programme note to the first concert performance of *A Thin Halo of Blue* (dedicated to the composer's wife, Philomena) offer a useful introduction to this most programmatic of Buckley's compositions. The Latin and English texts were compiled by

---

[84] Cian Gleeson, 'Sheer Composure', *Sunday Times,* 4 June 1995.
[85] Pat O'Kelly, *Irish Press,* 25 February 1994.

the composer. The latter comprise a series of commentaries made by astronauts on their departure from the earth and their subsequent experiences, which were published in a book entitled *The Home Planet*.[86] The Latin text comprises a list of place names on the moon:

Mare serenitatis	Sea of serenity
Mare tranquillitatis	Sea of tranquility
Mare imbrium	Sea of rain
Mare vaporum	Sea of vapours
Mare spumans	Sea of foam
Mare crisum	Sea of crisis
Mare frigoris	Sea of cold
Mare nectaris	Sea of honey
Mare nubium	Sea of clouds
Palus somni	Marsh of sleep
Lacus somniorum	Lake of dreams
Sinus iridum	Bay of rainbows
Sinus roris	Bay of dew
Mare felicitatis	Sea of happiness
Oceanus procellarum	Ocean of storms
Aurora Borealis	Aurora Borealis
Mare humorum	Sea of moisture
Mare foecunditatus	Sea of fertility

There are two anomalies here: Aurora Borealis is not a place name on the moon but is, of course, the Latin name for the Northern Lights, and the 'Mare felicitatis' (Sea of happiness) does not in fact exist. It is a hidden tribute to Felix Hamel who was born while the work was being composed. Felix is the son of Buckley's friend and colleague, the German composer Peter Michael Hamel.

A Thin Halo of Blue falls into four sections. These sections are not determined by distinct structural divisions dictated by logical formulations of the music, but rather by the shift in emphasis of the text to which the music is a close commentary. They are divided as follows:

---

[86] Kevin W. Kelley, *The Home Planet* (London: Queen Anne Press, 1988).

Fig. 14: *A Thin Halo of Blue*, structural sub-division

1) Opening to I (p. 22):	Personal thoughts/preparations for lift-off/lift-off
2) (p.22) to O+3 (p.32):	Weightlessness/silence
3) O+4 (p. 32) to Y (p.52):	Light/visions of Earth/Aurora Borealis
4) Y (p.52) to end:	Observations from afar/descriptions of earth/ astronauts speaking during flight

[Note: the score does not have bar numbers. It uses rehearsal markings every two pages or so. Therefore, O+3 (p. 32) signifies the third bar of O on page 32.]

1) Personal thoughts/preparations for lift-off/lift-off (Opening to I)

> Before leaving the house we sat at the kitchen table. By tradition there was bread, salt and water. When we drove away I looked to the balcony and saw mother wiping away the tears. I waved to her; she did not see me./ A fine morning, a clear sky, sunny, bright. Only in my soul is there something unquiet./ Then they closed the hatch; it went clang like a dungeon door./ I could hear the sound of pipes whining below me as the liquid oxygen flowed into the tanks and a vibrant hissing noise as they were supercooled by the Lox. Through a mirror mounted near the window I could see the blockhouse and across the Cape. Through the periscope I looked east at the Atlantic along the track I would follow./ It seems I am leaving the planet forever and there is no power can bring me back.

The opening ephemeral flourishes on harp, percussion (glockenspiel, xylophone, vibraphone, celesta) and piano played over strings provide a predominant sound motif of the score and immediately establish the mood for a work inspired by space and weightlessness. Two piccolos outline the first melodic ideas, which appear to such an extent throughout the work that they may be viewed as motifs. These motifs return in the closing bars providing a frame for the entire work.

Ex. 33: *A Thin Halo of Blue*, opening bars (piccolo parts)

Starting at bar 4, the choir speaks the Latin words (below) with lines superimposed giving a strong sense of the populated Earth. The section is, in effect, a meditation on the moon's constant presence in the human psyche.

Fig. 15: Distribution of Latin words (bar 4)

Sopranos	Mare serenitatis, Mare tranquillitatis, Mare foecunditatis, Sinus iridum.
Altos	Mare nectaris, Mare imbrium, Mare nubium, Palus somni.
Tenors	Mare humorum, Mare vaporum, Mare crisum, Lacus somniorum.
Basses	Mare spumans, Mare frigoris, Sinus roris, Oceanus procellarum.

At B+5/6/7 (page 4) the choir sings the Latin words 'Mare serenitatis' (Sea of serenity) in a series of slow, rising scales. By this stage, the use of rising scales has become an identifiable feature of Buckley's compositional style, and the technique has been discussed in previous works such as *Time Piece* and *Symphony No. 1*. Rising scales on strings and harp return to announce the fourth section (at Y+3 page 52).

Throughout *A Thin Halo of Blue*, the music enhances the text by providing sonic equivalents to the imagery. The following examples highlight Buckley's consummate skill in this regard. When the text describes 'A fine morning, a clear sky, sunny, bright', the music paints the image of brightness starting at D (page 8) with its rustling flashes of pitched percussion over tremolo strings. The mood of the music immediately shifts with the words 'Only in my soul is there something unquiet'. The orchestra responds with wild flourishes and aggressive pronouncements from the choir (D+7 page 10 to E+4, page 12). When the hatch clangs 'like a dungeon door' Buckley imitates the sound of that image with *ff* timpani, brass, strings, piano, harp and bassoon playing under exuberant scale passages on the woodwind.

As if to make the sound 'of pipes whining below [...] as the liquid oxygen flowed into the tanks', Buckley employs a series of aleatoric sound strata which, when superimposed, combine to make gurgling sounds extraordinarily suitable to the text. At G page 17, he divides the forces into seven separate aleatoric entities, each of which has a different tempo. Performed at the dynamic markings *mp* and *p*, this combination of carefully judged linear entities creates a perfect sense of flowing liquid and demonstrates Buckley's complete control over his use of restricted aleatoricism.

At the words 'It seems I am leaving the planet forever and there is no power can bring me back,' Buckley's programmatic skill mimics rocket boosters sending the craft away from the Earth (see G+2 page 18), while an immediate sense of weightlessness is portrayed by the sustained choir lines on the word 'Mare' at H page 19.

2) Weightlessness/silence (I to O)

> Weightlessness comes on abruptly. I soared as if I were inside a soap bubble. Like an infant in the womb of my spacecraft, still a child of my Mother Earth./ You experience a strange dreamlike sensation of freedom. You can spread out your arms and legs as if soaring in the clouds./ What struck me most was the silence. It was a great silence, unlike any I have encountered on Earth; so vast and deep that I began to hear my own body. My heart beating; my blood-vessels pulsing; even the rustle of my muscles moving over each other seemed audible.

Upon arrival into space, the choir takes up the words 'Mare nectaris, mare nubium', etc., which are set to the (slightly altered) piccolo motifs from the opening bars (see Ex: 33 above). The motivic importance of these melodies is enhanced when they reappear at J (page 23) before transferring to the oboes at J+3 (page 24). From K-1 (page 24/5), Buckley has counterpoised cleverly the narrator's English text and the choir's Latin text in such a way that one enhances and amplifies the other: the narrator speaks of 'a strange dreamlike sensation of freedom' while the choir sings the words 'Palus somni, Lacus somniorum' (Marsh of sleep, lake of dreams).

Athough *A Thin Halo of Blue* is not composed in any given key, Buckley uses sustained pedal notes to emphasize tonal centres at certain moments in the work. The tonal centre of E is a recurring feature underpinning both the second and fourth sections. The piccolo motifs also are written over an E pedal. Furthermore, on the syllable 'som' (of the word 'somniorum') the harmony arrives at an E major sharpened 7th chord, giving the impression of restful peace.

Ex. 34: *A Thin Halo of Blue*, rehearsal mark L

Characteristically, this clear tonality is soon offset by arpeggiated commentaries on the piano and harp, the first three notes of which outline E, G and G♯ (A♭ in the harp). The conflation of G and G♯ within the context of an E-based harmony immediately imposes a major/minor binary on the tonality. The remaining notes of the arpeggios intimate other tonalities.

More examples of effective word painting can be observed at M (page 28). To the lines 'What struck me most was the silence ... (pause c. 2") ... It was a great silence ...', Buckley places delicate, almost imperceptible touches of harp harmonics and pitched percussion over *ppp* high tremolo strings. The resulting silence that is 'sounded' is most effective. Further subtle constructs of sound are orchestrated at 'even the rustle of my muscles moving over each other seemed audible,' where Buckley employs five aleatoric entities for glockenspiel, vibraphone, celesta, harp and piano played over sustained strings and sleigh bells at N-1 (page 30): the music looks and sounds like sinews and muscles gently twisting over each other. The piccolo motives return again at N+1, and are transferred to clarinets in altered versions. Their presence helps create a sense of continuity throughout the entire work.

3) Light/visions of Earth/Aurora Borealis O+4 to Y

> At 0600 hours we went into the shade. The station shone like an open door in a house in the countryside./ From behind the rim of the moon there emerges a sparkling blue and white jewel, a light delicate sky-blue sphere laced with slowly swirling veils of white, rising gradually like a small pearl in a thick sea of black mystery./ It takes more than a moment to fully realize this is Earth ... Home./ I shuddered when I saw a crimson flame through the porthole. Vast pillars of light were bursting into the sky, melting into it, and flooding over with all the colours of the rainbow./ A greenish radiance poured from Earth directly up to the station, a radiance resembling gigantic phosphorescent organ pipes, whose ends were glowing crimson and overlapped by waves of swirling green mist./ The intense and dynamic changes in the colours and forms of the pillars and garlands made me think of visual music. Finally we saw that we were entering directly into the Aurora Borealis.

The third section, which deals with the experience of entering the *Aurora Borealis* is descriptively intense and musically explosive. The 'sparkling blue and white jewel' is sonically depicted by fragmented and jagged arpeggios intermixed in the woodwind, percussion (marimba, vibraphone), piano and harp played over wild glissandi harmonics in the strings (see Q+3 page 37). The sudden shock of seeing the Earth from afar ('It takes more than a moment to fully realize that this is Earth...Home') is perfectly captured when the busy orchestra suddenly stops at R-1 (page 39). At this point, the music represents a shift in the consciousness of the observer and ingeniously suggests fluctuations of psychological states.

The 'vast pillars of light' are evoked strongly at S (page 41) where eighteen separate lines of aleatoric material, with *ff* dynamics, are projected over tremolo strings and a held choir chord. The effusion of light is caught perfectly in the orchestral interplay at T (page 42). When the narrator finally sees that he is 'entering directly into the Aurora Borealis', the music reaches a climax of great intensity at X (page 50) where twenty-two separate lines of aleatoric music converge over sustained double-basses and trombones with accented and rhythmically shifting *ff* outbursts from the choir repeating the words 'Aurora Borealis'. This aggregate of hugely diverse components lasts seventeen seconds and, along with the swirling and glistening orchestration that emerges at X, represents the timbral and colouristic climax of the entire work before bringing the section to a theatrical close.

4) Observations from afar/descriptions of earth/tape of astronauts (Y to end)

> The first day or so we all pointed to our countries. The third or fourth day we were pointing to our continents. By the fifth day we were aware of only one Earth – indescribably beautiful with all the scars of national boundaries gone./ You see clouds towering up. You see their shadows on the sunlit plains. A ship's wake in the Indian Ocean. Brush fires in Africa. Reds and pinks of the Australian desert./ Plankton blooms off the coats of Chile. Transverse sandbars in the Mosambique Channel. Madagascar, green with tropical forest Glacial lakes in the Canadian Shield of Quebec. Dasht-i-Kavir salt desert in Iran with the great swirls of reds and browns and whites. Orange dust cloud over Western Sahara./ You see parallel sand dunes in the Algerian desert. The mouths of the Ganges in Bangladesh. Cumulonimbus clouds over the Atlantic, east of Acension Island./ Linear dunes in the Namibian desert southeast of Walvis Bay. Tidal estuaries, islands, and mangrove swamps in the Bay of Bengal. Snow cover in Desolation Canyon along the Green River of Utah. Sunset over the coastal ranges of Yukon and British Columbia. Spring thaw along the Hudson Bay.

Having depicted the emotional experience of penetrating the *Aurora Borealis*, the fourth section describes how a critical distance from the Earth offers the observer a new and unique perspective. As a central theme of the text, this shift of perspective diminishes the significance of all so-called boundaries and makes the fragility of the Earth more easily felt. Ultimately, humanity can be understood as a whole rather than as a multitude of warring factions. Buckley reflects the significance of the text by weaving another series of slowly rising scales, which holds the attention on the moment while acting as a prelude for the music which follows.

The rising scales (played on strings and harp harmonics at Y+3 page 52) are subject to aleatoric processes. The harp scales are performed at crotchet = 60, first violins play at crotchet = 52, second violins play crotchet = 60, while the violas play at crotchet = 66. Some of the strings' scales have short fermatas (pauses), further imposing a blurred and arhythmic character on the music. This blurring effect is most apt as it parallels the merged nations of the Earth as seen from the vantage point of the outer-space observer. All the individual scales finish on d'''. Arriving at different times, they eventually merge into a sustained unison. The transformation of the numerous to the singular is a perfect sonic equivalent to the disappearance of the multitudinous nationalities of the Earth into one humanity as depicted by the speaker when the spacecraft is moving further away – 'By the fifth day we were aware of only one Earth...'. This epiphany is captured by the orchestral warmth and the new glowing brightness embodied by the tonal centre of E, which has been a central element throughout the entire work.

This sustained E pedal remains a dominant feature of the section despite the incongruity of the shifting harmonic webs which hover above it. The piccolo motif heard at the opening of the work returns. Its melodies are spread throughout the woodwind, ensuring its prominence in this section to the very end. Following the thirty seconds of archive tape recording featuring astronauts talking over an intercom, the duo of piccolos is played over strings and crotales and accompanied by the choir intoning the words 'Palus somni, Lacus somniorum' (Marsh of sleep, lake of dreams). This also marks a surprising harmonic shift in the strings to a B♭ pedal (at FF page 60) that gives the music a floating, ethereal quality and brings the score to a dream-like finish.

Ex. 35: *A Thin Halo of Blue*, two bars before rehearsal mark FF

The programmatic nature of *A Thin Halo of Blue* is not typical of Buckley, who is more at home in abstract forms. Where programmatic themes have previously been addressed in such works as *Oileáin, Boireann* and *Taller Than Roman Spears*, Buckley's approach sublimates the thematic source material into abstracted soundscapes that suggest a detached atmosphere rather than anything of an overtly depictive nature. However, the particularly descriptive quality of the text for *A Thin Halo of Blue* presented Buckley with a unique opportunity to flex more overtly his illuminative and programmatic skills and permitted him to respond directly to words. The result is a *tour de force* of orchestration, timbral and harmonic control and a finely judged sense of formal structure.

The Words Upon the Window Pane

In 1991, Buckley was presented with his first opportunity to compose an opera. To mark the occasion of Dublin becoming the European City of Culture in 1991, Opera Theatre Company (OTC) invited applications from composers and commissioned four chamber operas. These works were to be performed in one production and have as a common thread a connection to Dublin. The operas were as follows: *The Poet and his Double* (text and music by Raymond Deane); *Hot Food with Strangers*, text by Judy Kravis and music by Marion Ingoldsby; *Position Seven*, text by James Conway and music by Kenneth Chalmers; and *The Words Upon the Window Pane* with a libretto by Hugh Maxton, adapted from the play by William Butler Yeats, and music by Buckley.[87] They were all premiered on 17 October during the Dublin Theatre Festival at Lombard Street Studios. Dublin is one of the few European capitals without an opera house or a permanent professional opera company. The decision by OTC, therefore, to commission four new operas by Irish and British composers was at the time (and even by today's standards) a brave and innovative project given Ireland's general failure to nurture the genre over the previous fifty years.

The poet Hugh Maxton (who, under his real name, W.J. McCormack, is also well known as a literary historian and cultural commentator) was Buckley's choice as librettist. It was a happy collaboration as they agreed almost immediately that Yeats's play would be the most suitable vehicle for them. As Maxton explains:

> I submitted to him [Buckley] several outlines for original plots, one for an opera based on the death of a distinguished Irishman of the past, and a brief summary of *The Words Upon the Window Pane*. The play has long fascinated me; I have directed it twice, and acted in it once. He jumped at the idea of adapting Yeats's play.[88]

Yeats wrote the play in 1930. Dedicated to Lady Gregory, the premiere was given later that year in the Abbey Theatre. Given the

---

[87] See Appendix IV for libretto.
[88] Hugh Maxton, programme note for *The Words upon the Window Pane* (Dublin: Opera Theatre Company, 1991).

terms of the commission to compose a twenty-minute opera, Maxton compressed the text to the central episode, deleting all subsidiary elements.

Though he never actually appears in the play, *The Words upon the Window Pane* is dominated by Jonathan Swift and his complex relationship with two women – Ester Johnson, known as Stella, and Hester Vanhomrigh whom he called Vanessa. Swift's lifelong affection for Stella resulted in his rejection of Vanessa in acrimonious circumstances. This episode lies at the core of the play and the opera.

The setting is a sparsely furnished room in an eighteenth-century house in Dublin, which once belonged to friends of Stella. Mrs Henderson, a famous medium, has been brought over from London by the Dublin Spiritualist Society to conduct a series of séances in the room. Amongst the participants are Robert Corbet, a sceptic and something of an expert on Swift. Mrs Henderson's attempts to contact the other world are interrupted by the spirit of Jonathan Swift, causing her to re-enact the central episodes with Stella and Vanessa. This play-within-a-play takes place entirely in the mind of Mrs Henderson. Furthermore, Stella and Vanessa are portrayed through the memory and imagination of Swift. The layering of echoes and memories suggests a Russian nesting-doll structure. These scenes represent the core of the play and the opera. Stella's poem to Swift is heard in full, and the words are etched upon the window pane.

> You taught how I might youth prolong,
> By knowing what is right and wrong;
> How from my heart to bring supplies
> Of lustre to my fading eyes

The séance is regarded as a failure and all the characters leave except for Corbet, who is astonished by what he has witnessed, but is still dubious about the metaphysical world. He is inclined to believe that Mrs Henderson is a skillful actress who has created the whole scenario. It is clear from Corbet's questioning that Mrs Henderson has absolutely no idea who Swift was. And yet, at the end of the opera, she is left alone on stage quoting his turbulent words: 'perish the day on which I was born.'

Yeats is an abiding presence for Buckley, although this was the first opportunity he had to engage directly with the poet's work (he subsequently responded to Yeats's poetry in 1993 with the piano piece *The Silver Apples of the Moon, The Golden Apples of the Sun* and his choral setting of 1995, *He Wishes for the Cloths of Heaven*). It was the dramatic and musical possibilities inherent in the characterization and setting of *The Words Upon the Window Pane* that offered Buckley great potential for development.

He was attracted by the central role of Mrs Henderson, which requires a highly virtuosic control and command as it must embody numerous characterizations in rapid succession. Buckley correlates this feat to a concerto soloist, and this innovative correlation was a pivotal concern when he embarked upon the opera. 'The virtuosic role of Mrs Henderson', he explains, 'suggested for me parallels with the concerto medium, which was to be a central element of my work from that time onward. In some figurative sense, it was my first concerto.' Ex. 36 demonstrates the typical declamatory nature of Mrs Henderson's vocal style. Her elaborate cadenza-like solos illustrate the quasi-instrumental characteristics of the vocal line:

Ex. 36: *The Words Upon the Window Pane*, bars 158-164 (Mrs Henderson)

The drama, however, is rather subdued in atmosphere where it does not concern the central figure of Mrs Henderson. Buckley has created an altogether individual approach to operatic writing, relying on his ability to compose brilliant gestures of predominantly colouristic and textural interest, rather than concentrating on the traditional underpinning of stage action or delineating in music the sequence of precise emotional states that the opera canon has reinforced.

Buckley's 'instrumental' approach to vocal writing extends to all characters in the opera. Using this tactic, he critiques the operatic canon by reducing the traditional importance of the pure vocal line and by diffusing the relationship between text and voice through the redistribution of the power relations between the vocal writing and the orchestral music that normally accompanies it, giving the latter a more predominant role than it has enjoyed previously. As Buckley points out: 'the instrumental music is not intended as a mere accompaniment to the voices, but rather as an independent commentary, which simultaneously amplifies the emotions inherent in the text.'[89] Hans Keller (in the context of Schubert's conflict-ridden relationship to opera) made this connection as far back as 1979 when he pointed out that:

> It is in the field of instrumental music pure and complex which, just because it has absorbed musical drama in its sonata thought, seems furthest removed from stage drama – and within that field, it is, of course, the string quartet and its relatives (such as the string quintet) which, *ceteris paribus*, present the richest and subtlest expression of sheer musical drama.[90]

A specific example from *The Words Upon the Window Pane* demonstrates this diffused relationship between word and music: when Robert Corbet becomes greatly excited by the words upon the window pane, his passion for Swift is reflected in his music – widely spaced intervals, and an elaborately decorated melodic line. This highly embellished vocalization reduces our ability to hear the words clearly, thus compromising their import. The reduction of the textual clarity in favour of an abstract vocal brilliance which verges on the instrumental is echoed in one critic's observation that, 'the other [...] roles were mainly recitative and [...] much of the colour was provided by the orchestra.'[91]

Given the complex and layered nature of the play in relation to both characterization and theme, Buckley's twenty-minute opera skillfully manages to contain and present the structural intricacies of the text. *The Words upon the Window Pane* is obsessed with the metaphysical, the surreal, death and the passage of time, and Buckley's approach elevates the action to a timeless interplay of present reality and remembered past. The play's structure (and consequently the opera's) comprises a number of scenes that cross with ease the thresholds between temporal and spatial paradigms. Yeats's sophisticated use of language further enhances the idea of layers. It is not only *his* language we hear, but also Swift's voice, Vanessa's voice and Stella's voice – all through the voice of Mrs Henderson. Thus, ideas of resonance and

---

[89] John Buckley, 'like a bell with many echoes: drama and opera', in *Mirror Up to Nature: The Fourth Seamus Heaney Lectures*, ed. Patrick Burke (Dublin: Carysfort Press, 2010), p.94.
[90] Hans Keller, 'Introduction: Operatic music and Britten', in *The Operas of Benjamin Britten* ed. David Herbert (London: Hamish Hamilton, 1979), xiii/viv.
[91] Mary MacGoris, '20-minute operas a success', *Irish Independent*, 18 October 1991.

memory are embedded in the very words of the play. Yeats himself, in his introduction to the play, highlighted this essential characteristic when he referred to it as being 'like a bell with many echoes.'[92] The transcendental quality of the play manifests itself through the interplay of layers occupying spatial and temporal domains.

This counterpoint resonates with Buckley's own views on the importance of time, both situated and suggested, in relation to the live performance of music and theatre: 'Drama and all forms of music, but especially opera, are best experienced in performance.' He explains:

> While text and score may undoubtedly have intrinsic value as literature, it is how they are transformed and realised through performance that is of interest to me here. In drama and opera, gesture, expression, tone of voice, physical posture, subtle nuances of timing and emphasis, are not added in narrative form as they are of necessity in a novel, but embody an essential element of the experience. Drama and music unfold and can only be experienced through time. In a very real sense the canvas of the dramatist and composer does not so much consist of words and musical sounds, as it does of time. It is through the control and manipulation of time with the words or the music that the art is created and experienced.[93]

Buckley has placed an emphasis on time as a means to negotiate and reflect the intricate *mise-en-abyme* structure that is this play-within-a-play-within-a-play.

Concerto for Organ and Orchestra

After decades of debate and delay, President Patrick Hillary opened the National Concert Hall on 9 September 1981. Prior to the opening, no purpose-built auditorium for classical music existed in Dublin, and there was no appropriate home for the two main national orchestras. They were forced to present their concerts in a variety of mostly unsuitable venues such as the Gaiety Theatre or Saint Francis Xavier Hall. Thus, the opening of the National Concert Hall at Earlsfort Terrace marked a milestone in the history of classical music in Ireland. The National Concert Hall was not a purpose-built complex, and its transformation from the examination hall of University College Dublin was overseen by the Office of Public Works under its principle architect, Michael O'Doherty. The main auditorium has a capacity of 1,200. The

---

[92] W.B. Yeats, *The Words Upon the Window Pane* (Dublin: The Cuala Press, 1934), Introduction p. 2.
[93] John Buckley, 'like a bell with many echoes: drama and opera,' in *Mirror Up to Nature: The Fourth Seamus Heaney Lectures*, ed. Patrick Burke (Dublin: Carysfort Press, 2010), p.83.

renowned acoustics expert Dr V.L. Jordan of Copenhagen, best known for his work at the Sydney Opera House and the Metropolitan Opera House, New York, oversaw the acoustic arrangement. The installation of the new organ, built by Kenneth Jones & Associates of Bray, Co. Wicklow in 1991, represented the final stage in the outfitting of the hall. The organ was inaugurated in 1991 in a concert given by Gerard Gillen.

In 1992, the board of the National Concert Hall and the Arts Council of Ireland, in association with RTÉ, commissioned a major new work for the instrument. This commission was awarded by competition, and Irish composers submitted their scores under a *nom de plume*. The board of assessors consisted of the composer Jane O'Leary, organist Gerard Gillen, and the distinguished American composer and Pulitzer prizewinner, Charles Wuorinen. The commission was unanimously awarded to Buckley. The resultant *Concerto for Organ and Orchestra*, the first such work ever written by an Irish composer, was first performed on 26 June 1992 as part of the Seventh Dublin International Organ and Choral Festival by the National Symphony Orchestra of Ireland, conducted by Robert Houlihan, with soloist Peter Sweeney. The work, dedicated to the composer's father-in-law, Hugh McGinley, is scored for three flutes, three oboes, three clarinets, two bassoons, contrabassoon, four horns, three trumpets, two trombones, bass trombone, tuba, two sets of timpani, a wide range of percussion and strings.

One of Buckley's principal concerns in this concerto is the balance between the orchestra and organ, which, in a sense, is like a second orchestra. Frequently, the interplay of the musical material takes the form of a dialogue, with organ and orchestra counterpoised in equal force and measure. The intricate organ solos have corresponding passages in the orchestra: elsewhere organ and orchestra unite and enhance each other's material. The orchestral writing is often of an audacious nature, making the work a concerto for orchestra as much as for organ. It brings together, perhaps more than any other composition of Buckley's, all the developments of the past and all the potentialities of the future. The taut monolithic aggressiveness and structured rhythmic vitality of its outer sections hark back to the raw (if less formal) canvasses of *Boireann* and *Oileáin*, while the improvisatory structures and svelte sheen of the orchestration of its inner section point towards the harmonic refinement dominating all his works from this period onwards. One reviewer commented, 'The fast sections make much use of glassy surfaces irregularly spattered with clustery chords from the organ and with sliding orchestral lines that evoke the soaring and swooning world of the ondes Martenot, so beloved of Messiaen and other French composers.'[94]

Structure

Structurally, this work is similar to *Concerto for Alto Saxophone and String Orchestra*, which Buckley composed five years later: both are single movement works that divide into an A-B-A1 form, the centre section of which provides the majority of the musical argument. In *Concerto for Organ and Orchestra* the outer frames are alike in character; the music is rhythmic, highly energetic and tightly structured. They bookend the more extended material of the B section, which is through-composed, structurally ambiguous and in a constant state of change.

Section A lasts up to the slow rising strings at 25 (page 43) that immediately follow the timpani and organ pedal duo (page 43). This opening section lasts approximately five minutes. The A1 section starts at 61 (page 110) where the orchestra starts re-investing rhythmic energy into the music, preparing it for the recapitulation of the opening A material. This section also lasts just under five minutes. Large portions of these outer sections comprise the same material.

[Note: the score does not have bar numbers. It uses rehearsal markings every two pages. Therefore, rehearsal mark 15+2 (p. 31) signifies two bars after rehearsal mark 15 on page 31].

Fig. 16: Outline of recurrence of material from Section A to A1

Section A	Rehearsal mark 4 (p. 9) to 15+2 (p. 31) is repeated exactly at section A1: 67 (p. 116) to 78+5 (p. 138) [88 bars]
Section A 1	Rehearsal mark 19+6 (p. 39) to 21+6 (p. 41) is repeated exactly at section A1: 78+11 (p. 139) to 80+6 (p. 141) [14 bars]

---

[94] Michael Dervan, 'Coruscating brilliance', *The Irish Times*, 30 June 1992.

A total of 102 bars of material from section A is repeated in section A1. The re-use of material is a technique Buckley employs to secure rhythmic, melodic and motivic continuity and signifies a growing concern with tighter structural blocks. He significantly expanded upon this approach in *Concerto for Alto Saxophone and Orchestra*.

The B section of *Concerto for Organ and Orchestra* lasts almost twenty minutes, approximately double the lengths of sections A and A1 taken together. This imbalance makes for a curious formal structure and the outer framing music struggles to contain the extended dialogues of the inner material, suggesting that the central section may be too elongated for a cogent structural plan. In the B section, the music largely comprises a series of orchestral commentaries interspersed with enigmatic solos for the organ, which, because of their quasi-improvisatory nature, defy any formal assessment. A third element can be identified where organ and orchestra fuse into a unified entity. The following plan charts these interactions. The extensive B section encompasses numerous developmental references to the more flamboyant material of the opening.

The intensely rhythmic phrases of the outer sections all derive from the core motif in the work.

Ex. 37: *Concerto for Organ and Orchestra*, rehearsal mark 4 (organ part)

This energetic and repeated rhythmic cell recalls previous works such as *Guitar Sonata No. 1*, while elsewhere Buckley has reached extraordinary levels of refined simplicity as in rehearsal mark 55+6 to 56 where a profound and delicate sense of repose demonstrates his complete absorption of a rarefied French aesthetic into his harmonic language.

Ex. 38: *Concerto for Organ and Orchestra*, rehearsal mark 55+6 to 56

A refinement of orchestral control is further shown by the slowly rising strings (with pitched percussion providing extra colour) that initiate the central B section (rehearsal mark 25, page 43). Buckley retains this signature musical technique from a number of earlier pivotal works including *Time Piece*, *Symphony No. 1* and *A Thin Halo of Blue*. More delicately controlled than in previous incarnations, the rising strings demonstrate a consummate control of colouristic effects.

Another distinctive aspect of the *Concerto for Organ and Orchestra* is the close relationship between the organ and the two sets of timpani, the latter functionally allied to the soloist's material. This unusual coalition operates at significant moments in the work. The timpani repeat the prominent hemiola rhythm of the organ's opening motif (see Ex. 37 above) acting as a reinforcing element. The duologue between organ pedal and timpani gradually diminishes the rhythmic drive of the A section (page 43), thereby creating a transition to the middle section. Furthermore, in the B section, the timpani are regularly called upon to reinforce numerous sustained notes played on the organ pedals that appear at the end of long virtuosic melodic phrases. Striking the same notes as the organ, the timpani tonally underpin the given pitch centre. Fig. 17 highlights where the timpani colour the sustained pedal points on D and C.

Fig. 17: Points where timpani reinforce organ pedal notes

1) Rehearsal mark 25 page 43 on C
2) Rehearsal mark 42+7 page 80 on D
3) Rehearsal mark 57 page 103 on C
4) The bar before Rehearsal mark 59 page 107 on D

Although this note enhancement does not imply a return to traditional functional harmony, the selected pitch centres give a tonal implication to chosen points in the score. Each of these pedal points is autonomous in that they are neither linearly nor structurally connected. In this regard, they serve a similar function to the sustained pedal notes featured in *Symphony No. 1*, providing momentary tonal anchors for the music, which otherwise functions atonally within light timbral and colouristic filigrees.

Other anchors are employed at specific points. Cascading atonal organ music, coloured by the orchestra, arrives at rehearsal mark 49 on the note D♭. This pitch is enharmonically reinforced by the timpani on C♯, providing a momentary tonal focus in the score. From this point, the orchestra (again free from any tonal categorization) immediately bounces its scales energetically in an ascending direction. The atonal music, therefore, is moulded in a U shape, the lowest point of which is suddenly and briefly given a strong D♭ emphasis. If these tonal 'points' serve to anchor the music, they do so transiently. At the very least, they offer brief respites from the extended atonal arguments dominating the entire work and represent curious anomalies within an otherwise homogeneous atonal palette.

Despite these small incongruities and the work's structural curiosity, the *Concerto for Organ and Orchestra* demonstrates Buckley's absorption of all the diverse processes that have influenced him since the late 1970s. From this work onwards, the more traditional lyrical and rhythmic gestures of his own musical character merge seamlessly with the atonally-dominated timbral constructs. The resulting musical formations are both stylistically homogeneous and unique.

6 | Towards a New Refinement (1997-2005)

The Late 1990s and the New Millenium

In 1998, Buckley responded to an invitation from guitarist John Feeley by composing *Guitar Sonata No. 2*. His recent concern with greater formal discipline is readily appreciated by comparing the styles of the two guitar sonatas. The fantasia-like opening of *Guitar Sonata No. 1* is essentially a *tour de force* of improvisatory writing. Its second movement has an uncharacteristic emotional lyricism of a kind not found elsewhere in Buckley's music, while the third movement is an exercise in sheer rhythmic verve, where the stability of the structure is undermined by sporadic outbursts of violent percussive energy in the utilization of extended techniques. The work as a whole makes considerable demands on the virtuosity of the performer and can be considered an unabashed technical showpiece. In contrast, the four tightly knit movements of *Guitar Sonata No.2* (1998), though no less technically demanding than the earlier score, afford few opportunities for similar overt virtuosic display. Buckley devoted nine months to the composition of this piece: 'I was determined not to write the first Guitar Sonata again,' he remarks. But his new manner would have prevented this replication in any case, as the emphasis was now on achieving a greater simplicity of contour and transparency. As Buckley explains: '*Guitar Sonata No.2* focuses on a tighter structural plan with fewer flamboyant gestures.' The key to the second guitar sonata is restraint, and the consistent subordination of the melodic and textural content to the formal design results in music that explores an inwardness of feeling rather than bravura gestures and extrovert showiness. Buckley composed yet another work for the instrument in 2004 when he wrote *In Winter Light* (alto flute and guitar) for John Feeley and William

Dowdall, former principal flautist of the RTÉ National Symphony Orchestra and Professor of Flute at the Royal Irish Academy of Music. This series of important guitar works undoubtedly establishes Buckley as one of Ireland's foremost composers for the instrument.

Buckley's next work was composed in response to a commission from Camerata Ireland. Founded in 1999 by the Irish pianist Barry Douglas, the orchestra's personnel consists of musicians from both parts of the island of Ireland. It enjoys the joint patronage of the heads of state of Ireland and the United Kingdom. The impetus to establish this cross-border orchestra arose out of the new political and cultural possibilities resulting from the Good Friday Agreement, the first major accord eventually leading to peace in the Six Counties. The idea that music can serve as a perfect medium to bring opposing forces together had already met with considerable success in the even more polarized context of the Israeli-Palestinian conflict. The West-Eastern Divan Orchestra, comprised of Israeli and Palestinian musicians, was established by Daniel Barenboim and Edward Said. As Barenboim elucidates,

> [In music] no element is entirely independent because it is by definition in a relationship of inter-dependence [...] In music we know and accept the hierarchy of a main subject, we accept the permanent presence of an opposite, and sometimes even of subversive accompanying rhythms.[95]

Camerata Ireland aspired to create musical experiences within an all-Ireland context. For its inaugural concerts, the orchestra commissioned Ian Wilson (from the Six Counties) and Buckley (from the Republic) to compose a pair of works. Wilson's piece, *What We Can See of the Sky Has Fallen*, takes its title from the poem of the same name by Londoner Lavinia Greenlaw, while Buckley's *A Mirror Into the Light* (a title suggested by Wilson) is taken from a line in the same poem. The gentle lamenting quality of Wilson's piece, featuring a prominent oboe part, is well complemented by Buckley's more overtly exuberant work. Both pieces were premiered at Stormont Castle, Belfast, in April 1999. Given the utopian implication of the title, the orchestral sheen of *A Mirror into the Light* was likely intended to symbolize the new optimistic developments taking place in cross-border relationships as epitomized by the Good Friday Agreement.

The remainder of 1999 was occupied with the composition of *Quattuor* – a large-scale work commissioned by Dublin Youth

---

[95] Daniel Barenboim, 'West-Eastern Divan Orchestra' in website: http://www.west-eastern-divan.org/press/press-release.html (cited 3 August 2005).

Orchestras (DYO) or Ceolfhoirne na nÓg Átha Cliath. DYO is a member of the Irish Association of Youth Orchestras and through IAYO is linked to the European Association of Youth Orchestras – a network of eleven countries. *Quattuor* (which is Latin for 'four') is a colossal work written for the DYO's four youth orchestras – the DYO Symphony Orchestra, the DYO Transitional Orchestra, the DYO Intermediate Orchestra and the DYO Junior String Orchestra, which were conducted by John Finucane, Ronan O'Reilly, John Page and Vanessa Sweeney respectively. The work, which was completed on New Year's Eve 1999, was commissioned as part of the millennium celebrations in Ireland and was premiered in the National Basketball Arena on 9 April 2000. Composing for four youth orchestras, ranging from junior strings to full symphony orchestra, presented Buckley with some very specific challenges. Not least of these was the necessity of creating music appropriate for the technical ability of the players. Another challenge related to the practical necessity of coordinating the four orchestras when they played together. Buckley partially tackled these problems by giving each orchestra a movement of its own and by organizing the material so that the remaining three movements share music, taking the spatial layout into consideration. The seven movements were therefore arranged as follows:

Fig. 18: *Quattuor*, movement layout

Intrada	Junior, Intermediate, Transitional and Symphony Orchestras
Air and Dance	Junior Orchestra
Scherzo	Transitional Orchestra
Interlude	Intermediate, Transitional and Symphony Orchestras
Elegia	Intermediate Orchestra
Finale	Symphony Orchestra
Coda	Junior, Intermediate, Transitional and Symphony Orchestras

Though *Quattuor* undoubtedly has a semi-pedagogical function, it still makes a completely satisfactory concert work. However, given the particularity of its forces, it is hard to see how this work could ever have 'a life beyond the occasion', as Buckley would wish.

Two more large-scale works were written in the following two years: *Strings in the Earth and Air* of 2000 (the title is taken from one of the poems in James Joyce's collection *Chamber Music*), commissioned by the Chamber Orchestra of the European Union, and *Concerto for Bassoon and Orchestra* of 2001, commissioned by the National Symphony Orchestra of Ireland and Michael Jones, who is its principal bassoonist. By now Buckley had come to realize that the concerto form held a special attraction for him. He had always been interested in writing for solo instruments and, at the other extreme, had produced an extensive output of orchestral music. The concerto form seemed a natural result of these two interests. A central feature of any concerto is virtuosity, and *Concerto for Bassoon and Orchestra* makes great technical demands on the soloist 'While I have never deliberately set out to write technically demanding music for its own sake, virtuosity is a highly important aspect of my compositional approach', explains Buckley. Virtuosity is certainly a requirement of the *Concerto for Bassoon and Orchestra*, whose Haydnesque orchestral proportions guarantee a freedom from problems of balance. Not long after completing *Concerto for Bassoon and Orchestra*, Buckley felt compelled to reconsider the nature of his professional activities. In its sheer scale, *Quattuor* was typical of the kind of work he had been commissioned to write in recent years, and he now felt that the time had come for him to reassess his position. 'I wanted to write fewer pieces, and think longer about them,' he said. '*Quattuor* with its almost six hundred pages seemed to me to be an excess of notes.'

In 2001, Buckley decided to accept a post as lecturer at St Patrick's College, Drumcondra. Although it meant giving up his independence as a freelance composer, the new position gave Buckley the opportunity (perhaps for the first time of his professional career), to concentrate exclusively on works of higher artistic quality. He drew the Aosdána *cnuas* between 1985 and 2001, but continued to deliver lectures during that period, as well as educational workshops and other programmes for a wide variety of organizations, including RTÉ, the National Concert Hall, the Music Association of Ireland, the National Chamber Choir, People's College, Forás Éireann, the Arts Council, Samhlaíocht Chiarraí and Ennis Composition Summer School. Taking up the post in St Patrick's College in 2001 simply consolidated all that freelance educational work in one place with a proper salary structure and therefore represented continuity in his career rather than any major turning point. He remains a member of Aosdána.

His new responsibilities certainly did not inhibit his creative spirit. Indeed, if anything, it secured him the time to concentrate on fewer works but of greater artistic depth, as perusal of his catalogue from

2004 testifies. Major works composed since 2004 include *In Winter Light* (for alto flute and guitar, 2004); *endless the white clouds...* (for harp, 2005); *Campane in Aria* (for orchestra, 2006); *Flute Concerto* (2006); *Violin Concerto* (2008); and *Constellations* (for multiple flutes, 2009). In some respects, the move to St Patrick's completed a cycle in his career: having begun as a primary-school teacher, he now returned to his *alma mater* to help educate a new generation of young people for the teaching profession.

SELECTED ANALYSIS

Concerto for Alto Saxophone and Strings

Composing for the saxophone occupied Buckley's creative energies during 1997 when he was finally able to fulfill a long-cherished ambition to compose a concerto for Kenneth Edge. He had always felt that *Arabesque* was a 'concerto in embryo' as he put it. Edge's engagement as artist-in-residence at the University of Limerick in 1996, together with the fact that the Irish Chamber Orchestra was also affiliated with the University, created the propitious circumstances that finally allowed Buckley to realize his ambition. Edge and the Irish Chamber Orchestra jointly commissioned the work, and *Concerto for Alto Saxophone and String Orchestra* was first performed in the concert hall of the university on 27 September 1997. It was described as 'a virtuosic piece ... showing the same sort of instrumental brilliance as the composer's *Organ Concerto* and conveying at times a distinct French flavour in the string writing, a sort of homage, perhaps, to the saxophone's country of origin.'[96]

Henri Dutilleux stands as a major influence on Buckley's string sound. Compositions such as *Timbres, Espace, Mouvement* (1976) provide the model *par excellence* for the glistening and ephemeral sound that so attracts Buckley. At the time of composition, the Irish Chamber Orchestra consisted of sixteen strings with the following arrangement: five first violins, four second violins, three violas, three cellos, and one double bass. In many sections of the work, Buckley's sub-division of these small forces results in only a single instrument per part, thereby creating a sense of transparency and evanescence. Buckley's music in the late 1990s saw a substantial refinement of timbral constructs paralleled with an ever-tightening grip on formal structure. This development is a central feature of the *Concerto for Alto Saxophone and String Orchestra*, where the repetition (either exactly or in inversion) acts as a pivotal process in the development of material and structural planning. The single-movement work falls into three parts, A-B-A1 (giving it a similar physiognomy to that of the *Concerto for Organ and Orchestra*).

There are no themes as such in *Concerto for Alto Saxophone and String Orchestra*. There are, however, substantial sections of music that

---

[96] Michael Dervan, *The Irish Times*, 29 September 1997. Dervan's point regarding the French flavour of the music is apt, though Adolphe Sax was, in fact, Belgian.

are repeated exactly, or in inversion, a process most commonly used by Buckley to provide familiarity and to develop his material coherently.

Fig. 19: *Concerto for Alto Saxophone and String Orchestra*, plan of selected repeated sections

From Section A	No. of bars	Type of repeat and Section	Rehearsal Mark
First 8 bars	(8 bars)	exact repeat in A1 at:	68+5 to 69+2
Rehearsal mark 3 to 4	(7 bars)	exact repeat in A at:	16+6 to 17
Rehearsal mark 4 to 6	(15 bars)	inversion in A at:	17 to 18+5
Rehearsal mark 6 to 6+4	(4 bars)	(almost) exact repeat in A at:	18+6 to 18+9
Rehearsal mark 6+6 to 8+6	(20 bars)	inversion in A at:	19–1 to 21–2
Rehearsal mark 6+5 to 13+4	(73 bars)	exact repeat in A1 at:	56+11 to 63+4
Rehearsal mark 6+6 to 8+6	(20 bars)	inversion in A1 at:	55–1 to 56+7
Rehearsal mark 14+7 to 16+4	(18 bars)	exact repeat in A1 at:	66 to 67+4

This simple approach to prolongation and development of musical material is substantially different from the repeated sections found, for example, in much Baroque music where binary and tertiary forms dominate. Performance practice in this period required that repeats were to be embellished with ornaments and extemporizations in a way that completely altered the music in a material and rhetorical manner. In *Concerto for Alto Saxophone and String Orchestra*, the exact repeats (or inversions) signify a different application of form and structure. For this highly rigorous approach to creating structure and maintaining motivic consistency, Buckley repeats entire blocks of music. Section A1 is almost completely comprised of blocks of music extracted from section A (though not exclusively). Fig. 19 shows that, of the 200 bars making up A1, 119 bars (or almost 60%) derive from section A.

Buckley's manipulations of the repetitions can be found in correlating inverted sections. These inversions are almost identical. However, Buckley colours them differently by shifting the musical material from instrument to instrument: a given melodic phrase which originally appears on, say, the second violin, now emerges on the viola or cello in the repetition, giving the same melodic phrase a new colour and texture. Examples 39a (showing a 7-bar segment from 6+7 in section A) and 39b (highlighting its retrograde repeat from 55 in section A1) demonstrate Buckley's alteration of the timbral qualities of the repeated material and the exact preservation of its formal structure.

Ex. 39a: *Concerto for Alto Saxophone and String Orchestra*, rehearsal mark 6+7 to 7+3

Ex. 39b: *Concerto for Alto Saxophone and String Orchestra*, rehearsal mark 55 to 55+7

This use of self-reflecting structures also lies at the heart of the figurative images of M.C. Escher and his experiments in Optical Art, which conceptually divided the plane through repeated mirror-like and compatible figures.[97] Escher's images capture a sense of infinity. Though fixed in a finite structure, they suggest an impression of continuous rotation. Likewise, Buckley's use of block structures locates a space that is both temporal and static. The use of Escher-like mirrored structures and large quantities of previously heard material displays an approach to composition that values segment duplication and factors of recognition over an ever-flowing release of newly composed material. It implies a self-censorship of any impulses that might disrupt the formal contour of the work. Although this self-discipline can be recognized as a prominent attribute of Buckley's music from the late 1990s onwards, it is at its most rigorous in the outer sections of *Concerto for Alto Saxophone and String Orchestra*.

As if to counteract the total hegemony of formal structure over content in the A and A1 sections, Buckley creates something quite the opposite in the central section, a place where pure discourse takes precedence over mirrored and repeated segments. The central B section is the slow 'movement' and is, in fact, an amplification of the melodic material provided by *Arabesque* – the work Buckley wrote for solo alto saxophone some years earlier. The section roughly divides into four sections:

Fig. 20: *Concerto for Alto Saxophone and String Orchestra*, **structural division of B section**

Rehearsal mark 22 (p. 33)	Adagio – Cadenza
Rehearsal mark 27 (p. 42)	Adagio – più mosso – Adagio
Rehearsal mark 37 (p. 61)	Adagio – *accelerando*
Rehearsal mark 41 (p. 69)	Adagio – *accelerando* to 51 (p.83) [beginning of A1 section]

The recurrence of accelerations and decelerations determines the numerous zones of varying densities and tensions. In this section, the string orchestration most strikingly invokes the French school, with

---

[97] Maurits Cornelis Escher (1898-1972) is noted for his 'impossible structures' (*Relativity*, *Ascending and Descending*) and his transformation prints (*Metamorphosis I*, *Metamorphosis II*, *Metamorphosis III* and *Sky & Water I*). Fascinated by the regular division of the plane, his work was partially influenced by Islamic art and architecture.

wide intervals in the lower strings and an incremental tightening of the intervals as the range gets higher (see Examples 40 and 41 below). The central section does not conform to a linear harmonic plan. When the strings enter, typically in support of a sustained note on the saxophone (see Example 40), Buckley constructs a harmonic frame around the solo instrument that is pertinent only to the moment and locale it serves. The harmonic result is often the aggregate of a series of melodic motifs dispersed throughout the range of the strings. Buckley creates his harmonic sound directly from melodic fragments, frequently introduced by the saxophone.

From rehearsal mark 42, the strings develop a harmonic construct devised from a four-note motif comprising a minor 7th, a minor 2nd and a tone. The cellos and double bass outline their F♯, E, D♯, and C♯ motif, above which the violas play a transposition of the motif on B, A, G♯, and F♯. The second violins (top system) add a further transposition playing E, D, C♯ and B, while the first violins (top and centre stave) slightly alter the motif as C♯, A, G♯ and F♯. Having completed their motifs, all the strings sustain the last notes and the result forms the harmonic basis for the saxophone solo. The established motif is echoed by the saxophone at rehearsal mark 42+4 (page 71) in the first three notes of the first group of demisemiquavers.

Ex. 40: *Concerto for Alto Saxophone and String Orchestra*, rehearsal mark 42

Rehearsal mark 42+5 represents the aggregate of all these fragments. The final harmonic result offers an opportunity to see how Buckley structures his harmonic plane (see Examples 40 and 41).

Ex. 41: *Concerto for Alto Saxophone and String Orchestra*, harmonic structure of bar 42+5

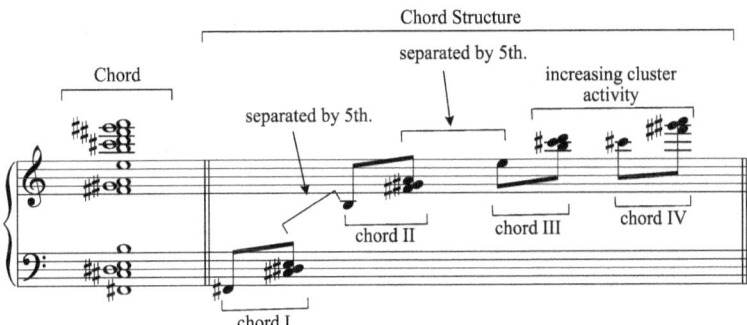

For this harmonic complex, Buckley has vertically superimposed four chords. Each chord is built upon a perfect 5th, the top note of which becomes the focus for a cluster of notes (typically with added major seconds and minor thirds). Chord I (on double bass and cellos) is built upon the 5th, F♯ and C♯ (the notes D♯ and E colour the upper C♯). Chord II (on violas) shows the 5th, B and F♯ (the upper note upon which is added a G♯ and an A, heard on the second violin). Chord III (on second violins) is built on the E above this, with a B creating the perfect 5th. This upper B is coloured by a C♯ and D, the former of which takes the root of the final and fourth chord (on a second violin and first violins). Above the C♯ is placed a G♯ (creating the perfect 5th), which is further coloured by a lower F♯ and a higher A. Buckley has constructed these chords so that the top note of each cluster is a perfect 5th below the root note of the chord above, so that each chord group is also separated by the interval of the perfect 5th, except for the two top chords, which are placed very close to each other, thereby increasing the cluster activity in the higher register. This heightened cluster formation offers that particularly French effect perfected by Dutilleux, while the 5th-based harmony provides the elusive open sound. Four 5th-based chords constructed one upon the other defy tonal categorization and reject a sense of harmonic movement in any traditional understanding of the term.

This 'in the moment' approach contributes to a sense of harmonic stasis and ambiguity. As in *Concerto for Organ and Orchestra*, the extended central section lasting over thirteen minutes tends to dominate the overall work, and the outer sections, which combined last only seven minutes, struggle to provide a convincing balance. Despite the internal conflict in this work between formal construction and free discourse, the overall result is consistently abstract. The distance in the language rejects sentimental indulgence and places the piece firmly within an objectivized neo-classicism. Furthermore, the harmonic consistency the work displays nominates it as among the most integrated in Buckley's *oeuvre* – formal structure and stylistic language interlock most convincingly.

Tidal Erotics

In 1998, Buckley embarked on a major collaborative venture with the Irish artist Vivienne Roche for an exhibition in the Hugh Lane Municipal Gallery of Modern Art in Dublin. The exhibition ran from April to June of the following year and subsequently showed at the Sirius Gallery in Cobh, County Cork, and the Galway Arts Centre. Roche was born in Cork in 1953 and studied at the Crawford College of Art and at the School of the Museum of Fine Arts in Boston. She had by this time acquired a considerable international reputation, particularly as a sculptor, and had participated in international group exhibitions in France, Finland, Sweden, England and the United States. She and Buckley first met about ten years previously in Norwich when they served on the European jury of *Pépinière*, a scheme designed to assist young artists of various disciplines, and the seeds of collaboration were sown at that time.

While both artist and composer were in the initial stages of planning the Hugh Lane Gallery project, an opportunity arose that allowed them to first work on a smaller project. The National Sculpture Factory in Cork commissioned a piece from Roche for presentation to Micheál Martin, TD, then Minister for Education and Science, in recognition of his support as a member of its board of directors. Buckley was asked to provide a piece of music that would complement Roche's work. This provided both artists with an opportunity to discuss the nature of their collaboration, and in a sense, rehearse for the larger project. The result was *Airflow*, and Buckley's music for solo flute was performed on the occasion of the presentation in April 1998 in Cork by William Dowdall. This initial collaboration set the framework within which the artists worked together:

> The concept for the work evolved through a series of discussions relating to common points of reference between sculpture and music; scale, tone, form, shape, line and gesture. Vivienne and I sought to create a dynamic interaction between the two art-forms.[98]

The collaboration for the Hugh Lane Gallery, however, was to be a much more elaborate affair. Since 1996, Roche had been attracted by the latent erotic associations of tidal motions, marine organisms, the spinal contours of sea-moulded sand and the interlaced and intertwined seaweeds cast upon the shore. *Tidal Erotics*, as the project was entitled, comprised a series of pencil drawings and bronze casts in which Roche attempted to capture these flowing ephemeral configurations, seeking to convey a sense of their motion while at the same time fixing them in place. The process of making bronze sculptures from living seaweed meant that the latter was completely destroyed. The writer Sebastian Barry tapped into the contractions implied by this process:

> The prime of life disappears into the permanence of bronze. They are no longer just the artefacts of the sea and the sea-tide, but of the artist. To the accident of the cycle of their true life is added the intervention, the virtuoso intent of the artist. It is interrupting their life to lend them further life, to banish them into human rooms – in this case four carefully structured rooms – where they will elicit meaning from anyone who sees them, and yet remain enigmatically themselves also.[99]

Buckley provided a score mirroring this captured movement in music. The realization of the idea engaged both artist and composer for a full eighteen months. In contrast to her earlier work, which had been on a much larger scale, *Tidal Erotics* represented a more intimate approach. In seeking to find an aural parallel for this intimacy, Buckley was constrained by the fact that the music was written not to be performed live but heard as recorded sound moments. Naturally, this mode of presentation altered his usual approach to both instrumental layout and structural organization, and Buckley found the challenge of this collaboration particularly stimulating. Roche echoes Buckley's view of the collaboration:

---

[98] John Buckley, 'In Lines of Dazzling Light' (liner notes to CD), *Black Box* (BBBM1210), 1999.
[99] Sebastian Barry, 'Tidal Erotics' in *Tidal Erotics* (Dublin: The Hugh Lane Municipal Gallery of Modern Art, 1999), p.6.

In terms of abstraction, John and I share a very similar language and a way of talking about our work, and this common language was why I invited him to work with me. What happened was an absolute collaboration in which we extended our vocabulary to accommodate the other, but did not cross over to each other's forms.[100]

The installation was divided into four separate spaces, each of which was given a title – *Soundings, Tidal Erotics, The amen of calm waters* and *Ever drifting*. The visitor's trajectory through the exhibition was carefully judged by the artists. The initial presence of the observer triggered a tam-tam sound (lasting one minute), which suggested the distant sound of the sea. The exhibition, staged in different rooms, provided different experiences. In one room, the music was generated when a person entered or left; in two further rooms, the music alternated with varying periods of silence, while in the fourth, music played when the observer approached the sculpture. 'In *Tidal Erotics*, we wanted to give the observer some control in determining how much music they heard,' Buckley comments. 'The interplay of various observers in the gallery provided a unique sonic experience at any given time suggesting echoes of Cage's chance operations though within tightly controlled parameters.' Ciaran Bennett has observed that 'the engagement of visual and aural pattern explores the harmonics of the space and interacts to manifest a complete statement of multi-dimensional achievement.'[101]

Buckley created a score comprising sixteen discreet movements (plus the tam-tam sound used as an entrance and exit) ranging from twenty seconds to three and a half minutes). Occasionally, the score insists on the doubling of instruments, which is achieved in the recording studio by the process of multi-tracking. Five instruments were used – flute, horn, cello, piano and percussion – which were deployed in various combinations. The different groupings of instruments were designed to correlate with the particular type of sculptures and drawings shown in each room. The first space, *Soundings*, for example, contained a series of artworks that were organized in pairs and complemented by a series of instrumental duets, ten in all. This first space functioned as a kind of anteroom to the second space, *Tidal Erotics*, which was much larger and held a combination of sculptures and drawings. Here, Buckley provided a series of trios, which reflected the correspondingly more complex aspects of

---

[100] Katy Deepwell, *Dialogues: Women Artists from Ireland* (London: IB Tauri, 2005), p.165.
[101] Ciaran Bennett, 'Triangular Palimpsest' in *Tidal Erotics* (Dublin: Hugh Lane Municipal Gallery of Modern Art, 1999), p. 15.

Roche's work. The third space, *The amen of calm waters*, contained a series of large drawings and a single large sculpture. In a parallel gesture, Buckley reserved the full forces of his quintet for this space. A second quintet (adapted from a slow movement from one of Buckley's earlier works, *In Lines of Dazzling Light*) complemented the artwork of the final space, *Ever drifting*, which suggested the stillness of water left behind after the tide has receded. On leaving the gallery, the observer again triggered the tam-tam, thereby closing the journey with the sound of the distant sea once more.

Fig. 21: *Tidal Erotics*, structural plan

Entrance:	percussion (tam-tam)	00.58	Entrance
I:	horn and piano	00.52	Space I: *Soundings*
II:	percussion and piano	00.51	
III:	flute and piano	00.20	
IV:	cello and piano	00.40	
V:	horn and percussion	01.07	
VI:	flute and horn	00.35	
VII:	horn and cello	00.30	
VIII:	multi-tracked flute and percussion	00.41	
IX:	multi-tracked cello and percussion	00.21	
X:	flute and cello	00.48	
XI:	flute, horn and piano	00.53	Space II: *Tidal Erotics*
XII:	flute, cello and multi-tracked percussion	01.39	Exit
XIII:	cello, percussion and piano	00.54	
XIV:	horn, cello and piano	00.52	
XV:	flute, horn, cello, percussion and piano	03.21	Space III: *The amen of calm waters*
XVI:	clarinet, bassoon, horn, percussion and piano	02.35	Space IV: *Ever drifting*
Exit:	percussion (tam-tam)	00.58	Exit

The timings of the individual movements betray a Webernesque penchant for brevity correlating to the ephemeral nature and reduced size of the subject matter to which the music responds. In many cases the musical material has been condensed to concise instances – sometimes even one momentary gesture, which has forced Buckley to imbue the music with a highly-charged energy. Harmonically, however, these watercolours are more akin to Takemitsu's subtle surfaces than to Webern's semantic constructions. Buckley's increasing exploration of timbre, his ecstatic outbursts and apparently spontaneous eruptions are, finally, controlled by his allegiance to formal design and structure.

Ex. 42: *Tidal Erotics*, movement II (full score)

'Piece 2' covers a span of only eight bars and though initial hearings give the impression that it is freely-composed, Buckley's sense of structure and form never loses authority. The entire piece is built upon a descending three-note semitone figure in the lower register of the piano – C♯/C/B, which divides the piece into three short gestures. This downward motion is imitated in contrary motion by the treble clef piano material at bars 1 and 2 – G♯/A♯ (middle stave) rising to A/B, and F♯/G♯ to G/A. The crotales, vibraphone and tam-tam might, at first perusal, seem to offer a mere improvisation over the piano's three-part structure. But the percussion echoes the downward movement of the piano's C♯-C-B bass line with its own F♯, F and E descent (see Ex. 42: *Tidal Erotics*, movement II). This echo is suggested not as a strictly semantic and pitch-centred imitation, but rather as a timbral paraphrase of the central structural contour of the short work. The percussion hovers above the germinal material in empathetic resonance.

Movement XII from *Tidal Erotics* displays Buckley's consummate control of his materials, while also demonstrating his refinement of a harmonic technique he had been exploring since his early works. Since *Oileáin* (1979), Buckley had been investigating the idea of fundamental tonal strata around which commentaries emanating from distant tonal spheres would be woven – a technical devise very much in the style of Messiaen's *Vingt Regards sur l'Enfant Jésus* or Ives's *The Unanswered Question*. Movement XII is harmonically structured on a series of overlapping perfect 5^{ths} based on a B♭ fundamental. The glockenspiel provides a counterpointing melody that fits harmonically within the established harmony. It is left to the cello and flute to create strata representing distant harmonic entities. Although both instruments enter on a D♭, giving the initial impression that they are homogeneous with the established harmony, at bar 5 they suddenly spurn both the mood and key, and the flute music explodes in a flame of dissonance.

The tonal centre shifts enharmonically at bar 6, the G♭/D♭ becoming F♯/C♯, which now acts as the fundamental of a new cycle of 5^{ths}. In bar 9, the cello escapes the pull of the harmony in a rapid flurry into a distant atonal arena. The glockenspiel creates a sense of escalating movement. The vibraphone always maintains its minim pace, but the glockenspiel steadily increases its rhythmic ratios starting with minims and increasing to semiquavers in bar 12, creating in the process a driving energy in the music. In these fourteen bars Buckley has perfected his craft; he displays complete control over his harmonic devices and skilfully determines the pace of the work. The spontaneous outbursts are allowed only within the correcting order of his contours. Sound is liberated, but form always has the last word.

In Winter Light

After a two-year hiatus between 2002 and 2003 during which he established and consolidated his work at St Patrick's College, Buckley started composing again in 2004. The first work he wrote was *In Winter Light* (released on the *Celestial Harmonies* label), which dispenses with much of the vivid colouring of his earlier work.[102] He remembers, 'I had written so many pieces full of orange and silver and gold that I now wanted something more muted, various shades of grey and white.'.Since then, he has produced *endless the white clouds...*, in which the imagery of 'various shades of grey and white' clearly persists.

In Winter Light (2004) falls into two highly contrasted movements. The first movement's reference to *Toward the Sea* by Toru Takemitsu extends beyond the mere choice of instrumentation of alto flute and guitar. Buckley's writing for the guitar, the interplay between instruments and the peculiar shape of the musical phrases all pay tribute to Takemitsu's unique approach to shading textures. Formally, the movement is through-composed and the constant reference to chromatic motifs creates continuity. Although two of these can be highlighted as predominant, Buckley employs them as ever-changing, flexible motifs whose shapes alter with repeats. Thematically motif II is a sequential use of motif I. Both motifs appear at bars 4 and 6 respectively.

Ex. 43: *In Winter Light*, movement I, bars 4-6 (alto flute part)

Both motifs centre around semitone intervals, motif II being a rhythmic variant of motif I. The first moves from a semitone (D♭ to C) to a tone (C to D), but the relationship between the first and third notes

---

[102] *In Winter Light: music for guitar and flute*, CD, Celestial Harmonies 13244-2, 2004.

remains a semitone (D♭ to D). The second motif is a descending (or ascending) four-note chromatic scale (though occasionally it appears as a two- or three-note figuration), often embellished with ornaments. The movement is saturated with these motifs and their variants. Dominating the alto flute music, motif I is reiterated numerous times after its initial appearance at bar 4. These can be seen, for example, at bars 17, 49, 64/5, 68, 72/3, 84 and 85/6.

The three-note motive is structurally significant as it always appears at the opening of a phrase, and its constant recurrence helps anchor the otherwise freely-composed music. Motif II also appears regularly but in many guises (sometimes with extra notes placed inside the established motif figuration). It continues to make its presence felt throughout the movement, which ends with a slow ascending version in minims over three bars (see bars 87-89, page 10). Sometimes Buckley intricately weaves motif I into more complex gestures, ensuring that, at least subliminally, it maintains an influence on the melodic and harmonic material. Ex. 44 offers some illustrations:

Ex. 44: *In Winter Light*, **movement I, bar 27 (analysis of embedded motifs in flute part)**

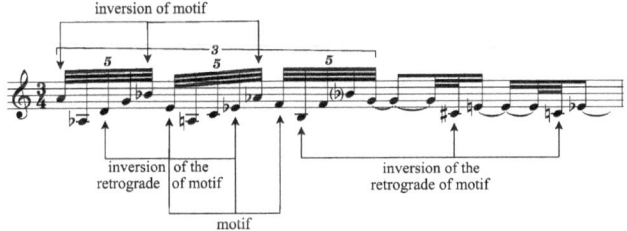

The second movement recalls the tight rhythms, repeated sequences and exact recapitulations exemplified in Buckley's recent scores, such as the framing music of *Concerto for Alto Saxophone and String Orchestra* and *Concerto for Organ and Orchestra*. Structurally paraphrasing these works, the second movement of *In Winter Light* falls into a simple A-B-A1 form, with the A sections containing fast and rhythmic music, while the B section contains a free *Adagio* quite reminiscent of the first movement. In a device crystallized in *Concerto for Alto Saxophone and String Orchestra*, most of the musical material from section A is repeated in section A1.

160   Constellations: The Life and Music of John Buckley

The predominant 6/16 metre of this movement brings to mind the similar bounce of *Concerto for Alto Saxophone and Orchestra*. Here, however, Buckley has rhythmically counterpoised the guitar against the flute so that its 6/16 pattern is accompanied by the guitar playing a 'walking bass' (the continuous jazz bass style) in four dotted semiquavers per bar.

Ex. 45: *In Winter Light*, movement II, bars 10-13

The sequences prominent in *Concerto for Alto Saxophone and Orchestra* are also recalled here, most notably in the section from bar 94 to 97, which is presented again at bar 102 to 105 in an altered version.

Ex. 46: *In Winter Light*, bars 94-97 superimposed on bars 102-105

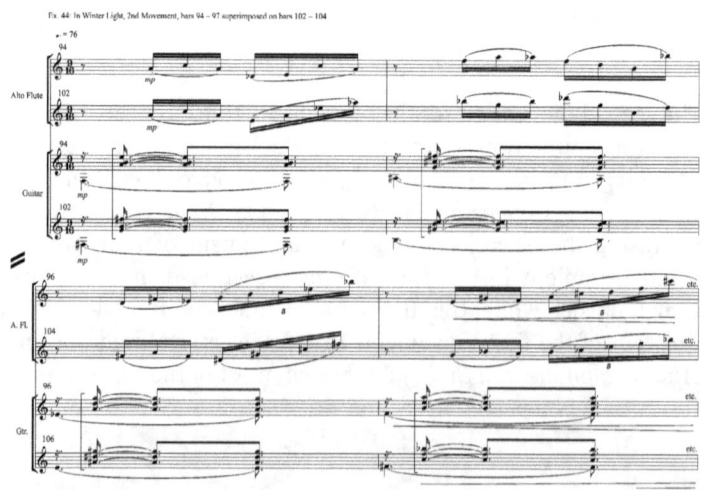

By superimposing the two sequences, we note how Buckley creates them without reverting to exact replicas. The rise in the guitar music is obvious enough – the bass notes (at the start of each bar) have risen from F, A♯, E♭, F to F♯, B, E, F♯. The chords above these bass notes have also shifted, but not necessarily in a systematic fashion. The change can, however, be observed in the lowest note of each chord rising initially from A, G, A, B to G, A♯, A♯, C. In an attempt to avoid an obvious sequential shift, Buckley has altered the flute music so that, though a sequence is at play, it remains difficult to define exactly how. He has achieved this by altering the shape of each figuration. Although they may have shifted position within the figuration, key notes also have risen, thus achieving the effect of the shifting sequence. The sequence is further enhanced by the repetition of dynamic markings and phrase marks at correlating positions. A highly sophisticated way of creating formal structure for his material without detracting from the musical argument, this fluid technique also features in *Concerto for Alto Saxophone and String Orchestra*, where it is used to great effect.

In Winter Light displays the two main characteristics of Buckley's music between the years 1995 and 2005. On the one hand, the first movement embodies that highly refined, French-influenced, through-composed style in which timbre and colouristic textures play an important role. On the other hand, the second movement typifies the highly rigorous approach to structure and formal design that Buckley insisted upon in his works from this period: movements are tightly knit, rhythmically taut, structured in relatively simple frames of the A-B-A1 type, and developed through the often exact repetition of previously heard material. Through a process of objectivization, he has distilled a harmonic sound world uniquely his own. Allied to a rigorous concern for structural resilience, this dual approach has allowed Buckley to nurture a compositional path, which, though original and contemporary, is always acutely aware of its historical precedents.

7 | Constellations (2005-2010)

as far as the eye can see...

Subtle developments in Buckley's works occur in the years between 2005 and 2010, which display a more lucid, free approach to structural forms, while allowing spatial elements to vie with timbral factors as significant characteristics. The work *endless the white clouds...* typifies this latest stylistic development. This is the first piece Buckley has written for solo harp and it was commissioned for Geraldine O'Doherty by the Ninth World Harp Congress Dublin 2005. Buckley worked very closely with O'Doherty during the compositional process. As he recalls:

> The challenges were not only technical, because it's a very difficult instrument to write for, even more so than the guitar, but also aesthetic. Do you write music conducive to the harp as an instrument, or something new that may or may not suit the instrument's idiosyncratic nature? Geraldine and I both agreed that we wanted a harp piece. Not because of the Congress for which it would be written, but simply because it was what we wanted. I didn't find that restrictive in any way.

The title of the work has an unusual genesis. Around the time of composition, Buckley had been asked to give a talk on Mahler's symphonic song cycle, *Das Lied von der Erde* (1908), based on translations of ancient Chinese texts, made by the German poet Hans Bethge (1876-1946). In the last movement of this work, 'Der Abschied' (The Farewell) by Wang Wei (699-795), Mahler made a number of changes to Bethge's translation, as seen below.

1) Original text with translation:[103]

Ich werde nie mehr in die Ferne schweifen, –
Müd ist mein Fuss, und müd ist meine Seele,
Die Erde ist die gleiche überall,
Und ewig, ewig sind die weissen Wolken...

[Never more shall I wander far abroad,–
My foot is weary, weary is my soul;
The earth is everywhere the same,
And endless, endless the white clouds...]

Altered text with translation:

Ich werde niemals in die Ferne schweifen.
Still ist mein Herz und harret seiner Stunde.
Die liebe Erde allüberall
Blüht auf im Lenz und grünt aufs neu'!
Allüberall und ewig blauen licht die Fernen.
Ewig...Ewig...

[Never more shall I wander far abroad.
My heart is quiet, waiting for its hour.
Everywhere the dear earth
Blossoms in springtime and burgeons again!
Everywhere and evermore the blue distance beckons,
Evermore...Evermore...]

Regarding these alterations, Buckley adds: 'Mahler made his own amendments, and omitted the beautiful line 'endless the white clouds'. I realized that these words summed up exactly what I was trying to achieve with my piece, and I thought that if Mahler didn't want these words, maybe I could have them.' The piece was conceived to function like a cloud: minute fragments emerge, develop, form and dissipate. Buckley explains that 'the piece lasts the same length of time it takes for a cumulus cloud to form and dissolve.' This imagery suggests a through-composed format, where the inter-relationships of the growing melodic and harmonic particles create the structural stability in the work. *endless the white clouds...* was recorded by Cliona Doris in 2007.[104]

Another work written in 2005 served a more sombre function – to commemorate the death of Buckley's teacher and friend, James Wilson. Curiously, Buckley links *A Few Notes for Jim*, for solo violin, with *endless the white clouds...*, though clearly for emotional reasons rather than musical ones. 'It links very closely with the harp piece', he recalls, 'because the last time I met Jim we were both having a harp piece

---

[103] Kurt Blaukopf, trans. Inge Goodwin, *Mahler* (London, Futura, 1973), p. 237.
[104] Cliona Doris (harp), *A Pale Yellow Sky*, CD: RTÉ Lyric fm, CD115, 2008.

performed.[105] My wife and I went off to Australia for the summer and he died while we were there.' The title, *A Few Notes for Jim*, is clearly ironic, as the work is suffused with notes. Indeed, much of its material was drawn from *Violin Concerto*, which Buckley was also writing at this time. *A Few Notes for Jim* was written for and first performed by violinist Darragh Morgan at Airfield House, Dundrum (Dublin), on 24 November 2005.

2006 was dominated by two major works for orchestra – *Campane in Aria* (three flutes, three oboes, three clarinets, three bassoons, four horns, three trumpets, three trombones, one tuba, timpani, four percussion and strings), and *Flute Concerto – In Winter Light* (solo flute/alto flute, harp, percussion and strings), a version of the alto flute and guitar work of the same title. *Campane in Aria* was commissioned by the National Concert Hall (Dublin) to mark the occasion of its twenty-fifth anniversary, making it another of Buckley's 'official' works. This explains its jubilant character. 'Campane in Aria' (Bells in the Air) is a direction occasionally given to the horn section in the orchestra indicating that the bells of the instruments, which normally face away from the audience, should be raised in the air. This resonant and exhilarating sound can be observed in the closing moments of the work. Buckley explains that 'the title also refers to the sense of celebration associated with the bells ringing and the tintinnabulation of the glockenspiel and vibraphone, along with marimba and xylophone, is a prominent feature of the middle section of the work.' Although through-composed, the work seamlessly falls into three sections, with a slow central part flanked by two outer energetic sections. Dedicated to the National Concert Hall and 'to everyone who has worked so hard for its outstanding success', it was premiered there on 9 September 2006, by the RTÉ National Symphony Orchestra with Gerhard Markson conducting.

Flute Concerto – In Winter Light provides a tremendous contrast to the outwardly celebratory *Campane in Aria*. RTÉ commissioned Buckley to write a flute concerto. As a shortage of time prevented him from embarking on a new work, Buckley proposed a concerto version of the alto flute and guitar work, and RTÉ agreed to this solution. *Flute Concerto – In Winter Light* has two movements and a cadenza, and lasts seventeen minutes. It was premiered by William Dowdall (to whom it is dedicated) and the RTÉ National Symphony Orchestra, with Christian Gansch conducting. Buckley had always felt that the original

---

[105] Buckley's *endless the white clouds...* and Wilson's *Serenade*, for violin, cello and harp.

flute and guitar piece had the potential to be expanded. Given the delicate nature of that work, it is no surprise that the orchestration is relatively light. The harp plays the role of the guitar, with the strings given the function of sustaining the sonorities and of exploring the higher partials of the music, while the percussion (marimba in the first movement, bongos and congas in the second) adds a more dynamic, rhythmic element. The one totally new section in the work is the cadenza, which Buckley subsequently transformed into a solo work aptly entitled *Winter Echoes*. This new solo work, which was written two years later in 2008, is a further reflection on light, the prevailing theme of much of Buckley's mature music. The composer has described this work as:

> a musical reflection on the extraordinary magical qualities of light during an Irish winter. This can vary between the startling luminous brilliance of the low sun at midday and the muted twilight, as shadows softly merge into a late November evening. This short piece attempts to capture and interpret these moods through a combination of virtuoso brilliance and lyrical reflection.[106]

As can be seen, the latter half of the decade saw the ongoing collaboration with flautist William Dowdall produce a number of important new works for the flute. Furthermore, Buckley was among the first composers to respond to Dowdall's innovative work in the promotion of the newly-constructed glissando head-joint for the flute. *Sea Echoes*, which is meant as a companion piece to *Winter Echoes*, was composed in July 2008, and dedicated to Dowdall. The most striking aspect of the sliding head-joint is its ability to play a true glissando. From the start, however, Buckley wanted to avoid writing a piece that might be conceived of as a 'bag of tricks':

> I was determined not to create a series of special effects, but to compose a piece where the new possibilities arose naturally as an extension of the musical argument. As the title suggests, the work is inspired by the undulating shape of the waves, the sibilant whispers as they arrive and retreat from the shore and the distant suggestion of bird and whale song.[107]

Buckley's important work of the decade is undoubtedly *Violin Concerto*, written in 2008. Written for the violinist Gwendolyn Masin, the work awaits a premiere performance. It is a large-scale concerto and, like *Symphony No. 1*, had a long gestation period, taking up to six years to be completed. Conscious of the vast canon of violin concertos,

---

[106] John Buckley, e-mail message to author, 28 September 2010.
[107] John Buckley, e-mail message to author, 28 September 2010.

Buckley embarked on an in-depth study of the genre, looking closely at the concertos of Berg, Szymanowski, Shostakovich, Carter and, perhaps most importantly, Dutilleux. 'The Dutilleux probably had the most profound influence on me, although I hope my work is very different.' Technical control was an essential feature of Buckley's preparation and composition of the piece: 'As with all the concertos I have written, I am concerned with the balance between orchestra and the solo instrument. That is a key issue; it is not just a matter of balance of dynamics, but a balance of the relationship between the material and its development.' *Violin Concerto* lasts about twenty-five minutes and represents something of a change of direction as far as formal design is concerned. The vast majority of Buckley's large-scale orchestral works (including concertos) have adopted the standard A-B-A format. This work transcends that simple contour for a more seamless flow between fast and slow tempi. Indeed, it assumes some of the qualities of Elliot Carter's Quartets in its surreptitious modulation between varying tempi. As Buckley describes it:

> The opening slow section leads to a showy faster movement with bravura passages. This moves to a slow middle section, and then to a large scale cadenza. The entire work tapers out into a slow, ephemeral finish. The tempo modulates in a way that is something new in my work; sometimes two tempi run at the same time. It is not sectional like my earlier works; it is more organic in that sense. The sections flow in a more seamless manner.

This softening of the contour, somewhat in the style of *endless the white clouds...* suggests a more sophisticated approach to structural schemata. The integrated manner of the unfolding material becomes the formalizing device.

Buckley's connection with music education is further underscored with the second composition he wrote in 2008, *as far as the eye can see*, for alto saxophone, oboe, horn and piano. This one-movement work, lasting just six minutes, was written for the WhistleBlast Quartet and was premiered by them at the Linenhall Theatre, Castlebar, Ireland, on 11 June 2009. Its initial commission was built around an educational project whereby school children would compositionally respond to the images emitted by Buckley's work, though the composer insists that *as far as the eye can see* has a life of its own and can be performed as such. The title is inspired by the sweeping landscape and seascape of the west of Ireland, especially in Mayo, where the WhistleBlast Quartet is based, implying that spatial elements are now an important influential factor in Buckley's music of the last few years.

Spatial and timbral factors are central to Buckley's most innovative and dynamic flute work, *Constellations* (2009), which once again was written at the instigation of William Dowdall, who premiered it on 17 October 2010 at the Hugh Lane Gallery on the occasion of the Irish launch of the CD on which it is featured.[108] Steve Reich's *Vermont Counterpoint* (1982) sets a precedent for multiple flutes on tape against a solo flute. Buckley's *Constellations*, however, is not so much concerned with the rhythmic interplay of these instruments, but rather centres on the exploration of motivic transference and the timbral potential of the various combinations of the instruments. The latter element is brought to an extraordinary degree of sophistication as Buckley employs bass flutes, alto flutes, flutes in C and piccolos in various combinations (starting with the lower register instruments and steadily moving up the range). In many ways, *Constellations* represents the epitome and culmination of Buckley's latest style. The control of 'orchestration' and the attendant timbral results make for a work rich in texture and colour (at its most dense, the work uses up to fourteen flutes simultaneously). The inter-relationship between the parts renders spatial elements equally important to the melodic, harmonic and timbral aspects of the work. Dowdall's significant contribution to Buckley's latest music has been noted. It should not be surprising, however, that Buckley has returned to his own instrument to explore the facets of music that appeal to him so much, and which he crafts with such exceptional skill.

Coda

Reviewing his career, Buckley finds it relatively easy to measure the distance he has travelled in terms of stylistic development. He has reached a point where his principal desire is to concentrate his creative energies and to ensure that each piece he undertakes will contribute to the fuller realization of his artistic vision. Although he has not yet written a work for string quartet, he expresses a growing enthusiasm for the medium. Whether concerto form or string quartet, Buckley is keen to explore the potential of cycles of works: 'The idea of writing a series of concertos appeals to me. I certainly want to write a set of string quartets – but I don't feel that I'm old enough for that yet.'

---

[108] William Dowdall (flutes), *Breathe: New Notes for Flute from Ireland and New Zealand*, 1979-2010, on ATOLL, ACD 111, 2010.

He admits to being prepared for a change of style if it becomes necessary. However, he maintains that previous stylistic changes have arisen from an organic process of development:

> Composers who insist on working in a style whose expressive potential has been exhausted tend to write dry and rather academic music that has no real heart and no real truth in it. If I find that my current approach is no longer adequate to my expressive needs, I hope I will have the courage to explore new directions.

Despite his frequent recourse to impressionistic titles, Buckley maintains that they do not correlate to any equivalent elusiveness in form or design, but rather to the sound world enclosed within those structures. The music is essentially abstract in quality. Overtly, its principal concern is with itself and with its own unfolding processes. As timbre and texture have become ever more central to his musical identity, formal structure has correspondingly assumed a more significant controlling function. The continuing emancipation of pure timbre and the exploration of sound as elusive variants of shade had to be contained within the beneficial paradigm of a controlling structure. Buckley's music certainly has few, if any, personal or biographical connotations, and scarcely relates to contemporary social or political events. 'On the other hand,' he insists, 'I would say that almost every single note I have written is autobiographical.'

The late 1990s saw a major development in Buckley's career when a number of commercial recordings became available for the first time. These included *Concerto for Organ and Orchestra, Symphony No. 1*, and the complete piano music on the Naxos/Marco Polo label (performed by Anthony Byrne, a leading exponent of Buckley's work), while Black Box music issued *Concerto for Alto Saxophone and Strings* and a selection of chamber works.

Buckley's academic career was further enhanced when he was awarded a PhD by the National University of Ireland, Maynooth in 2002. He was subsequently awarded a DMus in 2007 by the same institution. Alongside his ongoing work as lecturer in St Patrick's College, Buckley continues to make significant contributions to music education. His most recent publication with Yvonne Higgins is *The Right Note* – an innovative resource in support of the revised primary-school music curriculum. He has displayed a great commitment to the support of new music in Ireland and to his fellow composers. Over the past forty years he has served on numerous committees, including those of the Music Association of Ireland, Music Network, the Irish Music

Rights Organization, the Dublin Festival of Twentieth-Century Music and the Toscaireacht of Aosdána.

A major breakthrough came in 2002 when Eckart Rahn's CD label, *Celestial Harmonies*, and its associated publishing company, *ERP Musikverlag Eckart Rahn*, added Buckley's works to its catalogue. Amongst the scores published to date are an album of flute music, *endless the white clouds...* and *Guitar Sonata No. 2*. CD releases include, *in winter light*, the complete works for flute and guitar, and *William Dowdall – Works for Solo Flute*, featuring *Sea Echoes* and *Winter Echoes*. *Celestial Harmonies* is committed to publishing Buckley's complete *oeuvre*.

If we are to include *Constellations*, John Buckley's catalogue extends to an impressive one hundred works spanning almost forty years of creative production. He has composed music in practically every genre from the simplest of pedagogic pieces to the most advanced and expanded orchestral forces. Coming from a farming background with little financial support, he has emerged as one of the leading voices in Irish music. If we were to consider his contribution to Irish music education alone, his reputation would be immense. When we add to this achievement his central involvement in the transformation of the landscape of Irish art music with an array of highly original compositions, many of which will remain as a lasting testament to his craft and musical imagination, we begin to realize the stature of this composer. That Buckley continues to be a relatively obscure figure outside Ireland can only be attributed to the ongoing problems in relation to contemporary music and Irish cultural identity. Ireland's historical relationship with classical music is complex and subject to various interpretations, colonial, social, cultural, political and economic. That this relationship continues to be plagued with difficulties and obfuscations at the beginning of the 21st century is a silent scandal.

The creative urge of Irish composers over the past century has forged an art genre that can be seen, despite its eclecticism, as a coherent body of creative energy. Buckley, who emerged in the 1970s helped forge, alongside his contemporaries, a new modernism that exhibited Irish musical creativity in terms of a broader European and world context. The work of Irish composers paralleled the political and economic transformation of the island. As the aesthetic expression of this new musical modernism and the ensuing diversity it engendered in the younger generations was largely free of historical, colonial and political impediments (a claim that may only be made for Irish literature with some difficulty), it was, and remains, a fresh and vital expression of Irish cultural consciousness. The music of John Buckley, with its abstracted refinement, its unabated joy in pure sound and its finely honed contours, stands as one of the finest expressions of this new cultural consciousness.

Bibliography

Books, Book Chapters and Periodicals:

Barry, Sebastian, et al., *Tidal Erotics Catalogue Brochure* (Dublin: Hugh Lane Municipal Gallery of Modern Art, 1999).

Bartolozzi, Bruno, *New Sounds for Woodwind* (London: Oxford University Press, 1967).

Blaukopf, Kurt, *Mahler*, translated by Inge Goodwin (London: Futura, 1974).

Bodman Rae, Charles, *The Music of Lutoslawski* (London: Omnibus Press, 1999).

Boydell, Brian, *Rotunda Music in Eighteenth-Century Dublin* (Dublin: Irish Academic Press, 1992).

Burke, Patrick, ed., *A Mirror Up to Nature: Fourth Seamus Heaney Lectures* (Dublin: Carysfort Press, 2010).

Cage, John, *A Year from Monday* (London: Marion Boyars, 1968).

Clarke, Heather, *The Ulster Renaissance: Poetry in Belfast, 1962-1972* (London: Oxford University Press, 2006).

Cox, Gareth, Axel Klein, and Michael Taylor, eds. *The Life and Music of Brian Boydell* (Dublin: Irish Academic Press, 2004).

Deane, Basil, *Alun Hoddinott – Composers of Wales 2*. Edited by Roy Bohana (Cardiff: University of Wales Press, 1978).

Deepwell, Katy, *Dialogues: Women Artists from Ireland* (London: IB Tauris, 2005).

Dervan, Michael, 'Thinning Out the Textures'. *Irish Times*, 26 June 1986.

---, 'Taking the Strain'. *The Bridge*, Winter 1986.

Devine, Patrick F. and Harry White, eds. *Irish Musical Studies (4) – The Maynooth International Musicological Conference 1995* (Dublin: Four Courts Press, 1996.

Dudley Edwards, Ruth, *Patrick Pearse – The Triumph of Failure* (London: Faber & Faber, 1979).
Gillen, Gerard and Harry White, eds. *Irish Musical Studies (3) – Music and Irish Cultural History* (Dublin: Irish Academic Press, 1995).
Eliot, T.S, *Four Quartets* (London: Faber & Faber, 1944).
Ernst, Bruno, *The Magic Mirror of M.C. Escher* (Köln: Taschen, 2007).
Feehan, Fanny, 'Shortsightedness is the only word'. *Irish Independent*, 1978.
Ferris, Timothy, *Coming of Age in the Milky Way* (London: Vintage, 1990).
Fleischmann, Ruth, ed., *Aloys Fleischmann – A Life for Music in Ireland Remembered by Contemporaries* (Cork: Mercier Press, 2000).
Forster, Leonard, ed., *The Penguin Book of German Verse* (Middlesex: Penguin, 1957).
Gardner, Helen, ed., *The Metaphysical Poets* (Middlesex: Penguin, 1957).
Gillen, Gerard, Harry White, eds., *Irish Musical Studies (3) – Music and Irish Cultural History* (Dublin: Irish Academic Press, 1995).
Glacken, Brendan, 'Culture, sex and lobsters'. *The Irish Times*, 4 May 1995.
Gleeson, Cian, 'Sheer Composure'. *Sunday Times*, 4 June 1995.
Griffiths, Paul, *Olivier Messiaen and the Music of Time* (New York: Cornell University Press, 1985).
---, *The Contemporary Composers – György Ligeti*. London: Robson Books Ltd., 1997.
Hamel, Peter Michael, 'Der irische Komponist John Buckley'. *MusikTexte 20* (1987).
Harrison, Bernard, ed., *Catalogue of Contemporary Irish Music* (Dublin: Irish Composers' Centre, 1982).
Hayward, John, ed., *The Penguin Poets – John Donne* (Middlesex: Penguin, 1950).
Keller, Hans, 'Introduction: Operatic music and Britten'. In *The Operas of Benjamin Britten*, ed., David Herbert (London: Hamish Hamilton, 1979).
Kelley, Kevin W, *The Home Planet* (New York: Queen Ann Press, 1998).
Klein, Axel, *Irish Classical Recordings – A Discography of Irish Art Music* (Westport, Connecticut: Greenwood Press, 2001).
Lourié, Arthur, 'Oedipus Rex' in *La Revue musicale*, 8 (1927).
Manning, Jane, *New Vocal Repertory 2* (Oxford: Oxford University Press, 1998).

Mansergh, Nicholas, *Britain and Ireland* (London: Longmans, Green and Co., 1942).
Maxton, Hugh, Programme Note for *The Words Upon the Window Pane* (Dublin: Opera Theatre Company, 1990).
McCarr, Pat, *A Musical Journey – Purcell to Buckley* (Kilkenny: J & G Print, 1989).
Ó Buachalla, Brendán, *Aogán Ó Rathaille* (Baile Átha Cliath: Field Day Publications, 2007).
Ó Canainn, Tomás, *Traditional Music in Ireland* (London: Routledge and Kegan Paul, 1978).
O'Kelly, Pat, *The National Symphony Orchestra of Ireland – A Selected History* (Dublin: Radio Telefís Éireann, 1998).
Pakenham Longford, Frank, and P. O'Neill, *Éamon de Valera* (London: Hutchinson, 1970).
Pine, Richard, *Music and Broadcasting in Ireland* (Dublin: Four Courts Press, 2005).
Pine, Richard and Charles Acton, eds., *To Talent Alone, The Royal Irish Academy of Music 1848-1998* (Dublin: Gill & Macmillan, 1998).
Rees, Alwyn, and Brinley Rees, *Celtic Heritage – Ancient Tradition in Ireland and Wales* (London: Thames and Hudson, 1961).
Shakespeare, William, *A Midsummer Night's Dream* (London: Oxford University Press, 1986).
Steinitz, Richard, *György Ligeti – Music of the Imagination* (London: Faber & Faber, 2003).
Walcott, Derek, *Omeros*, (London: Faber & Faber, 1990).
Walsh, Stephen, *Stravinsky – A Creative Spring* (London: Pimlico, 2002).
---, *Stravinsky – Oedipus Rex* (Cambridge: Cambridge University Press, 1993).
Williams, William Carlos, *Paterson* (New York: Penguin, 1983).
Yeats, W.B., *The Words Upon the Window Pane* (Shannon: Irish University Press/T.M (MacGlinchey Publisher, 1970).

Newspaper Reviews:

Acton, Charles, *The Irish Times*. 19 September 1979.
Adams, Martin, *The Irish Times*. 16 February 1998.
Brachtel, Karl Robert, 'Einfallsreiche Dialoge'. *Münchner Merkur*. 10 March 1987.
Dervan, Michael, *The Irish Times*. 7 October 1987.
---, *The Irish Times*. 4 June 1988.
---, 'Coruscating brilliance'. *The Irish Times*, 30 June 1992.

---, *The Irish Times*. 29 September 1997.
MacGoris, Mary, '20-minute operas a success'. *Irish Independent*, 18 October 1991.
---, *Irish Independent*. 4 June 1988.
O'Kelly, Pat, *Irish Press*. 27 July 1978.
---, *Irish Press*. 31 July 1981.
---, *Irish Press*. 17 July 1989.
---, 'Festival winner returns to city'. *Evening Press*, 22 January 1990.
---, *Irish Press*. 30 October 1992.
---, *Irish Press*. 25 February 1994.
Pine, Richard, *The Irish Times*. 21 July 1989.
Sealy, Douglas, *The Irish Times*. 12 June 1983.
---, *The Irish Times*. 22 November 1995.
---, *The Irish Times*. 14 October 1997.
---, *The Irish Times*. 30 November 2000.

Papers:

Kinsella, Tina, Interview transcripts for M.Phil thesis: *Aosdána and the Female Visual Artist*. September 2008.

Websites and E-mail Correspondence:

Barenboim, Daniel, 'West-Eastern Divan Orchestra' in website: http://www.west-eastern-divan.org/press/press-release.html (cited 3 August 2005).
Corcoran, Frank, Introduction web site www.frankcorocran.com (cited 23 August 2006).
Buckley, John, E-mail message to author, 28 September 2010.
Corcoran, Frank, E-mail message to author. 11 February 2008.
Arts Council of Ireland: http://aosdana.artscouncil.ie
Association of Irish Composers: www.composers.ie
Contemporary Music Centre (Ireland): http://www.cmc.ie
Corcoran, Frank: http://www.frankcorcoran.com
Deane, Raymond: http://www.raymonddeane.com
Dwyer, Benjamin: www.benjamindwyer.com
---, *Interview with Raymond Deane*. Recording in the CMC sound archives; transcript on: www.benjamindwyer.com/articles
International Society for Contemporary Music: http://www.iscm.org
People's College, Dublin: http://www.peoplescollege.ie
Royal Irish Academy of Music: www.riam.ie
Salesians of Don Bosco: www.salesians.org

St Patrick's College, Drumcondra:
http://www.spd.dcu.ie/main/index.shtml

CD Recordings

Buckley, John, *In Lines of Dazzling Light*. (CD: liner notes) (*Black Box–*BBBM1210) 1998.

---, 'Organ Concerto/Symphony No. 1'. CD: *Irish Composers Series* (Marco Polo–8.223876).

Doris, Cliona (hp), *A Pale Yellow Sky*. (CD: RTÉ *Lyric* fm, CD115, 2007).

Dowdall, William (fls), *Breathe: new notes for flute from Ireland and New Zealand, 1979-2010*. (ATOLL, ACD 111, 2010).

Dowdall, William (fl) and John Feeley (gtr). *in winter light: music for guitar and flute by john buckley*. (CD, Celestial Harmonies 13244-2, 2004)

Scores:

Mellnäs, Arne, *Transparence* (for orchestra: instrumentation:4444 4440 03 1 str, cel) (Stockholm: Phono Suecia, 1972).

Letter Correspondence:

Fleischmann, Aloys, Letter correspondence with John Buckley. 10 September 1988.

Appendices

APPENDIX I – CATALOGUE OF COMPOSITIONS

Unless otherwise specified, works are in a single movement. Durations are generally given to the nearest minute. Date of first performance refers to the first live or broadcast performance of the work, depending on which occurred first. Names of venues are given as at the time of the first performance. Names of performing groups are given as at the time of first performance, e.g. RTÉSO (RTÉ Symphony Orchestra), later NSO (National Symphony Orchestra), later NSOI (National Symphony Orchestra of Ireland and currently (2011), RTÉSO (RTÉ Symphony Orchestra).

Doubling instruments are indicated in brackets immediately after the principal instrument as follows, for example:
3fl(afl) indicates three flutes, one of which doubles on alto flute.
3fl(picc, afl) indicates three flutes, one of which doubles on piccolo and one of which doubles on alto flute.

Abbreviations of orchestral scores follow the conventional layout order: woodwind, brass percussion, strings. Thus the abbreviation below from Symphony No. 1 (Catalogue No. 49) indicates three flutes, two of which double on piccolo and two of which double on alto flute, three oboes, three clarinets, one of which doubles on bass clarinet, three bassoons, one of which doubles on contra bassoon, four horns, three trumpets, three trombones, one tuba, timpani, five percussionists, harp and strings.
3(2picc, 2afl)33(bcl)3(cbn)/4331/timp/5 perc/hp/str

ABBREVIATIONS

a	alto (voice)
AC	with financial assistance from The Arts Council
afl	alto flute
arr	arrangement
asax	alto saxophone
b	bass (voice)
bar	baritone (voice)
barsax	baritone saxophone
bcl	bass clarinet
brec	bass recorder
bn	bassoon
btbn	bass trombone
ca	cor anglais
cbn	contra bassoon
cel	celeste
cl	clarinet
CMC	Contemporary Music Centre
com	commissioned
cond	conductor
CPI	Cerebral Palsy Ireland
ct	counter-tenor
DCGTHL	Dublin City Gallery, The Hugh Lane
ded	dedicated to
dir	director
drec	descant recorder
dur	duration
eflatacl	E flat alto clarinet
eflatcl	E flat clarinet
fp	first performance
fl	flute
gtr	guitar

hn	horn
hp	harp
hpsd	harpsichord
HLG	Hugh Lane Municipal Gallery of Modern Art, Dublin
ICO	Irish Chamber Orchestra
irhp	Irish harp
JFR	John Field Room
min	minimum
mz	mezzo-soprano
NCH	National Concert Hall, Dublin
NICO	New Irish Chamber Orchestra
NSO	National Symphony Orchestra
NSOI	National Symphony Orchestra of Ireland
ob	oboe
opt	optional
orch	orchestra
org	organ
perc	percussion
pf	piano
picc	piccolo
pub	published
RDS	Royal Dublin Society
RIAM	Royal Irish Academy of Music, Dublin
RTÉ	Radio Telefís Éireann
RTÉCO	RTÉ Concert Orchestra
RTÉSO	RTÉ Symphony Orchestra
rev	revised
s	soprano (voice)
SPD	St Patrick's College, Drumcondra
srec	sopranino recorder
ssax	soprano saxophone
str	strings

syn	synthesiser
t	tenor (voice)
tape	tape recording
tbn	trombone
TCD	Trinity College Dublin
tr	trumpet
trans	translated by
trec	tenor recorder
trrec	treble recorder
tsax	tenor saxophone
tu	tuba
UCD	University College Dublin
va	viola
vc	cello
vn	violin

John Buckley Catalogue of Compositions

1   *Sonata for Cor Anglais and Piano* (1973)
    ca/p
    3 movements
    Dur: 9'
    Fp: 6 January 1974, Dublin Festival of 20th Century Music
    Lindsay Armstrong (ca), Gillian Smith (pf)

2   *The Seasonable Month* (1973)
    s/fl/pf
    Song cycle
    1 Birdsong (William Blake)
    2 How Sweet I Roam'd from Field to Field (William Blake)
    3 Ode to a Nightingale (John Keats)
    4 To Meddowes (Robert Herrick)
    5 The Solitary Reaper (William Wordsworth)
    Dur: 20'
    Fp: March 1974, TCD, Dublin Arts Festival
    Mary Sheridan (s), Doris Keogh (fl), Paul Dorgan (pf)

3   *Three Pieces for Solo Flute* (1973)
    Dur: 10'
    Fp: 26 April 1974, TCD
    Derek Moore (fl)

4   *Auburn Elegy* (1973)
    satb chorus/2fl/cl
    Dur: 12'
    Text: from 'The Deserted Village' (Oliver Goldsmith)

Fp: August 1974, RTÉ
RTÉ Singers, Doris Keogh (fl), Deirdre Brady (fl), Jaqueline Nolan (cl), Hans Waldemar Rosen (cond)

5   *Sequence* (1974)
    cl/bn/pf
    Dur: 12'
    Fp: January 1974, TCD
    John Finucane (cl), Carol Block (bn), Gillian Smith (pf)

6   *Brass Quintet No.1* (1974)
    hn/2tr/tbn/tu
    3 movements
    Dur: 11'
    Fp: 16 February 1976, RTÉ
    Georgian Brass Ensemble

7   *Three Pieces for Solo Cello* (1975)
    Dur: 10'
    Fp: 18 October 1975, University College, Cork
    Aisling Drury-Byrne (vc)

8   *Keoghal* (1975 rev 1997)
    srec/drec/trrec/trec/brec
    5 movements: 1 Ceo Draoidheachta (Magic Mist)
    2 Rosc (March)
    3 An Bunán Buí (The Bittern)
    4 Suantraighe (Lullaby)
    5 Caoineadh (Lament)
    Dur: 9'
    Fp: 2 May 1976, Project Arts Centre, Dublin
    Capriol Consort, Doris Keogh (dir)
    Ded: Doris Keogh

9   *Wind Quintet* (1976 rev 1985)
    fl/ob(ca)/cl/bn/hn
    3 movements
    Dur: 13'
    Fp: 11 June 1977, St Catherine's Church, Dublin
    Les Amis de la Musique

10   *Fanfare for a City* (1976)
     Wind Ensemble
     Dur: 5'
     Fp: 28 August 1976, Kilkenny Castle
     Band of the Curragh Training Camp, George Prendergast (cond)
     Com: Kilkenny Arts Week

11   *Taller than Roman Spears* (1977 rev. 1986)
     3(picc)3(ca)3(bcl)3(cbn)/4331/timp/2perc/str
     1 Samhain, 2 Imbolg, 3 Bealtaine, 4 Lughnasadh
     Dur: 22'
     Fp: 26 July 1978, St Francis Xavier Hall, Dublin
     RTÉSO, Colman Pearce (cond)
     Ded: Colman Pearce

12   *"Why not?" Mr. Berio* (1977)
     tbn/pf
     Dur: 8'
     Fp: 12 January 1978, TCD, Dublin Festival of 20th Century Music
     Sean Cahill (tbn), Veronica McSwiney (pf)
     Com: Dublin Festival of 20th Century Music

13   *Bean Dubh an Ghleanna* (1978)
     satb chorus
     Text: anon
     Dur: 6'
     Fp: 6 May 1978, Cork International Choral Festival
     Cantairí Avondale, Seán Creamer (cond)

14   *Five Two-Part Songs for Children* (1978)
     sa chorus
     1 Suantraí (Lullaby)
     2 Tá Cat Agam sa Bhaile (I Have a Cat at Home)
     3 An Gáirdín Álainn (The Beautiful Garden)
     4 Ceol Earraig (Spring Music)
     5 Sí Éire ár dTírse (Ireland Is Our Country)
     Text: Michael Hartnett
     Dur: 8'
     Ded: Mary O'Flynn

15   *Oileáin* (1979)
      pf
      1 An Island of Beasts like Horses
      2 An Island of Black Mourners
      3 An Island of Black and White
      4 An Island Whose People Shout 'It is They!'
      Dur: 17'
      Fp: 3 May 1979, University College Cardiff
      Martin Jones (pf)
      Com: University College Cardiff

16   *Missa Brevis* (1979)
      satb or saab chorus
      Dur: 8'
      Fp: 3 May 1980, Trinity College, Dublin
      Renaissance Consort, Albert Bradshaw (cond)
      Com: Albert Bradshaw

17   *Pulvis et Umbra* (1979)
      ssssaattbb chorus/pf
      Text: Horace, Odes Book Four, VII
      Dur: 14'
      Fp: 18 September 1979, National Gallery of Ireland
      RTÉ Singers, Gillian Smith (pf), Eric Sweeney (cond)
      Com: RTÉ

18   *Five Epigrams for Flute and Oboe* (1980)
      fl/ob
      Dur: 10'
      Fp: 13 May 1980, Berlin
      Madeleine Berkeley (fl), Helmut Seeber (ob)
      Com: Concorde Ensemble/AC

19   *Fornocht do Chonnac Thú* (1980)
      22(ca)22/4330/timp/2perc/pf/str
      Orchestral ballet score
      Dur: 15'
      Fp: 23 April 1981, RTÉ
      RTÉSO, Colman Pearce (cond)
      Ded: Joan Denise Moriarty
      Com: Irish Ballet Company/Irish Goverment

20   *Orpen, Mirror to an Age* (1980)
      Film score
      fl/ca/pf/vc/s/ssssaattbb chorus
      Fp: 21 January 1981, RTÉ (TV)
      Com: RTÉ

21   *Scél lem Duíb* (1981)
      ssssaattbb chorus
      1 Scél Lem Duíb (My Story for You)
      2 Aithne dam Deirghed mo Leaptha (I Know my Bed Has Been Prepared)
      3 Am Gaeth im-Muir (I Am Wind on Sea)
      Text: Anon, old Irish
      Dur: 8'
      Fp: 1 May 1981, Cork International Choral Festival
      RTÉ Singers, Colin Mawby (cond)
      Com: Cork International Choral Festival/AC

22   *Concerto for Chamber Orchestra* (1981)
      1202/2000/str (min: 44321)
      5 movements
      Dur: 21'
      Fp: 5 January 1982, TCD, Dublin Festival of 20th Century Music
      NICO, Seóirse Bodley (cond.)
      Com: New Irish Chamber Orchestra/AC

23   *Horns and Pipes* (1982)
      2fl(picc)/2ob/3cl/eflatcl/bcl/2bn/cbn /4hn
      1 Fanfare I, 2 Earthwind, 3 Fanfare II, 4 Winds of Change
      Dur: 10'
      Fp: 11 November 1987, Thomas Prior House, RDS
      The Dublin Chamber Orchestra, John Finucane (cond)
      Com: Robert Houlihan

24   *Time Piece* (1982)
      fl/cl/vc/pf
      Dur: 12'
      Fp: 26 November 1982, University College Cardiff
      Kathryn Lucas (fl), Edward Pillanger (cl), Justin Pearson (vc), Oliver Knussen (dir)

Com: University College Cardiff

25 *To Sleep* (1983)
    satb chorus
    Text: John Keats
    Dur: 4'
    Fp: 26 November 1983, Christ Church Cathedral, Dublin
    The Eric Sweeney Singers, Eric Sweeney (cond)

26 *Three Irish Folksongs* (1983) arr
    satb/pf
    1 The Sally Gardens
    2 Kitty of Coleraine
    3 My Lagan Love
    Dur: 9'
    Fp: 17 May 1984, Waterford Regional Technical College
    WRTC Choir, Eric Sweeney (pf), Patrick Kennedy (cond)

27 *Sonata for Unaccompanied Violin* (1983)
    3 movements
    Dur: 20'
    Fp: 8 November 1983, University College Cardiff
    James Barton (vn)
    Com: University College Cardiff/Welsh Arts Council

28 *Boireann* (1983)
    fl/pf
    Dur: 13'
    Fp: 11 January 1984, JFR, NCH, Dublin Festival of 20th Century Music
    Madeleine Berkeley (fl), Jane O'Leary (pf)
    Ded: Madeleine Berkeley
    Com: Mid West Arts/AC

29 *Suite for Harpsichord* (1983)
    1 Toccata, 2 Nocturne, 3 Interlude, 4 Sarabande, 5 Fantasia
    Dur: 20'
    Fp: 29 January 1984, HLG
    Gillian Smith (hpsd)
    Ded: Gillian Smith
    Com: Gillian Smith/AC

30 *God Rest Ye Merry, Gentlemen* (1983) arr
    mz/1111/1110/1perc/str
    Dur: 5'
    Fp: 23 December 1983, JFR, NCH
    Virginia Kerr (mz), Dublin Sinfonia, William York (cond)
    Com: William York

31 *The Watchword of Labour* (1984) arr
    satb chorus/wind ensemble
    Dur: 5'
    Com: Irish Labour Party

32 *Festive Suite* (1984)
    Wind Ensemble
    1 Air, 2 Fanfare, 3 Lullaby
    Dur: 10'
    Fp: 6 May 1985, Davitt College, Castlebar
    Westport Town Band, Mike Roberts (cond)
    Com: Galway/Mayo Regional Arts
    Ded: Mike Roberts

33 *Music when Soft Voices Die* (1984)
    saatb chorus
    Text: P.B. Shelley
    Dur: 3'
    Fp: 5 October 1985, Aula Max, University College, Galway
    Cois Cladaigh choir, Brendan O'Connor (cond)
    Com: Galway/Mayo Regional Arts
    Ded: Brendan O'Connor

34 *Fantasia No 1 on a theme from "Keoghal"* (1984)
    trrec or other treble instrument
    Dur: 3'
    Fp: November 1984, Royal College of Music, London
    Aideen Halpin (trrec)
    Ded: Doris Keogh

35 *Brasspiece* (1984)
    brass band
    Dur: 4'

Fp: 5 October 1985, Aula Max, University College, Galway
St Patrick's Brass Band, Tommy Joyce (cond)
Com: Galway/Mayo Regional Arts
Ded: Tommy Joyce

36 *Praise Him with the Sound of the Trumpet* (1984)
satb chorus/brass band
Text: Psalm 150
Dur: 3'
Fp: 5 October 1985, Aula Max, University College, Galway
Cois Cladaigh choir, St Patrick's Brass Band, Tommy Joyce (cond)
Com: Galway/Mayo Regional Arts
Ded: Helen Bygrove

37 *And Wake the Purple Year* (1985)
hpsd
Dur: 7'
Fp: 22 January 1985, Newpark Music Centre, Dublin
Paula Best (hpsd)
Com: Newpark Music Centre, Dublin/AC
Ded: Paula Best

37a *And Wake the Purple Year* (1986)
arr for piano
Fp: 13 October 1986, SPD
Gillian Smith (pf)

38 *The Woman who Married Clark Gable* (1985)
Film score
cl/vn/va/vc
Dur: 12'
Fp: 18 November 1986, Channel 4 TV
rian O' Rourke (cl), Mary Gallagher (vn), Seamus O' Grady (va), Brigid Mooney (vc)
Com: Brook Films

39 *At the Round Earths Imagin'd Corners* (1985)
org
Dur: 8'
Fp: 26 September 1985, St Murdoch's Cathedral, Ballina

Gerard Gillen (org)
Com: Ballina Arts Festival/AC
Ded: Gerard Gillen

40 *Murphy Down Under* (1986)
    Film score
    syn/tr
    Dur: 10'
    Com: Emdee Productions

41 *Brass Quintet No. 2* (1986)
    3 movements
    hn/2tr/tbn/tu
    Dur: 12'
    Fp: 24 October 2010, Rathgar Methodist Church, Dublin
    Dublin Brass
    Com: Irish Brass Ensemble/AC
    Ded: Joszef Csibi and the Irish Brass Ensemble

42 *A Summer Ghost* (1986)
    Film score
    fl/vc/pf
    Dur: 13'
    Fp: 24 May 1987, Channel 4 TV
    Com: Strongbow Productions Ltd.

43 *Fantasia No. 2* (1987)
    trrec
    Dur: 4'
    Ded: Doris Keogh

44 *I Am Wind on Sea* (1987)
    mz - 2 crotales, 2 woodblocks (played by singer)
    Text: Old Irish trans Buckley
    Dur: 8'
    Fp: 4 October 1987, Círculo de Belles Artes Madrid
    Aylish Kerrigan (mz)
    Com: Aylish Kerrigan/AC
    Ded: Niamh Buckley

45 *Sirato* (1987)
    va
    Dur: 4'
    Fp: 1 November 1991, JFR, NCH
    Niamh Ní Canainn (va)
    Com: Maria Kelemen
    Ded: Maria Kelemen

46 *Drip, Drop, Drip* (1987)
    Arts Education Project
    voices/perc/tape/pf
    Dur: 12'
    Fp: 11 December 1987, Holy Spirit Girls' School, Ballymun, Dublin
    Pupils of Holy Spirit Girls National School, John Buckley (cond)

47 *Millennium Fanfare* (1987)
    Wind Band
    Dur: 35"
    Fp: 1 January 1988, Mansion House, Dublin
    Garda band, Tommy Boyle (cond)
    Com: Dublin Millennium Committee
    Ded: Dublin

47a *Millennium Fanfare* (1988)
    arr for brass band

48 *Winter Music* (1988)
    pf
    Dur: 11'
    Fp: 16 March 1988, Purcell Room, London
    Anthony Byrne (pf)
    Com: Anthony Byrne/AC
    Ded: Anthony Byrne

49 *Symphony No. 1* (1988)
    2 Movements
    3(2picc, 2afl)33(bcl)3(cbn)/4331/timp/5 perc/hp/str
    Dur: 37'
    Fp: 3 June 1988, NCH
    RTÉSO, Albert Rosen (cond)

Ded: James Wilson

50 *The Eagle* (1988)
    1 Haiku Seasons, 2 The Eagle
    s/sa chorus/pf/opt perc and treble insts
    Text: Raizan, Shoha, Kyoshi, Kyoroku, Basho, Buckley, Old Irish, Bible, Kilvert, Tennyson
    Dur 14'
    Fp: 26 May 1989, Mount Sackville School Dublin
    Ann O' Byrne (s), Gillian Smith (pf), Mount Sackville School Choir, Aideen Lane (cond)
    Com: Music Association of Ireland/AC

51 *Guitar Sonata No. 1* (1989)
    3 movements
    Dur 14'
    Fp: 5 August 1989, Guitar Institute, New York
    Benjamin Dwyer (gtr)
    Com: Benjamin Dwyer/AC
    Ded: Benjamin Dwyer

52 *Three Lullabies for Deirdre* (1989)
    pf
    Dur: 7'
    Fp: 24 April 1989, Waterford Regional Technical College
    Eric Sweeney (pf)
    Ded: Deirdre Buckley

53 *Where the Wind Blows* (1989)
    picc/2fl/2ob(ca)/3cl/eflatcl/eflatacl/bcl/2bn/2asax/tsax/barsax/3tr/4hn/3tbn/tu/timp/4perc
    Dur: 12'
    Fp: 13 August 1989, Royal Hospital, Kilmainham, Dublin
    Irish Youth Wind Ensemble, James Cavanagh (cond)
    Com: Irish Youth Wind Ensemble/AC
    Ded: James Cavanagh and the Irish Youth Wind Ensemble

54 *Abendlied* (1989)
    s/pf
    Text: Clemens Brentano, Joseph von Eichendorff
    Dur: 11'

Fp: 14 June 1989, RIAM
Penelope Price Jones (sop), Philip Martin (pf)
Com: Penelope Price Jones and Philip Martin
Ded: Penelope Price Jones and Philip Martin

55   *A Thin Halo of Blue* (1990)
Satb chorus/2(2picc)222/4330/3perc/cel/hp/pf/str/speaker/tape
Text: compiled Buckley
Dur: 17'
Fp: Prix Italia 1991
Barry McGovern (speaker), Anthony Byrne (pf), Cantique Choir, RTÉCO, Colman Pearce (cond)
Fp: Live performance version 26 January 1992, NCH
Barry McGovern (speaker), Anthony Byrne (pf), Cantique Choir, Pro Arte Orchestra, Colman Pearce (cond)
Com: RTÉ, live version com by Dept. of the Environment

56   *Arabesque* (1990)
asax or cl
Dur: 5'
Fp: 1 November 1991, JFR, NCH
Kenneth Edge (asax)
Com: Kenneth Edge
Ded: Kenneth Edge

57   *The Words Upon the Window Pane* (1991)
Chamber Opera
s/mz/ct/t/bar/fl(afl)/cl(bcl)/hn/vc/pf/perc
Text: Hugh Maxton after W. B. Yeats
Dur: 21'
Fp: 17 October 1991, Lombard St. Studios, Dublin Theatre Festival
Opera Theatre Company: Anne O' Byrne (s), Collette McGahon (mz), Kevin West (t), Jonathan Peter Kenny (ct), David Gantly (bar), OTC Ensemble, John Finucane (cond)
Com: Opera Theatre Company/AC

58   *Concerto for Organ and Orchestra* (1992)
org/3(2picc)332/cbn/4331/2timp/4 perc/str
Dur: 29'

Fp: 26 June 1992, NCH
Peter Sweeney (org), National Symphony Orchestra, Robert Houlihan (cond)
Com: NCH, RTÉ and AC
Ded: Hugh McGinley

59 *Jim Singing* (1992)
pf
Dur: 3'
Fp: 25 July 1992, Coláiste Muire, Ennis, Co. Clare
Martin O'Leary (pf)
Ded: James Wilson on the occasion of his seventieth birthday

60 *De Profundis* (1993)
sa soli/satb chorus/opt unison children's choir/2(picc)222/2200/timp/str
Text: Psalms 130, 131
Dur: 25'
Fp: 25 March 1994, NCH
Penelope Price Jones (s), Deirdre Cooling Nolan (a), Tallaght Choral Society, Tallaght Boys Choir, RTÉCO, Proinnsias O' Duinn (cond)
Com: Tallaght Choral Society/AC

61 *Sonata for Solo Horn* (1993)
3 Movements
Dur: 10'
Fp:15 February 1994, JFR, NCH
Cormac Ó hAodáin (hn)
Com: Marion Doherty and Bernard Hayden
Ded: Cormac Ó hAodáin

62 *Rivers of Paradise* (1993)
2 speakers/3(2picc)332 cbn/4331/ timp/3 perc/pf/str
Text: Anon Irish trans Buckley, John Donne, John Henry Newman, Albert Einstein, Galileo Galilei, Johannes Kepler, William Shakespeare, William Carlos Williams, Christopher Marlowe, T.S. Eliot
Dur: 15'
Fp: 18 September 1993, University Concert Hall Limerick
ill Golding, Bernadette Comerford (speakers), NSO, Colman

Pearce (cond)
Com: University of Limerick/AC

63 *The Silver Apples of the Moon, The Golden Apples of the Sun*
    (1993)
    pf
    Dur: 5'
    Fp: 21 May 1994, NCH
    Paulo Cremonte (pf)
    Com: GPA Dublin International Piano Competition/AC

64 *In Lines of Dazzling Light* (1995)
    8 movements
    cl/bn/hn/vn/pf
    Dur: 20'
    Fp: 22 February, 1995, Schubertsaal, Konzerthaus, Vienna
    Ensemble Contrasts Wien
    Com: Ensemble Contrasts Wien/AC
    Ded: Ensemble Contrasts Wien

65 *Maynooth Te Deum* (1995)
    satb soli/satb chorus/satb chamber choir/tb choir/ 3(2picc)
    333(cbn)/4331/timp/5 perc/org (ad lib)/str
    Text: Te Deum
    1 Te Deum Laudamus, 2 Tu Rex Gloriae, 3 Tu ad Liberandum, 4
    Tu ad Dexteram Dei Sedes, 5 Te Ergo Quaesumus, 6 Aeterna
    Fac, 7 Salvum Fac Populum, 8 Per Singulos Dies
    Dur: 35'
    Fp: 16 November 1995, NCH
    Regina Nathan (s), Collette McGahon (a), Emmanuel Lawler (t),
    Eugene Griffin (b), Maynooth College Choral Society, Maynooth
    College Seminary Choir, Gerard Gillen (org), NSO, Colman
    Pearce (cond)
    Com: St Patrick's College, Maynooth on the occasion of its
    bicentenary.

66 *Three Preludes for Piano* (1995)
    pf
    1 The Cloths of Heaven, 2 Like Ghosts from an Enchanter
    Fleeing, 3 Jim Singing
    Dur: 10'

Fp: 15 March 1996, JFR, NCH
Anthony Byrne (pf)

67 *He Wishes for the Cloths of Heaven* (1995)
    ssatb chorus
    Text: W.B. Yeats
    Dur: 5'
    Fp: 3 May 1996, Cork International Choral Festival
    Cantique Choir, Blánaid Murphy (cond)
    Com: Cork International Choral Festival

68 *Jabberwocky* (1996)
    satb chorus
    Text: Lewis Carroll
    Dur: 5'
    Fp: 4 May 1996, Cork International Choral Festival
    Cantairí Avondale, Mary O' Flynn (cond)
    Com: Cantairí Avondale

69 *Collage* (1996)
    In collaboration with Martin O' Leary
    developments of themes by students of CPI
    str orch
    9 movements
    Dur: 16'
    Fp: 22 June 1996, NCH
    ICO, Seamus Crimmins (cond)

70 *Saxophone Quartet* (1996)
    ssax/asax/tsax/barsax
    1 Toccata, 2 Passacaglia, 3 Allegro vivace, 4 Elegia, 5 Scherzo
    Dur: 14'
    Fp: 14 April 1998, Concertgebouw de Doelen, Rotterdam
    Aurelia Saxophone Quartet
    Ded: Aurelia Saxophone Quartet
    Com: Aurelia Saxophone Quartet/AC

71 *Two Songs* (1997)
    1 Spring
    2 Lá Bréa Idir Dhá Nollaig (A Fine Day Between Two Christmasses)

sa chorus
Dur: 5'
Fp: May 1997, Cork International Choral Festival
Brackenstown Senior National School Choir, Áine Shields (cond)
Com: Brackenstown Senior National School Choir/AC
Ded: Brackenstown Senior National School Choir, Áine Shields

Spring (2000-2002) arr
71a   2fl
71b   2vn
71c   2va
71d   2asax
71e   2cl
71f   drec/trrec

72   *Concerto for Alto Saxophone and String Orchestra* (1997)
asax/str (min: 54331)
Dur: 20'
Fp: 27 Sept 1997, University Concert Hall Limerick
Kenneth Edge (asax), ICO, Fionnuala Hunt (dir)
Com: Kenneth Edge and the ICO/AC
Ded: Kenneth Edge

73   *Airflow* (1998)
fl
Dur: 5'
Fp: 27 April 1998, National Sculpture Factory, Cork
William Dowdall (fl)
Com: National Sculpture Factory

74   *There Is a Spot 'Mid Barren Hills* (1998)
satb chorus
Text: Emily Brontë
Dur: 4'
Fp: 16 October 1998, Gresham Hotel, Dublin
The People's College Choir, Paul Walsh (cond)
Ded: Sheila Conroy

75 *Toccata* (1998)
pf
Dur: 4'
Fp: 18 November 1998, NCH
Anthony Byrne (pf)
Ded: Anthony Byrne on the occasion of his 40th birthday

76 *Guitar Sonata No. 2* (1998)
4 movements
Dur: 16'
Fp: 6 June 1999, HLG
John Feeley (gtr)
Com: John Feeley/AC
Ded: John Feeley

77 *Tidal Erotics* (1999)
(in collaboration with Vivienne Roche)
fl/hn/vc/perc/pf
17 movements
Dur: 16'
Fp: 13 April - 6 June 1999, HLG
William Dowdall (fl), Philip Eastop (hn), William Butt (vc), Massimo Marraccini (perc), Anthony Byrne (pf), John Finucane (cond)
Com: HLG

78 *A Mirror into the Light* (1999)
2222/2200/timp/str
Dur: 6'
Fp: 24 April 1999, Stormont Castle, Belfast, Camerata Ireland, Barry Douglas (cond)
Com: Camerata Ireland/AC

79 *Quattuor* (1999)
Four youth orchestras
1 Intrada, 2 Air and Dance, 3 Scherzo, 4 Interlude, 5 Elegia, 6 Finale, 7 Coda
Dur: 20'
Fp: 9 April 2000, National Basketball Arena, Dublin
Dublin Youth Orchestras, John Finucane (cond), Ronan O' Reilly (cond), Vanessa Sweeney (cond), John Page (cond)
Com: Dublin Youth Orchestras/AC

80   *Ragamuffin* (2000)
     drec/pf
     1 Morning Song, 2 Hopscotch, 3 Sunny Afternoon, 4 Winter
     Bells, 5 Ragamuffin, 6 Evening Song
     Dur: 7'
     Com: CMC Publications 2000

81   *Strings in the Earth and Air* (2000)
     str orch
     2 movements
     Dur: 8'
     Fp: 4 March 2000, Ardhowen Theatre, Enniskillen
     Chamber Orchestra of the European Union, Lavard Skou Larsen (dir)
     Com: Chamber Orchestra of the European Union/AC
     Ded: Oisin Buckley

82   *Concerto for Bassoon and Orchestra* (2001)
     bn/2222/2220/timp/4 perc/hp/str
     3 movements
     Dur: 22'
     Fp: 20 April 2001, NCH
     Michael Jones (bn), NSOI, Alexander Anissimov (cond)
     Com: RTÉ
     Ded: Michael Jones

83   *Carillon* (2001)
     org
     Dur: 13'
     Fp: 31 August 2003, St Michael's Church, Dun Laoghaire
     David Adams (org)
     Com: Ludwigshafen Festival
     Ded: Beatrix Hermann

84   *Happy Birthday, Dear Doris* (2002) arr
     4 fl
     Dur: 2'
     Fp: 16 April 2002, Mansion House, Dublin
     Deirdre Brady (fl), Elizabeth Petcu (fl), Ellen Cranitch (fl), Anne Marie Liddy (fl)

Ded: Doris Keogh on the occasion of her 80th birthday

85 *In Winter Light* (2004)
    afl/gtr
    2 movements
    Dur: 14'
    Fp: 16 May 2004, DCG
    William Dowdall (afl), John Feeley (gtr)
    Com: William Dowdall, John Feeley/AC
    Ded: William Dowdall, John Feeley

86 *Two Fantasias for Alto Flute* (2004)
    afl
    Dur: 8'
    Fp: 1 Nov 2004, RIAM
    William Dowdall (afl)

87 *endless the white clouds...* (2005)
    hp
    Dur: 11'
    Fp: 27 July 2005, O'Reilly Hall UCD, 9th International Harp Congress
    Geraldine O' Doherty (hp)
    Com: 9th International Harp Congress
    Ded: Geraldine O' Doherty

88 *A Few Notes for Jim* (2005)
    vn
    Dur: 5'
    Fp: 24 November 2005, Airfield House, Dundrum
    Fp: 24 November 2005, Airfield House, Dundrum
    Ded: In memoriam James Wilson

89 *Campane in Aria* (2006)
    2/picc/332/cbn/4331/timp/4 perc/str
    Dur: 8'
    Fp: 9 September 2006, NCH
    RTÉNSO, Gerhard Markson (cond)
    Com: NCH on the occasion of its 25th anniversary

90   *In Winter Light - Concerto for Flute/Alto Flute and Orchestra* (2006)
     fl(afl)/hp/ perc/str
     3 movements
     Dur: 18'
     Fp: 17 November 2006, NCH
     William Dowdall (fl/afl), RTÉNSO, Christian Gansch (cond)
     Com: RTÉ
     Ded: William Dowdall

91   *Winter Echoes* (2008)
     fl
     version of cadenza from *In Winter Light - Concerto for Flute/Alto Flute and Orchestra*
     Dur: 3' 30"
     Fp: 12 November 2008, SPD
     William Dowdall (fl)
     Ded: William Dowdall

92   *Sea Echoes* (2008)
     fl with glissando headjoint
     Dur: 3' 30"
     Fp: 12 November 2008, SPD
     William Dowdall (fl)
     Ded: William Dowdall

93   *Concerto for Violin and Orchestra* (2008)
     vn/picc/2332/cbn/4330/timp/4 perc/hp/cel/str
     Dur: 25'
     Com: Gwendolyn Masin
     Ded: Gwendolyn Masin

94   *as far as the eye can see* (2008)
     asax/ob/hn/pf
     Dur: 6'
     Fp: May 2009, Linenhall Theatre, Castlebar
     WhistleBlast Quartet
     Com: Whistleblast Quartet/AC
     Ded: Whistleblast Quartet

95 *Three Preludes for Two Violins* (2009)
2vn
1 In a Leafy Glade, 2 Perpetuum Mobile, 3 Ebbing and Flowing
Dur: 9'
Fp: Lyric FM 25 April, 2010
Anna Fliegerova (vn), Michael Romanovsky (vn)
Com: *lyric* fm
Ded: Anna Fliegerova, Michael Romanovsky

96 *Constellations* (2009)
multiple flutes
Dur: 10'
Fp: 17 October 2010, DCGTHL
William Dowdall (flutes)
Ded: William Dowdall

97 *Dialogue* (2010)
vc
Dur: 5'
Fp: 3 February 2010, SPD
Clíodhna Ní Aodáin (vc)
Ded: Clíodhna Ní Aodáin

98 *Irish Melodies* (2010) arr
fl(afl)/2vn/va/vc/hp/Irhp/bar/perc
1 Danny Boy
2 Eleanor Plunkett
3 The Plains of Boyle
4 Down by the Sally Gardens
5 Air and Jig
6 My Lagan Love
7 Two Jigs
8 She Moved Through the Fair
9 Variations on the 'Gneeveguilla Polka'
10 The Streams of Bunclody
11 The Bard of Armagh
12 The Mason's Apron
Dur: 60'
Com: Celestial Harmonies

APPENDIX II: *ABENDLIED*

Clemens Brentano

Abendständchen
Hör', es klagt die Flöte wieder
Und die kühlen Brunnen rauschen,
Golden weh'n die Töne nieder;
Stille, stille, lass' uns lauschen!

Evening Serenade
Listen, the flute laments again
And the cool fountains rustle,
Golden the notes waft down;
Still, still, let us listen!

Joseph von Eichendorff

Der Abend
Schweigt der Menschen laute Lust;

Rauscht die Erde wie in Träumen
Wunderbar mit allen Bäumen,
Was dem Herzen kaum bewußt,

Alte Zeiten, linde Trauer,
Und es schweifen leise Schauer
Wetterleuchtend durch die Brust.

Evening
When the loud merriment of men is quiet;

The earth rustles as in a dream
Miraculously with all her trees,
What the heart is hardly conscious of,

Old times, gentle sadness,
And quiet tremors sweep
Like summer lightening through my breast.

Joseph von Eichendorff

Mondnacht
Es war, als hätt' der Himmel
Die Erde still geküßt,
Daß sie im Blütenschimmer
Von ihm nun träumen müßt'.
Die Luft ging durch die Felder,
Die Ähren wogten sacht,
Es rauschten leis die Wälder,
So sternklar war die Nacht.
Und meine Seele spannte
Weit ihre Flügel aus,
Flog durch die stillen Lande,
Als flöge sie nach Haus.

Moonlit Night
It was as though the sky
Had gently kissed the earth,
So that she in the glory of blossom
Now had to dream of him
The breeze went across the fields,
The ears of corn waved gently,
The woods rustled softly,
The night was so starry-clear.
And my soul stretched.
Wide its wings and
Flew through the still lands,
As though it were flying home.

APPENDIX III: TEXT – *RIVERS OF PARADISE*

'The University is a Paradise, Rivers of knowledge are there, Arts and Sciences flow from thence…; bottomless depths of unsearchable Councils there.' [John Donne]

'A University training is the great ordinary means to a great but ordinary end. Its art is the art of social life, and its end is fitness for the world.' [John Henry Newman: *The Idea of the University* (1852/1873)]

'Pleasant is the student's life,
engaged in his studies;
it is clear to all of you,
that his lot is the most pleasant in Ireland.

Without control from king or prince
nor lord however powerful
without rent to the chapter
without dawn-rising, without straining.

Dawn-rising or shepherding
are never his concern
his is not the worry
of the watchman in the night.

He spends a while at draughts,
and at the sweet harp
and yet another while at wooing
and courting a fair woman.

His plough-team shows good profit
at the coming of spring;
the harrow for his ploughing-team
is a fistful of pens.'
[Anon: Irish 17th Century. Translation John Buckley]

'The most beautiful thing we can experience is the mysterious. It is the source of all true art and science.'
[Albert Einstein: *What I Believe* (1930)]

'Philosophy is written in this grand book – I mean the universe – which stands continually open to our gaze, but cannot by understood unless one first learns to comprehend the language and interpret the

characters in which it is written. It is written in the language of mathematics, and its characters are triangles, circles, and other geometrical figures, without which it is humanly impossible to understand a single word thereof; without these, one is wondering about in a dark labyrinth.'
[Galileo Galilei: *Il Saggiatore* (1623)]

'How the subtle mind of Galileo, in my opinion the first philosopher of the day, uses this telescope of ours like a sort of ladder, scales the furthest and loftiest walls of the visible world, surveys all things with his own eyes, and, from the position he has gained, darts the glances of his most acute intellect upon these petty abodes of ours - the planetary spheres I mean - and compares with keenest reasoning the distant with the near, the lofty with the deep.'
[Johannes Kepler: *Letter to Galileo* (1610)]

'The poet's eye, in a fine frenzy rolling,
Doth glance from heaven to earth, from earth to heaven;
And, as imagination bodies forth
The forms of things unknown, the poet's pen
Turns them to shapes, and gives to airy nothing
A local habitation and a name.'
[William Shakespeare: *A Midsummer Night's Dream* (1595/6)]

'A cool of books
will sometimes lead the mind to libraries
of a hot afternoon, if books can be found
cool to the sense
to lead the mind away.

For there is a wind or ghost of a wind
in all books echoing the life
there, a high wind that fills the tubes
of the ear until we think we hear a wind,
to lead the mind away.

Drawn from the streets we break off
our minds' seclusion and are taken up by
the books' winds, seeking, seeking
down the wind
until we are unaware which is the wind and
which the wind's power over us
to lead the mind away.

and there grows in the mind
a scent, it may be, of locust blossoms
whose perfume is itself a wind moving
to lead the mind away.'
[William C. Williams: *The Library (Paterson, Book 3*, 1949)]

'Nature that framed us of four elements,
Warring within our breasts for regiment,
Doth teach us all to have aspiring minds:
Our souls, whose faculties can comprehend
The wondorous architecture of the world;
And measure every wandering planet's course,
Still climbing after knowledge infinite,
And always moving as the restless spheres,
Will us to wear ourselves and never rest,
Until we reach the ripest fruit of all,
That perfect bliss and sole felicity,
The sweet fruition of the earthly crown.'
  [Christopher Marlowe: *Tamburlaine the Great* (1689)]

'We shall not cease from exploration
And the end of all our exploring
Will be to arrive where we started
And know the place for the first time.'
[T.S.Eliot: *Little Gidding* (1944)]

APPENDIX IV: *THE WORDS UPON THE WINDOW PANE*

a chamber opera

Music by John Buckley

Libretto by Hugh Maxton,

(adapted from the play by W.B. Yeats)

LIBRETTO

Miss Le Fanu	Secretary to the Dublin Spiritualist Society
John Corbet	A student
Cornelius Patterson	A sporty type
Conway Mallet	A young man
Mrs Henderson	A medium

A lodging-house room, an armchair, a little table in front of it, chairs at either side. A fire-place and window. A kettle on the hob and some tea-things on a dresser. A door at back and towards the right.

(*Le Fanu leads Corbet into the room – lights rise as they enter*)

Le Fanu. Better sit down, your wrist-watch must be fast. Mrs Henderson is resting upstairs as she always does beforehand. She has come back from London to spread the movement here. A poor woman with the soul of an apostle.

Corbet. (*Handing his coat to Miss Lefanu*) This is a wonderful room, for a lodging house.

Le Fanu. This house...

Corbet. (*Interrupting*) Wonderful.

Le Fanu. This house in the eighteenth century belonged to friends of Jonathan Swift, or rather of Stella. (*She advances and points at the* *window*) Somebody cut some lines from a poem of hers upon the window pane.

Corbet. (*Coming forward*) I know these lines well – Stella wrote them for Swift's fifty-fourth birthday.
  'You taught how I might youth prolong
  By knowing what is right and wrong.'

Le Fanu. I've shown these lines to several people, but you are the first to recognise them.

Corbet. I am writing a thesis on Swift, a tragic life. All those great ministers that were his friends, banished and broken.
  (*Mallet and Patterson enter and take their seats*)

Le Fanu.   Ah! Here's Conway Mallet. (*To Corbet, while drawing him towards the seated figure*) And that's old Cornelius Patterson. He thinks they race horses and whippets in the other world and is so eager to know if he's right that he is always punctual.

Mallet. My parents were drowned at sea, but constantly speak to me through Mrs. Henderson.

Le Fanu. I am going to sit down beside Mister Corbet. (*Mrs Henderson enters during bass clarinet solo. She enters from the hallway and goes directly to stand behind her chair.*) Mrs. Henderson, may I introduce you to Mr. Corbet, a young man from Trinity, and a sceptic. (*Corbet stands and nods respectfully*)

Patterson. We were all sceptics once.

Le Fanu. (*To Corbet, both still standing*) Sometimes I think it is all thought-transference. Then at other times, I feel like Job. The hair on my head stands up.

Corbet. Do you feel like Job to-night? (*Le Fanu and Corbet sit*)

Henderson. (*Asserting her central role*) I am glad to meet my dear friends again and to welcome Mr Corbet amongst us. As he is a stranger, I must explain that we do not call up spirits. We make the right conditions, and they come. Miss Le Fanu, a verse of a hymn please, the same one we had last time.

(*Le Fanu indicates start. They sing the following lines from Hymn, 564, Dublin Church Hymnal*)
  'Sun of my soul, Thou Saviour dear,
  It is not night if Thou art near:
  O may no earth-born cloud arise
  To hide Thee from Thy servant's eyes'

(*By the end of the hymn, Mrs Henderson is leaning back in her chair, snoring softly*)

Henderson. (*In a man's voice, Jonathan Swift's*) How dare you write to her? How dare you ask if we were married?

Le Fanu. A soul in its agony – it cannot see or hear us.

Henderson. (*In Swift's voice*) You sit crouching there. (*Rises suddenly*) Did you not hear what I said? I found you an ignorant girl without intellect, without moral ambition.

Corbet. It is Swift, Jonathan Swift, talking to the woman he called Vanessa.

Henderson. (*In Vanessa's voice*) If you and she are not married, why should we not marry like other men and women. (*In Swift's voice*) I have something in my blood that no child must inherit. I have constant attacks of dizziness. O God, hear the prayer of Jonathan Swift, that afflicted man, and grant that he leave to posterity nothing but his intellect that came to him from heaven. (*In Vanessa's voice*) Can you face solitude with that mind Jonathan? (*In Swift's voice*) My God, I am left alone with my enemy. Who locked me in with my enemy? (*Mrs Henderson exhausted sinks into her chair and sleeps*)

Mallet. Another verse of the hymn. It will bring good influences. (*They sing*)

> 'When the soft dews of kindly sleep,
> My wearied eyelids gently steep
> Be my last thought...

(*During the hymn, Mrs Henderson has been murmuring 'Stella'. The hymn breaks off due to Mrs Henderson's interruptions*)

Henderson. (*Continuing in Swift's voice*) Beloved Stella

Corbet. Vanessa has gone, Stella has taken her place.

Henderson. (*Continuing in Swift's voice*) Have I wronged you? You have no children, no lover, no husband. A cross and ageing man for friend. But do not answer – you have answered already in that noble poem you wrote for me:

> 'You taught how I might youth prolong
> By knowing what is right or wrong.'

Corbet. The words, the words upon the window-pane.

Henderson. (*Continuing in Swift's voice*)

> 'How from my heart to bring supplies

Of lustre for my fading eyes.'

Because you know I am afraid of solitude, afraid of outliving my friends and myself, you overpraise my moral nature. Yes, you will close my eyes, dear Stella. You will live long after me, but you will close my eyes, dear Stella. (*She sinks back into her chair*)

(*in her own voice*) Go away, go away. (*She wakes up*) I saw him a moment ago, has he spoiled things again?

Patterson. Yes, Mrs Henderson

Le Fanu. Mrs Henderson is very tired. We must leave her. You did your best. No one can do more. (*Le Fanu and Mallet lay money on the table*)

Henderson. No, no, I cannot take any money, not after a séance like that.

Patterson. A jockey is paid whether he wins or loses.

Le Fanu. We must leave her to rest. (*All are leaving. Mallet and Patterson exit rear left. Corbet holds back at the last moment*)

Corbet. I know you are tired, but I must speak to you. (*He puts a pound note on the table*) This is to prove that I am completely satisfied.

Henderson. Nobody ever gives me more than ten shillings, and yet the séance was a failure.

Corbet. I do not mean I am convinced. I think that you created it all, that you are an accomplished actress and scholar. But there is something I must ask you. Swift embodied the intellect of his epoch. He foresaw its collapse. He dreaded the future. Did he refuse to beget children because of that dread?

Henderson. Who are you talking of, sir?

Corbet. Swift, of course.

Henderson. I know nobody called Swift.

Corbet. Jonathan Swift, whose spirit seemed present tonight.

Henderson. What? That dirty old fellow?

Corbet. He was neither old nor dirty, when Stella and Vanessa loved him.

Henderson. Now they are old, now they are young. They change all in a moment as their thought changes.

Le Fanu. (*At the doorway, coaxingly*) Come along Mr Corbet. Mrs Henderson is tired out.

Corbet. (*Reluctantly*) Good-bye Mrs Henderson. (*Corbet exits with Le Fanu*)

Henderson. How tired I am! I'll make a cup of tea. (*She counts the coins on the table, carefully wrapping them in the pound note given by Corbet. She stands to put the money in her skirt pocket. She goes right, finds the teapot and puts it on the shelf, looking around wearily for other utensils. Pauses. Recommences the chore, absent-mindedly. Suddenly she lifts up her hands, and counts her fingers with great deliberation*)

(*In Swift's voice*) Five great ministers that were my friends are gone. Ten great ministers that were my friends are gone. I have not fingers enough to count the great ministers that were my friends and that are gone. (*She wakes up with a start*)

(*In her own voice*) Where's the cup and saucer? (*She goes uncertainly to the shelf and finds the saucer*) But where's the cup? (*She moves as if to check the table for the cup. The saucer falls and breaks*)
(*In Swift's voice*) Perish, perish the day on which I was born.

Appendix V

Te Deum

1. Te Deum laudamus

Male voice choir, large chorus, soprano, contralto, tenor and bass soloists.

Te Deum laudamus:	We praise Thee, O God,
Te Dominum confitemur.	We acknowledge Thee as Lord.
Te aeternum Patrem	Thee, the Father everlasting,
omnis terra veneratur.	all the earth doth worship.
Tibi omnes Angeli,	To Thee all the angels,
tibi Caeli, et universae Potestates,	to Thee the heavens, and all the powers,
Tibi Cherubim et Seraphim	To Thee the Cherubim and Seraphim
incessabili voce proclamant;	cry out without ceasing:
Sanctus, sanctus, sanctus	Holy, holy, holy
Dominus Deus Sabaoth.	Lord God of hosts.
Pleni sunt caeli et terra	Full are the heavens and the earth
majestatis gloriae tuae.	with the majesty of Thy glory.
Te gloriosus Apostolorum chorus	Thee, the glorious choir of the apostles,
Te Prophetarum laudabilis numerus,	Thee, the admirable prophets,
Te Martyrum candidatus laudat exercitus.	Thee, the white robed martyrs praise.
Te per orbem terrarum	Thee throughout the world
sancta confitetur Ecclesia,	the holy Church doth confess:
Patrem immensae majestatis;	the Father of incomprehensible majesty;
Venerandum tuum verum et unicum Filium;	Thine adorable, true, and only Son,
Sanctum quoque Paraclitum Spiritum.	and the Holy Ghost the Paraclete.

2. Tu Rex gloriae
Large Chorus

Tu rex gloriae Christe.	Thou, O Christ, art the King of glory.
Tu Patris sempiternus es Filius.	Thou art the everlasting Son of the Father.

3. Tu, ad liberandum
Chamber choir, Soprano, Contralto, Tenor and Bass soloists

Tu ad liberandum suscepturus hominem,	Thou, in order to deliver man,
non horruisti Virginis uterum.	dids't not disdain the Virgin's womb.
Tu, devicto mortis aculeo,	Thou, having overcome the sting of death,
aperuisti credentibus regna caelorum.	hast opened to believers the kingdom of heaven.

4. Tu ad dexteram Dei sedes
Large Chorus

Tu ad dexteram Dei sedes	Thou sittest at the right hand of God,
in gloria Patris.	in the glory of the Father.
Judex crederis esse venturus.	Thou, we believe art the Judge to come.

5. Te ergo quaesumus
Large Chorus, Soprano, Contralto, Tenor and Bass soloists

Te ergo quaesumus,	We beseech Thee, therefore,
famulis tuis subveni,	to help thy servants whom Thou hast
quos pretioso sanguine redemisti.	redeemed with Thy precious blood.

6. Aeterna fac
Large Chorus

Aeterna fac cum Sanctis tuis	Make them to be numbered with Thy saints
in gloria numerari.	in glory everlasting

7. Salvum fac populum
Male voice choir, Chamber choir, Soprano and Contralto soloists

Salvum fac populum tuum, Domine,	O Lord, save Thy people,
et benedic hereditati tuae.	and bless Thine inheritance.
Et rege eos, et extolle illos usque in aeternum	And govern them, and exhalt them for ever

8. Per singulos dies
Male voice choir, Chamber choir, Large chorus, Soprano, Contralto, Tenor and Bass soloists

Per singulos dies benedicimus te;	Day by day we bless Thee.
Et laudamus nomen tuum in saeculum,	And we praise Thy name for ever;
et in saeculum saeculi.	and forever and ever.
Dignare, Domine,.	Grant, O Lord, this day,
sine peccato nos custodire.	die isto to keep us from sin.
Miserere nostri, Domine,	Have mercy on us, O Lord,
miserere nostri.	have mercy on us.
Fiat misericordia tua, Domine super nos,	Let Thy mercy, O Lord, be upon us,
quemadmodum speravimus in te.	as we have trusted in Thee.
In te, Domine, speravi;	In Thee, O Lord, have I trusted;
non confundar in aeternum.	let me not be confounded for ever.
Te Deum laudamus:	We praise Thee, O God,
te Dominum confitemur.	We acknowledge Thee as Lord.
Te aeternum Patrem	Thee, the Father everlasting,
omnis terra veneratur.	all the earth doth worship.

APPENDIX VI: JOHN BUCKLEY DISCOGRAPHY

John Buckley: Solo and Chamber Works, Goasco GXX 001-4 (1985) audio cassette

Sonata for Unaccompanied Violin, Boireann, Five Epigrams for Flute and Oboe, Wind Quintet, Alan Smale (vn), William Dowdall (fl), Gillian Smith (pf), Madeleine Berkeley (fl), Helmut Seeber (ob), Ulysses Wind Quintet

John Buckley: Sonata for Unaccompanied Violin CMC 001S-4 (1991) audio casette

Sonata for Unaccompanied Violin, Alan Smale (vn)

Dreaming, Anew NEWD 406 (1994)

Three Lullabies for Deirdre, Roy Holmes (pf)

Contemporary Music from Ireland, Vol 1, CMC CD01 (1995)

Sonata for Solo Horn (first movement), Cormac Ó hAodáin (hn)

LeFanu/Kinsella/Wilson/Buckley/Barber Songs, Altarus AIR-CD-9010 (1996)

Abendlied, Penelope Price Jones (s), Philip Martin (pf)

strings a-stray Black Box Music BBM 1013 (1998)

Concerto for Alto Saxophone and String Orchestra, Kenneth Edge (asax), Irish Chamber Orchestra, Fionnuala Hunt (dir)

Concerto for Organ and Orchestra, Symphony No 1, Peter Sweeney (org), National Symphony Orchestra of Ireland, Colman Pearce (cond)

John *Buckley: Piano Music,* Marco Polo 8.223784 (1999)
Three Preludes for Piano, And Wake the Purple Year, Three Lullabies for Deirdre, The Silver Apples of the Moon, The Golden Apples of the Sun, Winter Music, Oileáin, Anthony Byrne (pf)

in lines of dazzling light: John Buckley Solo and Chamber Works, Black Box Music BBM 1012 (1999)

Saxophone Quartet, Fantasias Nos. 1 & 2, Three Pieces for Solo Flute, Arabesque, Sonata for Solo Horn, Airflow, In Lines of Dazzling Light, Quartz Saxophone Quartet, William Dowdall (fl), Aideen Halpin (trrec),

Kenneth Edge (asax), Cormac Ó hAodáin (hn), Reservoir, Mikel Toms (dir)

Faces: Quartz Saxophone Quartet, Black Box Music BBM 1012 (1999)

Saxophone Quartet, Quartz Saxophone Quartet

Tidal Erotics, Hugh Lane Municipal Gallery of Modern Art (1999)

Tidal Erotics, William Dowdall (fl), Philip Eastop (hn), William Butt (vc), Massimo Marraccini (perc), Anthony Byrne (pf), John Finucane (cond), Reservoir, Mikel Toms (cond)

Where the Wind Blows, Irish Youth Wind Ensemble, IYWE01 (2001)

Where the Wind Blows, Irish Youth Wind Ensemble, James Cavanagh (cond)

abc# exploring classical music 2002 RTÉ.246CD (2001)

written and presented by John Buckley

National Symphony Orchestra of Ireland, Colman Pearce (cond)

in winter light: music for guitar and flute by John Buckley, Celestial Harmonies 13244-2 (2004)

Three Pieces for Solo Flute, Airflow, Two Fantasias for Alto Flute. Guitar Sonata No 1, Guitar Sonata No 2, Lullaby for Deirdre, In Winter Light, Willian Dowdall (fl/afl), John Feeley (gtr)

Völker hört die Signale, Thorofon CTH 2208 (2004)

The Watchword of Labour, IT&GWU band, Guinness Choir, James Cavanagh (cond)

A Pale Yellow Sky: new music for harp, RTÉ Lyric FM CD 115 (2008)

endless the white clouds... , Clíona Doris (hp)

Irish Contemporary Organ Music at the National Concert Hall Dublin, (2008)

Carillon, David Adams (org)

An Equal Music, Cois Cladaigh CCLCD002 (2009)

Music when Soft Voices Die, Cois Cladaigh, Brendan O'Connor (cond)

William Dowdall Works for Solo Flute, Celestial Harmonies 13253-2 (2010)

Winter Echoes, Sea Echoes, William Dowdall (fl)

Reservoir, Diatribe DIACDSOL001 (2010)

Three Preludes for Piano, Isabelle O'Connell (pf)

Contemporary Music from Ireland, Vol 9

The Contemporary Music Centre CMC CD09 (2010)

In Winter Light (first movement), William Dowdall (afl), John Feeley (gtr)

Breathe, Atoll ACD111 (2010)

Constellations, William Dowdall (fl)

Index

A

Abbey Theatre, 5, 18, 67, 129
Acton, Charles, 13, 23, 175
Adams, Martin, 57
Alcorn, Michael, 84-85
Aosdána, 4, 15, 19, 66, 84, 86-87, 99, 144, 170, 176
Armstrong, Lindsay, 23, 183
Arts Council of Ireland, 4, 37-38, 66, 68, 84-87, 96, 98, 110, 118, 134, 144, 176, 180, 188
Association of Irish Composers - AIC (also AYIC), 21-22, 176
Association of Young Irish Composers - AYIC (also AIC), 21-22, 38
Aurelia Saxophone Quartet, 2, 108, 197

B

Bainbridge, Simon, 85
Ball, Derek, 22
Barbirolli, John, 39
Barenboim, Daniel, 142, 176
Barry, Gerald, 1, 22, 38, 109
Barry, Sebastian, 153
Bartók, Béla, 24, 49, 79, 100, 102
Bartolozzi, Bruno, 26, 173
Barton, James, 64, 188
Beckett, Brian, 22
Beckett, Walter, 40
Beethoven, Ludwig van, 10, 12, 14
Belfast Group (the), 21
Benjamin, Arthur, 39
Bennett, Ciaran, 154
Bennett, Richard Rodney, 38
Berio, Luciano, 23, 26, 58, 65, 185
Bethge, Hans, 163
Blaukopf, Kurt, 164, 173
Bodley, Seóirse, 12, 19, 38, 40, 66, 71, 118, 187
Bodman Rae, Charles, 69, 173
Bohana, Roy, 39, 173
Boydell, Brian, 12, 18, 41, 95-96, 100, 173
Brachtel, Karl Robert, 96, 175
Brentano, Clemens, 62, 101, 193, 205
Britten, Benjamin, 100, 132, 174
Brosnahan, Eileen, 3

Buckley, John, *passim*
Burke, Patrick, 132-33, 173
Byers, David, 22
Byrne, Anthony, 101, 169, 192, 194, 197, 199, 216-17

C

Cage, John, 17, 68-69, 71, 74, 84, 154, 173
Cahill, Seán, 23, 185
Camerata Ireland, 142, 199
Capriol Consort, 13, 18, 184
Carson, Ciaran, 21
Carter, Elliot, 20, 167
Casken, John, 85
Ceoltóirí Chualann, 5
Chalmers, Kenneth, 129
Clarke, Heather, 21
Clarke, Rhona, 84
Contemporary Music Centre (Dublin) – CMC, 22, 96, 176, 180, 200, 216, 218
Conway, James, 129, 208
Corcoran, Frank, 1, 39, 41-42, 176
Cork International Choral Festival, 19, 65-66, 95, 97, 108, 185, 187, 197-98
Cork Opera House, 68
Coulson, Elizabeth Strean, 12
Cronin, Anthony, 118
Cross, Dorothy, 118
Cunningham, Merce, 68, 84

D

Danish Wind Quintet, 37
de Bromhead, Jerome, 1, 22
de Leeuw, Ton, 38
de Peyer, Gervase, 39
de Valera, Éamon, 1, 3-4, 20-21, 175
Deane, Basil, 39
Deane, Raymond, 1, 22, 38, 96, 99, 109, 118, 129, 176
Deane, Seamus, 21
Debussy, Claude, 28, 53, 101, 106, 117
Deepwell, Katy, 154, 173
Dervan, Michael, 23, 40, 68, 107, 117, 135, 146, 173, 175
Deutsch, Max, 97
Devine, Patrick F., 99, 173
Donne, John, 103, 106-107, 174, 195, 205
Doráti, Antal, 38
Doris, Cliona, 164
Douglas, Barry, 142, 199
Dowdall, William, 142, 153, 165-68, 170, 177, 198-99, 201-203, 216-18
Dowland Consort, 19
Doyle, Roger, 1, 22, 118-19
Dublin City Gallery, (see also Hugh Lane Gallery of Modern Art), 180
Dublin Festival of 20th Century Music, 12, 20-23, 37, 71, 183, 185, 187-88
Dublin Grand Opera Society (see also Opera Ireland), 99
Duff, Arthur, 40, 100
Dutilleux, Henri, 109, 146, 151, 167
Dwyer, Benjamin, 193

E

Edge, Kenneth, 106, 146, 194, 198, 214-15
Eichendorff, Joseph von, 62, 101, 193, 204

Einstein, Albert, 103, 195, 205
Eliot, T.S., 104, 174, 195, 207
Ennis Composition Summer School, 84-85, 95, 107, 144
Ensemble Contrasts Wien, 2, 196
Escher, M.C., 148-49, 174
Evening Press, 68, 102, 107, 176

F

Fallon, Pádraic, 41
Falun Blåsarkvintett (Sweden), 97
Feehan, Fanny, 38, 174
Feeley, John, 141, 177, 199, 201, 217-18
Finnissy, Michael, 85
Finucane, John, 143, 184, 187, 194, 199, 215
Fleischmann, Aloys, 12, 18, 65, 86-87, 116, 118, 174
Fleischmann, Ruth, 65
Fricker, Brenda, 87

G

Gaiety Theatre, 12, 133
Galilei, Galileo, 103, 195, 207
Gansch, Christian, 165, 202
Gillen, Gerard, 99, 104, 106, 134, 174, 191, 196
Ginastera, Alberto, 102
Glacken, Brendan, 84, 174
Gleeson, Cian, 119, 174
Goldsmith, Oliver, 18, 183
Goodwin, Inge, 164, 173
Graves, Charles, 12
Greenlaw, Lavinia, 142
Gregory, Lady, 129
Griffin, Eugene, 104, 196

H

Hallé Orchestra, 39
Hamel, Peter Michael, 85, 95-96, 109, 120, 174
Hammond, Phillip, 22
Handel, George Frederick, 10, 96
Hardebeck, Carl, 40
Hartnett, Michael, 5, 87, 185
Harty, Hamilton, 40, 100
Haughey, Charles, 19
Haydn, Joseph, 9
Hayes, Seán, 11
Heaney, Seamus, 21, 41, 132-33, 173
Henze, Hans Werner, 109
Herbert, David, 132, 174
Hillary, Patrick, 133
Hindemith, Paul, 15, 24
Hoddinott, Alun, 38-40, 50, 64, 65, 68, 105, 173
Hoffman, Paula, 97
Horan, John, 8
Hoskins, Bob, 87
Houlihan, Robert, 134, 187, 195
Huber, Klaus, 38
Hugh Lane Gallery of Modern Art (see also Dublin City Gallery), 152-54, 168, 173, 180-81, 217
Hyde, Douglas, 58-59

I

Ingoldsby, Marion, 84, 129
International Society for Contemporary Music (ISCM), 97, 176
Irish Ballet Company (see Irish National Ballet), 66, 186

Irish Chamber Orchestra, 71, 146, 181, 216
Irish Independent, 38, 117, 132, 174, 176
Irish Music Rights Organization (IMRO), 170
Irish National Ballet, 66-68
Irish Press, 42, 119, 176
Irish Times, The, 23, 37, 51, 57, 68, 84, 101, 107, 117, 135, 146, 173-76
Irish Youth Wind Ensemble, 96, 193, 215
Ives, Charles, 30

J

Johnson, Ester, 130
Jones, Martin, 51, 64, 186
Jones, Michael, 144, 200
Jordan, V.L., 134
Joyce, James, 144

K

Kelleher, Deborah, 13
Keller, Hans, 132
Kelley, Kevin W., 120, 174
Kelly, Denise, 22
Kennealy, Ginnie, 68
Kennelly, Brendan, 5
Keogh, Doris, 13, 18, 23, 26, 183-84, 189, 191, 201
Kepler, Johannes, 103, 195, 206
Kerrigan, Aylish, 57, 191
Kinsella, John, 12, 19, 66
Kinsella, Tina, 84
Knussen, Oliver, 76, 187
Kravis, Judy, 129
Kyllönen, Timo-Juhani, 85, 107

L

Larchet, John Francis, 18, 40, 100
Lawler, Emmanuel, 104, 196
LeFanu, Nicola, 86, 216
Lemass, Seán, 20
Levey, Richard Michael, 12
Liebig, Andreas, 106-107
Ligeti, György, 38, 71, 79, 95, 97, 174-75
Longley, Michael, 21
Lourié, Arthur, 59, 174
Lucas, Kathryn, 76, 187
Lutoslawski, Witold, 20, 49, 65, 68-69, 71, 109, 173
Lutyens, Edwin, 8

M

mac Cumhaill, Fionn, 43
mac Lir, Manannán, 43
Macaulay, William J.B, 37-38, 43
MacGoris, Mary, 117, 132, 176
Mahler, Gustav, 163-64, 173
Mahon, Derek, 21
Manning, Jane, 101, 174
Mansergh, Nicholas, 2, 175
Markson, Gerhard, 165, 201
Marlowe, Christopher, 103, 195, 207
Martin, Micheál, 152
Martin, Philip, 102, 194, 215
Masin, Gwendolyn, 166, 202
Maxton, Hugh, 129-30, 175, 194, 208
Maxwell-Davies, Peter, 109
McCabe, John, 38
McCarr, Pat, 9-11, 175
McGahon, Colette, 104, 194, 196

McGinley, Hugh, 134, 195
McGinley, Philomena, 17
McMahon, Bryan, 5
McSwiney, Veronica, 23, 185
Meehan, Paula, 118
Mellnäs, Arne, 85, 96-97, 110, 177
Messiaen, Olivier, 20, 51, 56, 102, 119, 135, 157, 174
Mise Éire, 5, 20
Moloney, Liam, 5
Morgan, Darragh, 165
Moriarty, Joan Denise, 66-67, 186
Morrison, George, 5
Muldoon, Paul, 21
Mulvey, Gráinne, 84
Music Association of Ireland, 12, 19-20, 37, 87, 144, 169, 193

N

Nathan, Regina, 104, 196
National Chamber Choir, 144
National Concert Hall, 2, 68, 88, 104, 109, 119, 133-34, 144, 165, 181, 217
National Symphony Orchestra of Ireland (see also RTÉ Symphony Orchestra), 88, 104, 134, 142, 144, 165, 175, 179, 181, 195, 216-17
National University of Ireland, Maynooth (see also St Patrick's College, Maynooth), 2, 83, 99, 104, 169, 173, 196
New Irish Chamber Orchestra (see Irish Chamber Orchestra), 71, 181, 187
Newman, John Henry, 103, 195, 205

O

Ó Buachalla, Brendán, 4, 175
Ó Canainn, Tomás, 58, 175
Ó Ceallaigh, Tomás, 37
Ó Duinn, Proinnsías, 38
Ó Gallchobhair, Éamonn, 40, 100
Ó Rathaille, Aogán, 4, 67, 175
O'Carroll, Al, 9
O'Doherty, Geraldine, 163
O'Doherty, Michael, 133
O'Leary, Jane, 1, 22, 87, 96, 99, 134
O'Leary, Martin, 83, 86
O'Sullivan, Thaddeus, 87
Ógra Ceoil, 12
Opera Ireland (see Dublin Grand Opera Society), 99
Opera Theatre Company, 129, 175, 194
Ormsby Vandeleur, James, 12, 21
Ormsby, Frank, 12, 21

P

Page, John, 143, 199
Panufnik, Andrzej, 20
Paterson, Paul, 85
Pearce, Colman, 13, 38, 43, 68, 104, 185-86, 194-96, 216-17
Pearse, Patrick, 12, 66-68, 174
Pearson, Justin, 76, 187
Penderecki, Krzysztof, 10, 12
Picasso, Pablo, 42
Pillanger, Edward, 76, 187
Pine, Richard, 6, 13, 101, 175-76
Potter, Archibald James, 13-15, 19-20, 40, 100
Price Jones, Penelope, 102, 194, 195, 214

Project Arts Centre (Dublin), 37, 184

R

Radio Éireann (RTÉ), *passim*
Radio Telefís Éireann (RTÉ), *passim*
Rasmussen, Karl Aage, 85
Rees, Alwyn, 50, 57, 175
Rees, Brinley, 50, 57, 175
Reich, Steve, 73, 168
Robinson, Joseph, 12
Roche, Vivienne, 152, 199
Rosen, Albert, 109, 117, 192
Rosen, Hans Waldemar, 22, 184
Royal College of Music, London, 189
Royal Irish Academy of Music, 12-13, 18, 102, 142, 175-76, 181
RTÉ (Radio Telefís Éireann, Radio Éireann), *passim*
RTÉ *lyric* fm radio, 83
RTÉ Singers, 22, 23, 184, 186-87
RTÉ Symphony Orchestra (see also National Symphony Orchestra of Ireland), 12-13, 19, 43, 68, 88, 109, 179, 181
Ruders, Poul, 85
Rural Electrification Scheme, 3

S

Said, Edward, 142
Salesian Order, 7-10
Scarlatti, Domenico, 96
Schubert, Franz, 9, 132
Schumann, Robert, 13, 101, 106
Scriabin, Alexander, 117

Sealy, Douglas, 37, 51, 57, 176
Shakespeare, William, 103, 175, 195, 206
Shostakovich, Dmitri, 167
Sibelius, Jean, 107, 117
Sliabh Luachra, 5
Smith, Gillian, 23, 183-84, 186, 188, 190, 193, 214
St Francis Xavier Hall, 12, 43, 185
St Patrick's College, Drumcondra, 144, 177, 181
St Patrick's College, Maynooth (see National University of Ireland, Maynooth), 2, 83, 104, 196
Stanford, Charles Villiers, 12
Stravinsky, Igor, 24, 42, 45, 59, 65, 175
Sunday Press, 68
Sweeney, Eric, 119, 186, 188, 193
Sweeney, Peter, 134, 195, 214
Sweeney, Vanessa, 130
Szymanowski, Karol, 167

T

Takemitsu, Toru, 112, 156, 158
Tallaght Choral Society, 103, 195
Tchaikovsky, Pyotr Ilyich, 16, 117
Tippett, Michael, 73, 100, 109
Toonder, Marten, 118
Travers, Pauric, 11
Trinity College Dublin, 13, 19, 26, 182
Tuatha Dé Danann, 44, 57

U

University College Cardiff, 39, 186-88
University College Cork, 18, 65
University of Limerick, 2, 103, 146, 196

V

Vanhomrigh, Hester, 130
Vaughan Williams, Ralfe, 13, 18, 23, 100
Victory, Gerard, 19
Vincentian Fathers, 11
Volans, Kevin, 118

W

Walcott, Derek, 59-60
Walsh, Stephen, 59, 65
Warren, Raymond, 65
Wei, Wang, 163
Weir, Judith, 85
Wellesz, Egon, 38
West-Eastern Divan Orchestra, 142, 176
Wexford Opera Festival, 99
WhistleBlast Quartet, 167, 202
White, Harry, 99-100, 173-74
Williams, William Carlos, 103, 195
Wilson, Ian, 142
Wilson, James, 15, 41, 85, 110, 164, 193, 195, 201
Wilson, John, 38
World Music Days, 97
Wuorinen, Charles, 134

X

Xenakis, Iannis, 20

Y

Yeats, William Butler, 62, 129-30, 132, 133, 175, 194, 197, 208

www.ingramcontent.com/pod-product-compliance
Lightning Source LLC
Chambersburg PA
CBHW051056230426
43667CB00013B/2319